Germaine de Staël Revisited

Twayne's World Authors Series
French Literature

David O'Connell, Editor

Georgia State University

TWAS 849

GERMAINE DE STAËL
Photo by Claude Berger, Genève from Collection Château de Coppet

Germaine de Staël Revisited

Gretchen Rous Besser

New School for Social Research

Twayne Publishers • New York
Maxwell Macmillan Canada • Toronto
Maxwell Macmillan International • New York Oxford Singapore Sydney

Twayne's World Authors Series No. 849

Germaine de Staël Revisited
Gretchen Rous Besser

Copyright © 1994 by Twayne Publishers

Twayne Publishers   Maxwell Macmillan Canada, Inc.
Macmillan Publishing Company   1200 Eglinton Avenue East
866 Third Avenue   Suite 200
New York, New York 10022   Don Mills, Ontario M3C 3N1

Macmillan Publishing Company is part of the Maxwell Communication Group of Companies.

Library of Congress Cataloging-in-Publication Data

Besser, Gretchen R.
    Germaine de Staël, revisited / by Gretchen Rous Besser.
        p.   cm.—(Twayne's world authors series)
    Includes bibliographical reference and index.
    ISBN 0-8057-8286-9
    1. Staël, Madame de (Anne-Louise-Germaine), 1766–1817—Criticism
    and interpretation.   I. Title. II. Series.
    PQ2431.Z5B47 1994   93-28437
    848'.609—dc20   CIP

The paper used in this publication meets the minimum requirements of American National Standard for Information Sciences—Permanence of Paper for Printed Library Materials. ANSI Z3948–1984.∞ ™

10 9 8 7 6 5 4 3 2 1 (hc)
10 9 8 7 6 5 4 3 2 1 (pb)

Printed in the United States of America

To the memory of Sidonya Menkes Rous,
my first "feminist" mentor

Contents

Preface

Increasingly, Germaine de Staël has become a subject for revision and reevaluation. Why is it necessary to rethink previous assessments of a writer who has been dead for nearly two centuries and whose most recent work was published in 1906?

There are two reasons for "revisiting" Staël. The changing perspective of feminist criticism has spawned an ever-increasing spate of articles, books, conference papers, and feminist-oriented studies that make abundantly clear the extent to which this remarkable and versatile woman writer was an anomaly for her era and a precursor of innovative and daring feminine achievement.

Secondly, the opening of Staëlian archives to researchers has enabled eminent critics like Pauline de Pange, Simone Balayé, Georges Solovieff, and Béatrice Jasinski to bring to light new documentation that has disproved, and caused the revision of, former data taken as gospel. For example, the massive undertaking of Lady Blennerhassett, who compiled the first biography of Staël in 1889, is now seen to contain innumerable factual misrepresentations. The publication of Staël's extant correspondence by Solovieff, Balayé, Pange, and especially Jasinski has provided new insights into her life and loves and has emended details of fact and date. Because of her meticulous and detailed research, I have relied on Béatrice Jasinski as the final arbiter of scholarly disputes. For example, she has corrected the impression perpetuated by Paul Gautier, Pierre Kohler, David Glass Larg, and most other biographers that Staël was expelled from Paris in mid-July of 1799, when in reality she left of her own free will. Jasinski also resolves the long-disputed publication chronology of the Genevan and Parisian editions of *Delphine* by offering a sheaf of documents to prove that the two editions appeared simultaneously in mid-December of 1802.

In the light of new data and a changing feminist perspective, I have attempted to analyze with clarity and without preconception the life, works, and contributions of Germaine de Staël.

Note on the References and Acknowledgments

For the sake of consistency, quotations from the majority of Staël's writings are taken from the first and only collected edition of her works published posthumously (1820–21), in accordance with her wishes, by her son Auguste de Staël and her son-in-law duc Victor de Broglie, with the help of August Willhelm von Schlegel, her longtime confidant. Reading and working from the first edition gave me a personal sense of contemporaneity with the author. Citations from other writings—*Le Journal de jeunesse* and "Un Ouvrage inconnu de Mme de Staël sur M. Necker"—are taken from the only sources where they appeared or, in the case of *Circonstances*, from the most recent and scholarly edition.

For access to the Frederick Lewis Allen Room of the New York Public Library—an oasis of tranquillity in a frenetic city—I am forever grateful to Wayne Furman, the library's administrative supervisor. For intellectual stimulation and encouragement, I shall always remember my Allen Room colleagues—Gloria and Ruth, John, Betsy, David, Ted, Phyllis, and Tony. The resources of the incomparable NYPL could have provided adequate documentation for a study five times as lengthy as this one. What few items the library did not own, its staff obtained from other institutions. I thank each anonymous librarian for patience, perseverance, and perspicacity in tracking down and making available a wealth of research material.

I am also deeply indebted to Jenny Buzas, secretary-general of the Château de Coppet, for graciously providing the frontispiece portrait, which represents a painting by François Gérard that hangs in the Château de Coppet, and for her kindness in tracking down other works of art that I was unable to locate.

Chronology: Germaine de Staël's Life and Works

Narbonne's son. Necker resigns permanently on 3
September. *Sophie* and *Jane Grey* are published in
October.

1792   On 10 August, Staël saves Narbonne, François de
Jaucourt, and Lally de Tollendal. On 2 September, nar-
rowly escapes massacre. Begins *De l'influence des passions*.
Gives birth on 20 November to second son, Matthias-
Albert (also Narbonne's).

1793   Louis XVI beheaded 21 January. From 20 January to
25 May, remains in England with Narbonne. In August
writes *Réflexions sur le procès de la reine*, which is published in early September. Marie-Antoinette executed
16 October.

1794   Begins liaison with Adolphe Ribbing. *Zulma* published
in April. Suzanne Necker dies 15 May. Robespierre
overthrown 27 July (9 Thermidor). Meets Benjamin
Constant 18 September. *Réflexions sur la paix* appears
anonymously in Switzerland.

1795   *Réflexions sur la paix* published in February under Staël's
name in Paris. In April or May, publishes *Recueil de
morceaux détachés*, including *Essai sur les fictions*. In July,
writes *Réflexions sur la paix intérieure* (not published).
Deputy Legendre denounces her to Convention on 18
August. Committee of Public Safety exiles her on 15
October.

1796   At Coppet, completes *Passions*, published September or
early October.

1797   Gives birth to Albertine de Staël, future duchesse de
Broglie, on 8 June (daughter of Benjamin Constant).
Coup d'état on 4 September (18 Fructidor).

1798   From June to October, composes *Des Circonstances
actuelles*. Begins *De la Littérature*.

1799   Napoleon Bonaparte coup d'état on 9 November (18
Brumaire) establishes consulate.

1800   *De la Littérature* appears on 25 April. Over the summer,
begins *Delphine*, learns German, and prepares second edition of *Littérature*, which appears in mid-November.
Obtains separation from husband in December.

1802   Staël-Holstein dies 9 May in Poligny en route to
        Coppet with his wife. On 2 August, plebiscite names
        Napoleon consul for life. *Delphine* published in mid-
        December in Paris and Geneva.

1803   Staël exiled 40 leagues outside Paris on 15 October.
        On 8 November, sets out on journey through
        Germany. From 13 December to 1 March 1804,
        sojourns in Weimar, meets Goethe and Schiller.
        Napoleon crowns himself emperor on 2 December.

1804   Necker dies 9 April at Coppet. Staël leaves Berlin pre-
        cipitously on 18 April. Learns on 22 April of father's
        death. Reaches Coppet on 19 May. Sets out on 11
        December for Italy with three children and Schlegel.
        Meets Vincenzo Monti in Milan.

1805   *Manuscrits de M. Necker*, preceded by "Du Caractère de
        M. Necker et de sa vie privée," go on sale in Paris in
        February. Staël accepted into Accademia dell'Arcadia
        in Rome on 14 February. From 21 February to 9
        March, stays in Naples, climbs Vesuvius, visits
        Pompeii. From 8 to 14 April, in Rome for Holy Week,
        meets Don Pedro de Souza. Spends the summer and
        fall in Coppet, meets Prosper de Barante. Begins
        Corinne and composes a play, *Agar dans le désert*.

1806   Finishes *Corinne* in November and corrects proofs.

1807   *Corinne* published 1 May; becomes immediate success.
        Coppet becomes mecca for European intelligentsia.
        Writes *Geneviève de Brabant* and *La Sunamite*. Returns to
        Vienna on 4 December to complete research for book
        on Germany.

1809   Publishes *Lettres et pensées du prince de Ligne*. Composes
        Signora Fantastici.

1810   Composes *Sapho*. Meets Fanny Randall, future secretary
        and confidante. On 24 September, police confiscate *De
        l'Allemagne* and exile Staël. In early November meets
        23-year-old Jean Rocca in Geneva.

1811   On 5 March, Staël and Jean Rocca swear solemn oath
        to marry when circumstances permit. Writes *Le
        Capitaine Kernadec* and *Le Mannequin*. Composes

Réflexions sur le suicide. Over the summer, begins *Dix années d'exil* and documentation for poem on Richard the Lion-Hearted.

1812   Gives birth secretly on 7 April to Louis-Alphonse (son of Rocca). Departs clandestinely for England on 23 May, via Austria, Russia, and Sweden. Begins *Considérations sur la Révolution française* and second part of *Dix années*.

1813   *Réflexions sur le suicide* published in January. Arrives in London on 18 June. Son Albert killed 12 July in duel. John Murray publishes *Allemagne* in October.

1814   Napoleon abdicates on 6 April. Staël returns to Paris on 12 May after 12-year absence. In May or June, appeals to Congress of Vienna to abolish slave trade. Works on *Considérations*.

1815   Announces Albertine's engagement to Victor de Broglie on 2 February. Flees to Switzerland on 10 March after learning of Napoleon's disembarkment. Napoleon defeated at Waterloo on 18 June. Staël leaves for Italy in September.

1816   Albertine de Staël and duc Victor de Broglie wed 20 February in a Protestant-Catholic ceremony in Pisa. Over the summer at Coppet, works on *Considérations* and *Dix années* (which children will publish posthumously). Secretly weds Rocca on 10 October.

1817   Suffers cerebral hemorrhage on 21 February. Albertine gives birth to a daughter on 1 March. Germaine de Staël dies peacefully in her sleep on 14 July. Interred 28 July in family crypt.

1818   Jean Rocca dies 30 January. Victor de Broglie and Auguste de Staël publish *Considérations sur la Révolution française*.

1820   *Dix années d'exil* and *Oeuvres complètes* published.

1821   *Réflexions sur la paix intérieure* published.

1827   Auguste de Staël dies; his only son, born posthumously, survives him briefly.

1838   Alphonse Rocca dies childless. Albertine de Broglie
        dies; her five children will spawn statesmen, writers,
        mathematicians, physicists, and eminent scholars
        devoted to her mother's works.

1906   *Des Circonstances actuelles* published.

Chapter 1
"Monsieur de Saint-Ecritoire"

A young girl of about 12 is seated on a low stool beside her mother's armchair. The child's towering coiffure, corseted bodice, and lady's hoopskirt form an improbable contrast with her parted lips, sparkling eyes, and primly folded hands.[1] Anne-Louise-Germaine Necker is raptly listening to the guests of her mother's Friday salon. The encyclopedists Denis Diderot, Jean d'Alembert, and abbé André Morellet are debating with the scientists Claude Helvétius and Georges Buffon; the writers Frédéric-Melchior Grimm and Antoine Thomas stifle a yawn as Bernardin de Saint-Pierre reads aloud from his new novel, *Paul et Virginie* (which was to be published in 1787); academicians, ambassadors, government dignitaries, and members of the great aristocratic families of Noailles, Crillon, Beauvau, and Lauzun mull over threats to the stability of the ancien régime, to which they owe prestige and position.

The child is exhibited, doll-like, to her mother's friends. At age five she once asked elderly Mme de Mouchy: "Madame la maréchale, what do you think about love?" Instead of playing with dolls, she reads Montesquieu's *Esprit des lois* (The Spirit of laws, 1748). Abbé Guillaume Raynal plans to insert her "Réflexions sur l'Edit de Nantes" in his 1770 *Histoire philosophique et politique des deux Indes* (Philosophical and political history of the two Indies) (d'Andlau, 11). Grimm will publish one of her early compositions in the *Correspondance littéraire* (Literary correspondence, 1753–90), which is read all over Europe.[2] "Mme de Staël was always young but was never a child," commented her cousin, Albertine Necker de Saussure, in her "Notice on the Character and Writings of Mme de Staël."[3]

From humble Swiss Calvinist origins, the parents of this infant phenomenon had themselves streaked like meteors to the stratosphere of Parisian wealth and power. The mother, Suzanne Curchod—born 2 June 1737 in the tiny Swiss village of Crassier—received a boy's education in Latin, Greek, physics, and geometry from her pastor father. Aspiring suitors in Lausanne founded a literary society in her honor, and for a brief but tumultuous period she was courted by young Edward Gibbon (the future author of *The History of the Decline and Fall of the Roman Empire*

[1776–88]), until his stern father broke off the match (a situation to be echoed in her daughter's novel *Corinne* [1807]).

Reverend Curchod's death in 1760 left his family pauperized. Suzanne was obliged to earn her living in the only two professions open to a woman of her time—first as a teacher (riding to pupils' homes on the back of a donkey) and then as a governess in the employ of a pretty French widow, Germaine de Vermenoux, who brought her to Paris in the spring of 1764. There, Cinderella's fortunes changed dramatically and permanently. Prince Charming was a stocky, 32-year-old Genevan named Jacques Necker, who had come to Paris in 1748 as an ambitious young assistant in Isaac Vernet's bank,[4] had recently founded the substantial banking firm of Thélusson and Necker, and was on his way to becoming the richest man in France.

Although Jacques Necker was courting Mme de Vermenoux at the time, the beautiful governess quite turned his head. Within a matter of months, he and Suzanne Curchod were married. The Necker union was unusual in being a marriage of love[5]—an ideal to which their daughter would aspire all her life. On 22 April 1766 Suzanne Necker gave birth to Anne-Louise-Germaine (named for her protectress Germaine de Vermenoux). Following Rousseauesque guidelines, the new mother was determined to nurse her baby but gave up the effort when, after four months, the child was found to be starving.

Mme Necker met another defeat in the educational program she foisted on the young girl in her determination to transform Louise (as she was known until her marriage)[6] into a living encyclopedia of mathematics, theology, modern and classical languages, history, and geography. The child suffered a mental and physical breakdown before she was 12,[7] whereupon the celebrated society doctor Tronchin prescribed rest and relaxation in a country setting. This decree demolished Suzanne Necker's glorious plans for her offspring. When Albertine Necker de Saussure complimented her sometime later on her daughter's prodigious distinction, the mother replied peevishly, "She's nothing, absolutely nothing, compared to what I wanted to make of her" ("Notice," xxxiv).

Louise had no playmates of her own age until she was 11, when Mme Necker finally invited a child of suitable background to visit. Catherine Rilliet Huber later described their first meeting: "Mlle Necker grasped my hand, . . . embraced me, told me she had been waiting for me for an eternity, she was sure she would love me till she died, I would be her only true friend, this moment would determine an everlasting affection."[8] And indeed, the two women were friends for the next 40 years.

As she recovered, Louise was soon frolicking in the terraced park of her parents' country estate at Saint-Ouen. Freed by doctor's orders from her constricting whalebone corselet, the child grew taller, stronger, and rosy-cheeked. Like woodland nymphs (and sometimes dressed as such), she and Catherine darted over the spacious grounds with bow and arrow, carved messages on trees, and staged comedies of their own composition for an indulgent audience of family and friends (Rilliet Huber, 6: 141, 145).

Although he adored his daughter and loved his wife deeply, Necker's principal occupation was amassing money. Speculating in corn after the Seven Years' War, he had piled up a tidy seven and a half million francs by the time he retired from banking in 1772. Necker made his wife steward of his immense fortune. She learned to buy and sell, farm, build, and oversee the family finances (as her daughter would do in her traces). Mme Necker also worked earnestly for philanthropic causes. The hospital she founded still bears her name.

Meanwhile, her husband was adding fame to fortune. Appointed minister of the Republic of Geneva to the Court of Versailles in 1768 and director of the French India Company the following year, he kept a splendid mansion on the rue de Cléry, where his wife presided over her Friday salon. In 1773 Necker published a monograph *Eloge de Colbert* (In Praise of Colbert), which received first prize for eloquence from the French Academy (an institution largely populated by habitués of the Necker salon) and contained the self-satisfied statement: "If men are made in the image of God, then the minister of finance, next to the king, must be the man who most closely approximates to that image."[9] Shortly after Louis XVI's coronation in May 1774, Necker published a pamphlet criticizing the economic program of Controller General Turgot, whom he replaced two years later. The only obstacle to his appointment was his religion. As a Protestant, Necker could neither attend the king's privy council nor be named controller general (though he might exercise that function). Louis XVI shilly-shallied for a year before appointing him director general of finance on 22 June 1777.

Upright, incorruptible, but inflexibly opinionated, Necker made substantial savings in a runaway budget during his four-year term as finance minister. To underwrite the costly American War, he proposed abolishing some of the court's 4,000 subaltern positions, which were customarily bought and sold at huge profits, and curtailing the farmer generals' share of taxes they collected for the crown. To enlist public opinion, he published for the first time in history a balance sheet of royal revenues and expenditures; within weeks, its 20,000 copies had sold out. "As much as

anything, the *Compte rendu* was an exercise in public education. Its deliberately simple language, and its effort to make a financial account read-
able by the common man, testifies to its attempt to form an engaged
citizenry" (Schama, 95). Blocked from attending the royal council,
Necker resigned on 19 May 1781 to work on a formidable treatise justifying his ministry, which his daughter hoped would secure his swift return
to power.[10] *De l'administration de M. Necker par lui-même* (The Administration of Monsieur Necker, by himself) was published in May 1791.

The family had returned in 1783 to Switzerland, where the following
year Necker purchased the property and château of Coppet for 500,000
francs. Built in 1257, the building consisted of three wings surrounding
an inner courtyard; flanking a wrought-iron gate on which Necker had
emblazoned the entwined initials "N.C." (Necker-Curchod) were two
asymmetrical towers, the older of which currently houses the Staël
archives. In spite of its magnificent location, the château was so situated
that only from the second-floor balcony could one glimpse the sparkling
waters of Lac Léman and the white-capped Jura mountains beyond.

The three Neckers were all indefatigable writers. Necker worked hard
at projecting his political and economic programs, defending his administration, and expounding his religious credo. His wife, whose literary
efforts he scorned and tried to suppress, was wont to jot down feelings
and impressions, which her repentant husband belatedly published in
the posthumous *Mélanges de Mme Necker* (Miscellany, 1798). In addition
to penning an anonymous tribute in 1781 to her father's *Compte rendu*
and competing with her mother in composing rival "portraits" of
Necker, Germaine kept a youthful journal during the summer of 1785.
Her *Journal de jeunesse* acknowledges Necker's dislike for women writers
and his wife's subordination to his wishes: "If mama had written, she
would surely have acquired a great reputation for wit; but my father
cannot abide a woman author, and during the four days he has seen me
writing his portrait, he has already been seized with apprehension, and
he calls me in jest: 'Monsieur de Saint-Ecritoire.'"[11] This facetious but
basically denigrating nickname conveyed Necker's indulgent dismissal of
his daughter's writing.

All her life Staël retained her early habit of writing on the fly and on
the sly. Invariably she carried with her a small green morocco folding
desk on which she would note ideas while riding in her carriage or even
conversing with friends. Erich Bollmann, the Hanoverian physician who
would later help Staël's lover Narbonne escape from the Reign of Terror,
described her writing habits: "Whilst her hair is being dressed, whilst

she breakfasts, in fact during a third of the day she writes. She has not sufficient quiet to look over what she has written, to improve it or finish it, but even the rough outpourings of her ever active mind are of the greatest interest."[12] It was not until after Necker's death that his daughter felt free to furnish her room at Coppet with a writing desk.[13]

In adolescence, Staël gravitated increasingly to her father for the approbation and love her mother withheld. The two often rebelled together against Mme Necker's rigidity. On one occasion, when the latter was called away from breakfast, she returned to find her husband and daughter prancing around the table, their napkins tied around their heads like turbans. Her look of astonished reproval sent them back to their seats without a word, "as ashamed as schoolboys caught in the act."[14]

The Neckers faced a dilemma in finding a suitable match for their daughter in Catholic France. During a court visit to Fontainebleau in 1783, they met a promising young Englishman from a noble Protestant family who, though not yet 24, had sat in the House of Commons for four years and would soon be prime minister of England. To her parents' consternation (and her mother's lasting recriminations), Louise Necker flatly refused to wed William Pitt or to live anywhere but in Paris. For this reason, she acquiesced to the courtship of Baron Eric-Magnus de Staël-Holstein—a womanizing courtier fettered with unpaid bills—with the proviso that she never reside in his native Sweden. After a year of negotiations over Necker's imposed conditions, the betrothal was finalized in September 1785.

In her *Journal de jeunesse*, the bride-to-be highlights the difference between her fiancé and her father. She recounts that she was dancing with the less-than-impetuous baron when her father interrupted: "Allow me, sir, to show you how a man dances with the lady he loves." Thereupon Necker, for all his great girth, whirled his daughter spiritedly around the floor. Despite her pangs, the young woman took herself firmly in hand. "M. de Staël is the only partner who suits me, for he is incapable of making me unhappy" (*Jeunesse*, 3:237)—a dubious prospect for repeating her parents' love duet.

The couple were wed with due splendor in the Swedish embassy chapel on 14 January 1786. As "ambassadress," Germaine Necker de Staël opened her own salon on the rue du Bac. Dolly Adams described her apartments, furnishings, and table as "the most elegant I have ever seen."[15] Foreigners, diplomats, and liberal French aristocrats were attracted by Staël's exuberance and wit. "In private, her conversation was extraordinary. . . . Her most accomplished pages and most eloquent

speeches fail to convey the persuasive power of her words when, free
from catering to a particular audience, she could play upon the unique
instrument that she had tuned herself. Then her great intellect spread its
wings and soared freely; then . . . more witness to than mistress of her
own inspiration, she exerted a supernatural force . . . over which, for
good or ill, she had little control" ("Notice," cclxvii). The subject's
father called her a "conversational phenomenon" (Jasinski, 4:441 n. 3),
and Adrienne de Tessé[16] declared: "If I were queen, I would order Mme
de Staël to speak to me always" (d'Andlau, 64). Mathieu de
Montmorency remarked that Staël sparkled best in conversation's "continual flux" of "dashing expressions, witty sallies, lively and profound
thoughts which . . . can only be inspired by inner conviction."[17]
Benjamin Constant spoke of her "marvelous and unique talent for conversation" that "clothed intimacy with indefinable magic."[18] According
to Charles Augustin Sainte-Beuve, "she was like that great Athenian
orator: when you admire and are moved by intelligent or burning
pages, someone can always say, what would you have thought if you
had heard her speak?"[19]

Staël's keen powers of observation, spiced with impish drollery, come
across in the juicy accounts of court life that she appended to her husband's official bulletins to King Gustav III. These narratives, composed
between March 1786 and December 1787, are a blend of court news,
scandal, love affairs, politics, balls, gambling debts, and dishonor, with
occasional references to more sober subjects like French criminal
jurisprudence, lettres de cachet, and the slave trade (of which Staël was a
lifelong opponent).

Among her admirers was the much-courted comte François-Apolline
de Guibert, who penned a laudatory portrait of Staël: "Zulmé is only
twenty years old, but already she is the most celebrated priestess of
Apollo. . . . Her large black eyes sparkle with the fire of genius, and her
jet-black tresses fall in rich ringlets on her shoulders. Her features are
more pronounced than delicate, and one senses in them something above
the normal destiny of her sex" (Bersaucourt, 106). When Guibert died
suddenly in May 1790, Staël composed his memorial.

Not everyone was smitten with Germaine de Staël. After she tore her
train curtsying to the queen at her formal presentation at court on 31
January 1786—an incident that caused her acute embarrassment—
barbed tongues pronounced the ambassadress clumsy and ill-dressed. La
Fayette's aunt, the comtesse de Boufflers,[20] who had helped engineer
Germaine Necker's marriage, was quick to criticize her to King Gustav:

"I hope M. de Staël will be happy, but I do not believe so. . . . [His wife] is imperious, obstinate, and possesses a self-assurance I have never witnessed in a person of her age. She passes judgment on everything indiscriminately and, although clever, she makes twenty-five ill-placed pronouncements for every corrrect thing she says" (d'Andlau, 21). The baronne d'Oberkirch disapproved of Staël unrelentingly: "Everyone considered her ugly, awkward, and self-conscious. She did not know how to comport herself and was obviously out of place amidst the elegance of Versailles" (Diesbach, 67).

Staël bore a daughter, named Gustavine in honor of the Swedish king, in July 1787.[21] The only one of Staël's children fathered by Staël-Holstein, she lived less than two years. Differences in age, taste, and temperament caused an eventual rift in the Staël-Holstein ménage. Staël wrote to her husband on 22 April 1794: "Do you want me to explain the everlasting misery of our situation? . . . You do not care for my friends, and I cannot live without them. A lively, witty conversation is unnecessary to you; without it, I fall asleep. You could exist pleasurably in the Swiss countryside; for my part, I should be better off in a coffin" (Jasinski, 2:628). As the couple drifted apart, Staël insisted on a separation, which she finally obtained in December 1800.

She had given vent to her marital disappointment in her earliest writings—the verse-plays *Sophie, ou les Sentiments secrets* (Sophie, or Secret feelings, 1786) and *Jane Gray* (1787). Her first important literary work was the *Lettres sur les écrits et le caractère de J. J. Rousseau* (Letters on the works and character of J. J. Rousseau) of 1788, published in a first edition of only 20 copies. By launching a book into the unknown, Staël was conscious of laying herself open to scrutiny and criticism, which she tried to parry in reams of self-justification.

One of the ministers who succeeded Necker accused him in April 1787 of a gross error in his *Compte rendu* of 1781 (a huge deficit instead of the surplus Necker had claimed). When the latter published a self-justifying memorandum, against the king's express order, he was exiled by a lettre de cachet 40 leagues outside Paris. The king recalled him to power on 26 August 1788, to popular acclaim, fireworks, and a spectacular rise in the money market. During his brief tenure, Necker convened the Estates General in May 1789, for the first time since 1614. On 17 June the Third Estate declared itself a National Assembly, and on 20 June, obliged to gather in the royal Jeu de Paume, it swore its so-called Tennis Court oath to meet wherever possible until a new constitution was implemented. Twice Necker tendered his resignation, and twice the

king signified him to remain. But at three o'clock on 11 July, Louis XVI
ordered him to leave the country surreptitiously. Pretending to set out
for a carriage ride with his wife, Necker departed in secrecy for Belgium.
By the time they reached Brussels, the Bastille had been stormed and
the first émigrés had left France. In a panic, the king recalled his minister. Necker's triumphal return to Paris (25–28 July) was, Staël said later,
her last completely happy moment. Her euphoria was short-lived. In
early October the angry populace descended on Versailles and brought
the royal family back to Paris in humiliation. Necker's hopes for a
British-style constitutional monarchy faded as revolutionary agitation
surged. So utterly had public opinion changed during his two-year term
that when Necker resigned on 3 September 1790, not a voice was raised
in his favor, though he had subsidized the royal treasury in 1777 with
2,400,000 pounds of his personal funds—half his fortune. (His daughter
was to badger the Directory, Consulate, Empire, and Restoration to have
this loan repaid.) Moreover, an angry mob pounced on him at Arcis-sur-
Aube and only released him by special order of the National Assembly.

Always generous to those in adversity (though Talleyrand accused her
of throwing people in the water for the pleasure of fishing them out),
Staël offered in 1792 to conduct the royal family to safety, but they
declined. Louis XVI had already attempted a bumbling escape with his
wife and young son, on 20 June 1791, only to be arrested in Varennes,
40 miles from the border, and brought back ignominiously to Paris.
From that day on, the royal family were prisoners of the state. It was
only a matter of time before the king was deposed, tried for treason, and
guillotined. France had already declared itself a republic on 21
September 1789, and all public acts were dated from year 1 of the new
regime. After the king's execution on 21 January 1793, Marie-
Antoinette was also put on trial. Staël wrote a courageous (albeit anonymous) defense of the unpopular Austrian queen, against whom the most
infamous charges had been brought. *Réflexions sur le procès de la reine*
(Reflections on the queen's trial, September 1793) constituted an
unavailing attempt to combat slander and placate Marie-Antoinette's
judges. Although Staël's effort failed, she had taken up cudgels as a
woman on behalf of a woman.

Toward the end of Louis XVI's reign, Staël had met and fallen in love
with the dashing comte Louis de Narbonne (rumored to be the incestu-
ous son of Louis XV and his daughter Adélaïde). Staël's liaison was a
secret from no one, except perhaps her husband. Her feat in securing for
Narbonne the post of war minister, in December 1791, prompted

Marie-Antoinette to remark, "What glory and pleasure for Mme de Staël to have the entire army . . . to herself" (Diesbach, 119). He lasted in office three months. On 31 August 1790, Staël had given birth to his son, Auguste de Staël. After the birth on 20 November 1792 of a second son, Matthias-Albert,[22] also Narbonne's, Staël stubbornly followed her lover to Surrey. She called the period from 20 January to 25 May 1793 "four months of happiness snatched from the shipwreck of life."[23] While staying at Juniper Hall, she met and took an immediate liking to the English writer Fanny Burney; Dr. Burney nipped their friendship in the bud by forbidding his 40-year-old daughter to visit a woman reputed to be both democratic and adulterous. (The insular conventionality of the British would long rankle Staël; like every good writer, she would turn it into literature.)

As the Revolution escalated, 100 heads a day rolled under Dr. Guillotin's humanitarian invention. Although Staël enjoyed a measure of inviolability as a Swiss citizen and Swedish ambassadress, a mob attacked her carriage on 2 September 1792 and brought her by force to the Hôtel de Ville. Saved from death by the intervention of the Communard Louis-Pierre Manuel, she promptly departed for Switzerland, from which haven she spirited dozens of émigré friends out of France by means of an ingenious but costly plan.[24] In this way Staël saved her lifelong friend Mathieu de Montmorency,[25] Mme de Laval (Mathieu's mother and Narbonne's former mistress), François de Jaucourt and his nephew Achille du Chayla, the duchesse Sophie de Broglie (whose son would marry Staël's daughter), the princesse d'Hénin (La Fayette's cousin), the marquise de Simiane (the love of La Fayette's youth), the maréchale de Beauvau, Narbonne's daughter, Malouet's mother and sister, the abbé de Damas, and many others.

Mme Necker, who had been slowly sliding toward death, expired on 15 May 1794 at age 57. Afraid of being buried alive,[26] she had made elaborate plans for a mausoleum at Coppet in which her body might be preserved indefinitely in a marble basin filled with spirits of wine. After Suzanne Necker's demise, her grieving husband visited her tomb daily for ten years, then took his place beside her in the basin of alcohol.

Ever a generous and devoted friend, Staël was a demanding and desperate lover. Seeking always to replicate her parents' perfect union, she passed from one passionate relationship to the next. While bombarding Narbonne with accusatory and cajoling letters, she allowed herself quietly to be comforted by the Swedish Count Adolph Ribbing, called "the handsome regicide" for his part in assassinating King Gustav III at a masked ball in 1792. During her affair with Ribbing, Staël met Benjamin Constant[27] on 18 September 1794. Twenty-six years old and desperately in love, Constant sent her five letters a day. "She is a Being apart," he wrote on 21 October, "the sort of superior Being who comes along once in a century" (Bornecque, xxxi). When Staël repulsed Constant's advances, he won her over by pretending to die from unrequited love. Their tempestuous relationship would bind them for 20 years.

Accompanied by Constant, Staël returned in May 1795 to Paris, where she reopened her salon to passionate debate about a new constitution for France. In February she had published *Réflexions sur la paix* (Reflections on peace), inspired by Robespierre's fall on 27 July 1794 and the possibility of new beginnings, and in April or early May she had brought out a *Recueil de morceaux détachés* (Collection of unrelated pieces), which included three novellas and the theoretical *Essai sur les fictions* (Essay on fiction). Her *Réflexions sur la paix intérieure* (Reflections on domestic peace) of July 1795 called for peace against Pitt's bellicosity and urged moderates of both republican and royalist parties to unite for France's common good; political troubles in early October convinced Staël not to publish the brochure. Invariably, she was misunderstood. On 18 August 1795, Deputy Legendre (her former butcher) denounced her to the Convention for plotting against the Republic, and the Committee of Public Safety enjoined Staël-Holstein to remove his wife from Paris.

While her father wrote a vast treatise on the Revolution, Staël worked in Coppet on a book she had begun in 1793, *De l'influence des passions sur le bonheur des individus et des nations* (The Influence of passions on the happiness of individuals and nations), composed under the shadow of both Narbonne's and Ribbing's defection. The latter's infidelity plunged her into the waiting arms of Benjamin Constant. In a curious document (probably dating from the spring of 1796, when they first became intimate), Constant signed a "contract" promising always to love the person "without whom there would no longer exist any interest for me on this earth" (Solovieff, 154).[28] A brief rapprochement with her husband provided legitimate grounds for the birth on 8 June 1797 of a daughter, Albertine—whose flaming red hair bore a compromising resemblance to Constant's.

In addition to collaborating with Benjamin on two political treatises, Staël played an important role (which she denied) in the intrigues that precipitated Bonaparte's coup of 18 Fructidor (4 September 1797) against the royalist majority. She was instrumental in having Talleyrand recalled from America and named minister of foreign affairs. When the government instituted reprisals against its adversaries, Staël again incurred disfavor by helping her friends. Inevitably, she ended up on the opposition side.

She first met Bonaparte at Talleyrand's invitation on 6 December 1797. Although he paid her scant attention, she was starry-eyed with admiration—a mistake she would regret and rectify (but, for some critics, would never live down). Staël modeled the protagonist of an unpublished tragedy of this period, *Jean de Witt*, on Bonaparte, whom she would later call "Robespierre on horseback" (Solovieff, 158). Visiting him unannounced at home one morning, she barged in on the general in his bath with the excuse, "Genius has no sex!" (Diesbach, 203). But when Bonaparte annexed Geneva in June 1798 and carried off Bernese gold to finance his Egyptian campaign, her enthusiasm evaporated. Before the French invasion, Necker burned his daughter's letters for fear they might compromise her. An old Swiss friend of the family, Charles-Victor de Bonstetten, noted that "nothing she published equalled the wit, force and eloquence of that correspondence" (Solovieff, 160). Staël spent the summer and fall of 1798 trying to eradicate her father's name from the émigré list and restore his two million–pound loan.

Sometime after Necker sold his mansion on the chaussée d'Antin to Jacques-Rose Récamier in October 1798, Staël met and was smitten by the banker's beautiful young wife.[29] Juliette Récamier, whom Staël called "the young sister of my choice" (Solovieff, 11), would become one of her closest friends (and would one day be loved by her son Auguste and her lover Benjamin).[30] Before the year's end, Staël put the finishing touches to *Des Circonstances actuelles qui peuvent terminer la Révolution et des principes qui doivent fonder la république en France* (On present circumstances that can end the Revolution and on principles that must underlie a republic in France), prescribing remedies for the country's political instability; because publication was deemed dangerous, she laid the book aside in favor of *De la littérature considérée dans ses rapports avec les institutions sociales* (The Influence of literature upon society), which came out in 1800. *Circonstances* did not appear until 1906.

Staël chanced to return to Paris on the evening of Bonaparte's coup d'état of 18 Brumaire (9 November 1799), which established the Consulate. Using her influence with Joseph Bonaparte to have Constant named to the Tribunate on Christmas Eve, she was attacked as responsible for the rash call for independence in his maiden speech of 5 January 1800 and was dispatched to Saint-Ouen by Police Minister Fouché.

Social acquaintances fled her company for fear of compromising themselves. At a reception given by Mme de Montesson, only Delphine de
Sabran Custine deigned to approach her. In gratitude, Staël named the
heroine of the book she was writing "Delphine" and introduced the incident twice into her tale. By February 1800 she was back in Paris, where
her house on the rue de Grenelle became a gathering place for the opposition. On 25 April her long-awaited book *De la Littérature* appeared.
Staël was soon at work on a second edition—with a preface designed to
draw the teeth of her critics—which appeared in mid-November and
sold out within a few weeks.

In January 1802 Bonaparte dismissed Constant and 19 other members of the Tribunate. Infuriated to hear that Staël had referred to him as
an "ideophobe," the first consul roared at his brothers Lucien and
Joseph: "Warn that woman not to try to bar my way or I will smash her,
I will crush her" (Solovieff, 198). A plebiscite on 2 August made
Bonaparte consul for life. Meanwhile, Staël-Holstein had died of a stroke
on 9 May en route to Coppet, leaving his affairs in such disarray that it
took his wife two years to pay off his creditors.

Her first novel, *Delphine*, came out in December 1802. Although a
huge popular success, it provoked the first consul's displeasure. After all,
the book defended divorce, espoused women's rights, undermined social
conventions, and glorified Protestantism just after he had signed a concordat with the Church of Rome. For the next nine months, Staël
remained prudently in Switzerland, where the stern Calvinists blamed
her for receiving company during her toilette and addressing male
acquaintenances by their first names. She took consolation in the friendship of her childhood playmate, Catherine Rilliet Huber, and her cousin
by marriage, Albertine Necker de Saussure,[31] of whom she said: "My
cousin possesses all the intellect that people ascribe to me and all the
virtues that I lack" (Solovieff, 248).

Staël was dedicated to her children and their education. As was the
practice with girls, she taught her daughter Albertine herself but
engaged a tutor for her sons. Albertine wrote to Necker de Saussure:
"When I was twelve years old, [my mother] conversed with me on an
equal footing, and nothing can describe the joy of spending half an hour
alone with her. . . . Her children always loved her passionately. From the
age of five or six, we used to quarrel over which of us loved her the most"
("Notice," ccli).[32]

Staël had been in residence near Paris for four weeks when, in
September 1803, a woman[33] told the first consul that all roads led to

Maffliers and Mme de Staël. Faced with the prospect of immediate banishment, she attempted to sweet-talk Bonaparte on 7 October: "If you wish me to leave France, give me a passport for Germany and grant me a week in Paris to settle my affairs and have a doctor attend to my six-year-old daughter, exhausted by her journey. In no country on earth would such a request be refused. Citizen Consul, it cannot be your intention to persecute a woman and two children: it is impossible that a hero should not protect the weak" (Jasinski, 5:14–15).[34]

On the afternoon of 15 October, an officer in mufti[35] galloped up with Bonaparte's signed order exiling her 40 leagues outside Paris; if she did not leave within 24 hours, police would escort her to the border. Retorting that recruits were treated in this way, not women and children, Staël demanded three days in Paris to wind up her affairs. The officer acceded. When he complimented her on her writings, Staël rejoined: "You can see the result of being an accomplished woman. I sugggest you advise the members of your family against it, when you have the chance" (Diesbach, 274).

When no reprieve was forthcoming, Staël set out disconsolately for Germany on 8 November 1803, accompanied by Benjamin Constant and her children Auguste and Albertine. Her initial reactions were mournful: "Material necessities in Germany—beds, food, heating—are unbearable . . . and even the most distinguished Germans are not part of the human species when it comes to habits and tastes," she wrote her father on 15 November (Jasinski, 5:109). She had complained the previous day to Charles de Villers (a French expatriate who had introduced her to Kantian philosophy): "Shall I tell you at the end of two days, like a true Frenchwoman, my impressions of a country I do not know? Stopping in a small town inn, I heard a piano being pounded in a smoky room where woolen garments were drying atop an iron stove. It is the same everywhere: a concert in a smoke-filled room" (Jasinski, 5:104). Six-year-old Albertine came down with scarlet fever in Frankfurt, and Staël feared for the child's life. But her spirits rose with her daughter's prompt recovery and the effusive welcome she received in Weimar and Berlin.

Her reputation as a writer had preceded her. Not only did the Duke of Saxe-Weimar entertain her splendidly, but Staël even won over the reticent Duchess Louise. Goethe alleged work and ill health to avoid meeting her but could not prevail against her persistence. He and Schiller were both agreeably struck by her intellect and conversation, although the latter complained that she was "the most active, combat-

ive, and voluble of all the human beings I have ever met"
(Blennerhassett, 3:59). Goethe provided an introduction to the 36-year-
old August Wilhelm von Schlegel[36] in Berlin. Schlegel would follow
Staël to Coppet and remain in her service until she died, as her children's
tutor, her own literary adviser and would-be suitor, and a "living
German encyclopedia" (Levaillant, 47) into which she could dip at
leisure.

If less stimulating than Weimar intellectually, Berlin was socially
more exciting. Staël was presented at court and feted in a whirlwind of
dinners, suppers, and card games, which she described breathlessly to
her father. Alas! when she received news of his illness on 18 April 1804,
he was already dead. She returned to Coppet in a paroxysm of despair.
"The grief of losing him afflicts my heart more deeply every day," Staël
wrote Gouverneur Morris on 16 August. "I have not lost my father but
my friend, my brother, my other and noblest half" (Solovieff, 281). She
wrote du Pont de Nemours on 13 November: "My religion on this earth
is my father's memory, and I know of nothing . . . I would not sacrifice
for a line written by his hand or an authentic word he spoke" (Solovieff,
333). Her sole comfort was to compile her father's papers into a book of
homage. *Manuscrits de M. Necker* (Monsieur Necker's manuscripts), preceded by his daughter's notice, "Du Caractère de M. Necker et de sa vie
privée" (Monsieur Necker's character and private life), was published the
following February.

Having failed in further attempts to have her banishment lifted, Staël
left for Italy on 11 December 1804 with her three children and Schlegel.
After crossing the Alps in deep snow, they spent a week in Turin and
another in Milan, where, according to the beautiful and clever contessa
Massimiliana Cicognara, all of society was eager to meet "the great man
known as Mme de Staël" (Diesbach, 323). Staël read the *Divine Comedy*
with the celebrated poet Vincenzo Monti, who afforded her an inside
view of Italian literature, politics, and social behavior. In Rome she was
received into the Accademia dell'Arcadia on 14 February under the
name of a woman poet of ancient Greece, Telesilla Argoica (a triumph to
be repeated, with flourishes, by her alter ego Corinne).

For two weeks Staël explored Naples and its environs, climbing
Vesuvius and visiting Pompeii, Herculaneum, and Cape Misenum, where
she situated Corinne's famous improvisation. Returning to Rome for
Holy Week, she encountered the sensitive and seductive Don Pedro de
Souza e Holstein, who like herself had just lost a father. They spent
romantic hours visiting the Roman ruins by moonlight. Although the

relationship never exceeded the bounds of a passionate flirtation, don Pedro served as the first model for Lord Oswald Nelvil in the novel *Corinne, ou l'Italie* (Corinne, or Italy, 1807)—the fruit of Staël's Italian trip, as *De l'Allemagne* (On Germany, 1813) would be the product of her travels through that country.

The second model for Nelvil was the future Duke of Palmella, the 23-year-old Prosper de Barante,[37] who joined Staël in the summer of 1805 at Coppet, where she began work on the novel that would occupy her until late 1806. Through Barante senior, who had discouraged his son's infatuation, Staël received permission to return to France. Residing with her retinue first in Auxerre, then in Rouen, then at the château of Acosta near Meulan, she managed at the same time to finish *Corinne*. To Fouché's suggestion that she slip in a few words in Napoleon's favor, Staël retorted that she would rather abandon publication than debase herself in this fashion. *Corinne* was an immediate international success with the public and a disaster with the emperor, who resented the author's praise of the English (with whom the French were at war) and her silence about his Italian conquests. "That woman is truly a crow," he wrote on 20 April 1807. "I acquire daily proof that no one is more evil than she. That woman is an enemy of the government and even of the France she claims she cannot live without" (Levaillant, 97). His exile order stood firm.

To mitigate the boredom of Switzerland, Staël invited visitors by the droves. The years 1807–10 marked the glorious period of Coppet, to which intellectuals of all backgrounds, ideas, and persuasions gravitated. The hostess often entertained 20 overnight guests and had 40 places set for dinner, where it was forbidden to discuss any fare other than food for thought. Conversation extended into the morning hours, Staël being an insomniac who could not sleep without opium. In addition to entertaining on a lavish scale, writing, conversing, and overseeing a large staff of servants, she administered her sizable fortune[38] and dispensed charity to the sick and poor of the region.

Among the visitors who frequented Staël's literary cenacle—many of whom composed important works in that heady intellectual climate—were close friends and admirers like Constant, Montmorency, Bonstetten, Juliette Récamier, Necker de Saussure, Simonde de Sismondi, the two Schlegel brothers, Vincenzo Monti, the Danish poet Frederika Brun, Pedro de Souza, Prosper de Barante and his father, the Englishmen Sir James Mackintosh and Lord Byron, as well as various acquaintances Staël met in her travels. She was wont to regale her guests with theatrical performances on the Coppet stage. A competent and compelling actress, she played the lead in Racinian tragedies and in her own plays—*Agar dans le désert* (Hagar in the desert, 1806), *Geneviève de Brabant* (Genevieve of Brabant, 1808), *La Sunamite* (The Shunammite, 1808), the soubrette in *Le Capitaine Kernadec* (Captain Kernadec, 1811)—while enlisting friends and children in supporting roles.

Accompanied by Albert, Albertine, and Schlegel, Staël spent the winter of 1807–8 in Vienna in order to complete the book she had projected writing since her first visit to Weimar. She was also eager to renew relations with Count Maurice O'Donnell, an Austrian of Irish descent whom she had met in Venice in 1805 and now barraged with the same kind of exigent letters she had once fired off to Narbonne and Ribbing.[39] None of her friends, except for Juliette Récamier, suspected her despair, just as Staël herself had no inkling that her fidgety "official" lover Constant had secretly married Charlotte von Hardenberg on 5 June 1808.

In September 1808, new guests descended on Coppet. The mysticism of Julian von Krüdener, author of *Valérie* (1804) (a feeble predecessor of *Corinne*), and of Zacharias Werner, a sexually obsessed dramatic poet, rubbed off on Staël's thinking. By now a matronly woman of 42 who habitually claimed she was several years younger (although her face revealed the ravages of opium abuse), Staël was nonetheless described as follows by the infatuated Werner: "Her body, although not as slender as that of a nymph, is voluptuously beautiful, especially the breasts and neck. She is unquestionably swarthy, and her face is not of perfect beauty, but all criticism is forgotten at the sight of her magnificent eyes, through whose fiery flashes shines a great and divine soul" (d'Eaubonne, 182).

The boom dropped in September 1810. Staël had left Geneva in May for the beautiful château of Chaumont—former residence of the Cardinal d'Amboise, Diane de Poitiers, Catherine de Médicis, and Nostradamus—in order to supervise publication of *Allemagne*. (It was here that she met an eccentric, heavyset British spinster with dyed hair, Fanny Randall, who would become her amanuensis and confidante.) Staël was correcting final proofs of her book when word came on 24 September that Napoleon's new police minister, René Savary, duc de Rovigo—more punctilious and hostile than his predecessor Fouché—had ordered the manuscript and galley sheets confiscated and its author banished from France within 48 hours. (This action bankrupted the publisher Nicolle, whom Staël generously reimbursed.) In a breathless tale of deception and daring, she smuggled three copies of her book out of the country. One was to follow Staël across Europe to England, where

Allemagne was published in June 1813 and immediately translated into English and German. It did not appear in France until 1814, after Napoleon's downfall. She describes the vicissitudes of this flight, with its material discomforts and police harshness, in the posthumous *Dix années d'exil* (Ten years of exile, 1820).

During her enforced stay in Geneva, Staël met the scion of one of that city's prominent families, the 23-year-old Albert-Michel-Jean Rocca, who fell madly in love with the chatelaine of Coppet. Tongue-tied in her presence, he would gallop his stallion Sultan up the steep cobbled streets, make the horse kneel beneath Staël's window, and tell anyone who would listen, "I will love her so much, she will marry me."[40] Persistence paid off. On 5 March 1811, in the presence of a Protestant pastor and Fanny Randall, Staël and Rocca, 22 years her junior, swore a solemn oath to wed when circumstances might allow.

The following fall and winter, she was deeply depressed. "Nothing interests me or gives me pleasure any more," Staël wrote Juliette Récamier on 31 October. "Life for me is like a ball after the violin has stopped playing" (Solovieff, 420). Her despondency and physical malaise (diagnosed as dropsy) were doubtless caused by her fifth pregnancy, from which she never fully recovered. On 7 April 1812, as she neared her 46th birthday, Staël secretly gave birth to a retarded child, Louis-Alphonse, whom she and Rocca nicknamed "Petit Nous" and spirited away to be raised by a country pastor. They did not see him again until 1814. None of her other children, residing at Coppet at the time, were aware of the birth.

Less than seven weeks later, on 23 May,[41] Staël set out in an open carriage (much as the Neckers had done in 1789), ostensibly for an afternoon drive, but in reality for London (via Austria, Russia, and Sweden). By the time Napoleon's spies discovered her escape, she was out of reach. Passing through Zurich, Saint-Gall, Tyrolia, and Salzburg (where Albert and Rocca caught up with her), Staël arrived in Vienna on 6 June. Austrian police hastened her journey through Galicia (24 police reports document her progress between 21 June and 10 July). She crossed the Russian border on 14 July.

Because of the simultaneous advance of Napoleon's Grand Army, Staël and her party had to detour by way of Kiev, Moscow, and Novgorod to reach Saint Petersburg. There, she met twice with Czar Alexander, who recognized her potential influence on comte Bernadotte, a man they both hoped would head a liberal monarchy in France. Letters to Thomas Jefferson, the Duke of Wellington, Bernadotte, and General

Victor Moreau attest to Staël's attempts to help defeat Napoleon and place Bernadotte on the French throne. An epigram circulating at the time referred to the three great European powers as "Russia, England, and Mme de Staël" (d'Eaubonne, 224).

When Staël reached Stockholm on 24 August 1812, Bernadotte greeted her like an old friend, gave Albert a commission with his hussars, engaged Schlegel as his secretary, and promised to take Auguste on as his aide-de-camp. In June 1813 she moved on to London, where John Murray paid the unheard-of sum of 1,500 guineas to publish *Allemagne* that October. Lionized by the court and by English society, Staël found Byron "the most captivating man in England." He in turn wrote of her in his journal: "I do not like her political ideas. . . . But she is an extraordinary woman, who has accomplished more intellectually than all the rest put together; she should have been a man" (Solovieff, 465).

Staël received a severe blow in July 1813 when her son Albert—always hotheaded and fractious—was killed by a Cossack officer in a duel over a gaming quarrel. After a 12-year absence, she returned to Paris on 12 May 1814 and reopened her salon to such eminent figures as Czar Alexander, Charles Augustus of Saxe-Weimar, Friedrich Gentz, the Duke of Wellington, Talleyrand, Fouché, and La Fayette. Once Bernadotte's candidacy for the French throne was out of the question, Staël rallied to the Bourbon cause. Her major preoccupations were Rocca's failing health and marriage prospects for Albertine, who had grown into a freckle-faced beauty. Staël spent the summer entertaining guests at Coppet, conceiving a poem about Richard the Lion-Hearted (for which she made plans to visit the Orient that never came to fruition), and writing *Considérations sur les principaux événements de la Révolution française* (Considerations on the principal events of the French Revolution, 1818), which would not appear in her lifetime. In mid-September she was back on the rue de Grenelle in Paris.

Hope of recovering Necker's fortune under Louis XVIII enabled Staël to announce Albertine's engagement to duc Victor de Broglie[42] on 2 February 1815. These plans were vitiated when news reached Paris of Napoleon's escape from Elba and disembarkment on French soil on 1 March. Victor de Broglie noted his future mother-in-law's reaction: "She saw at once what that meant. . . . The army in complete revolt, the country submissive, royalty abolished, the Emperor in the Tuileries. . . . She made her own plans with equal speed" (Blennerhassett, 3:530). On 10 March Staël and her family left for Switzerland; ten days later, Napoleon was in the Tuileries.

During the Hundred Days, Constant proved to be a self-serving opportunist. On 19 March he published a violent article against Napoleon, but within the month he had so changed his stripes that Napoleon appointed him to the Council of State on 19 April and had him help draft a new constitution (dubbed *la Benjamine*). Constant eluded Staël's repeated entreaties to repay the substantial sum he owed her so that she might marry off Albertine. In spite of the mother's renewed antagonism, Constant's relationship with his daughter remained smoothly affectionate (although no hint has come down that Albertine ever acknowledged him as her father).[43] After obtaining the pope's dispensation, Albertine married Victor de Broglie in Pisa on 20 February 1816 in a dual Catholic-Protestant ceremony. Staël's sole remaining wish, as she had written on 14 January, was to see Auguste married to a nice English girl with whom he could eventually preside over Coppet "in her father's name" (Solovieff, 516).

Staël spent her "farewell" summer at Coppet entertaining many English visitors, among them Lord Byron, who occasionally rowed across the lake from the Villa Diodati, where he was staying. As if aware her time was short, she worked feverishly on *Considérations* and *Dix années*, which her children published posthumously. On 10 October 1816, Staël legitimized Alphonse and her relationship with Rocca in a secret marriage witnessed only by Fanny Randall and Jean's brother Charles.

Back in Paris, Staël suffered a cerebral hemorrhage on 21 February 1817 while leaving a party given by Interior Minister Decazes. On 1 March Albertine gave birth to a daughter. Receptions continued at the rue Royale, with Albertine playing hostess, while chosen guests conversed with Staël in her bedroom. She told Chateaubriand (to whom she introduced Juliette Récamier, the autumnal love of his life): "I have always been the same, lively and sad; I have loved God, my father, and liberty" ("Notice," ccclxiii). Sometime later, she was transported to Sophie Gay's house on the rue Neuve-des-Mathurins, where she could be wheeled into the garden. (Her hostess named her daughter Delphine in Staël's honor.) Although semiparalyzed, Staël maintained a lively correspondence via Albertine and Fanny Randall. Her last letter (to Mary Berry, on 26 June) was a mixture of discouragement and faith as she wrote of suffering from severe cramps, losing the use of her hands and feet, and having to lie on her back for 90 days, like a turtle, "but with far more agitation of the mind and suffering of the imagination than that animal" (Solovieff, 534).[44]

Gangrene set in on 13 July. During the night of 14 July, after requesting an extra dose of opium, Germaine Necker de Staël-Holstein died peacefully in her sleep. Victor de Broglie and Benjamin Constant (whom Biondetta had refused to see) watched over her body. She was interred on 28 July in the family crypt at Coppet, which was then sealed forever. On the tomb could be seen a bas-relief that Staël had ordered from Friedrich Tieck in July 1808, depicting her mother leading her father by the hand to heaven, while he gazes fondly on a kneeling, veiled figure—herself.

Jean Rocca would outlive his wife by six months. Louis-Alphonse, always sickly, would be raised by his stepsister Albertine, marry a granddaughter of Louis de Narbonne, and die childless before he reached 30. After lecturing fervently for the abolition of slavery, Auguste was to die in 1827; his only son would survive him briefly. It was through Albertine that Germaine de Staël's and Benjamin Constant's spiritual heritage would be transmitted. A pious mother of five, she died the same year as Petit Nous, at the age of 41. She and her brother Auguste were scrupulous in respecting their mother's memory. Taking pains to erase all traces of her private life, they embarked on a campaign to amass—and burn—all her private correspondence.[45] Posterity has thus lost all Staël's letters to Benjamin Constant, Juliette Récamier, and Prosper de Barante, as well as correspondence she had saved from Narbonne, Ribbing, and Constant.[46]

Staël's first biographer was her favorite cousin, Albertine Necker de Saussure. The latter's "Notice" prefacing the first (and only) complete edition of Staël's works, published in 1820 by Auguste de Staël, is a loving, selective, and bowdlerized account of the writer's life, work, and character. The Staël archives, housed in the château at Coppet, were eventually made public (in partial installments) by her descendants, some of whom concentrated on perpetuating her legacy: in particular, comte Othenin d'Haussonville (Albertine's grandson); comtesse Jean de Pange (née Pauline de Broglie, Albertine's granddaughter), who founded the Société des Etudes Staëliennes in 1924; the latter's son, Victor de Pange; Robert de Luppé, a direct descendant of Albertine; and comtesse Elisabeth Le Marois (a d'Haussonville) and her daughter, comtesse Béatrix d'Andlau.[47] The groundwork of Staëlian scholarship was laid and has been continued by her progeny.

Chapter 2

Apprenticeship

From early youth, Germaine Necker was either listening open-mouthed to the literary and political conversations that swirled around her or penning the "follies" (tales where the heroine goes mad with love), portraits, and encomiums then in vogue. The moral lessons implicit in her first writings, the conscious elaboration of maxims and rules of conduct, were a natural heritage of the Enlightenment and of her mother's stern orthodoxy. Staël's revolt lay in the very act of writing—a deliberate challenge to the paternal interdiction that had forced Mme Necker to abandon her book on François de la Mothe-Fénelon.

At the same time, while contravening his wishes, her lifework was an unceasing attempt to vindicate her father. Beginning with the *Journal de jeunesse*, few of her works lack his imprint.[1] These diary entries (16 June–17 August 1785) are self-conscious meditations on religion, death, nature, and the writer's impending marriage, bathed in near-incestuous adulation of her more-than-perfect father: "He would like me to love him like a lover, and yet he speaks to me like a father; I would like him to long for me like a lover, and yet I behave like a daughter. . . . Of all the men in the world, he is the one I would have wanted for a lover." She envisions the kind of woman who might have compensated her father for sacrificing ambition and talent. "Find repose on my bosom, glory in my admiration, and happiness in my passion. . . . All man's faculties are fulfilled when he loves" (*Jeunesse*, 2:159). The dream of being loved so completely that a man surrenders all other interests to immerse himself entirely in her is a wish patently impossible of fulfillment. And yet, this is the utopia that Staël would vainly seek in her various love affairs and would erect as an unachievable ideal for the doomed heroines of her fiction. The corollary—happiness through married love—is the other side of this coveted, if counterfeit, coin.

While deploring her father's denigration of women writers, she is ready (temporarily) to echo his patriarchal injunction that "women are not meant to pursue the same career as men, to compete and provoke jealousy far different from that which love inspires." She pays lip service to the conventional idea that love is the be-all and end-all of a woman's life (but does she not prescribe the same ideal for her father?):

No, our happiness is loving, our glory is to admire the man whom fate or choice has destined for us; cursed are we when we upset the order of nature! If she endowed us with talents superior to those of our sex, how sweet it would be to reveal them only to the man we love, to be able to say, I could have sparkled on the world's stage. . . but you are my sole interest on earth . . . and paeans of praise do not equal a gaze that says: "I find you worthy of being loved by me." (*Jeunesse*, 3:236)

This false humility is consonant with the role expected of eighteenth-century woman, who had no claims to property in her own name, no rights of citizenship, no recourse to divorce, and often no say in choosing a husband or bringing up children. Her enforced dependency on a man—father, husband, brother—meant that the only way she could shape her future was by gaining ascendancy through love. But love enslaves woman even more than man. This is the catch-22 that Staël's fictional heroines have to face. From Mirza to Corinne, they exhibit a willingness to sacrifice talent (as Suzanne Necker did) for love.

In the last entry of the *Journal de jeunesse*, Staël baldly hypothesizes that if her father were recalled to govern France, and her mother by some misfortune should be no more . . . his daughter would devote her life to making him happy (*Jeunesse*, 3:242). With one stroke of the pen, she has erased and replaced Mme Necker. This unresolved mother-daughter conflict finds expression in Staël's first play, *Sophie, ou les Sentiments secrets* (Sophie, or Secret feelings, 1786). Written in the rhymed alexandrine couplets of seventeenth-century tradition, this piece is of interest primarily for its autobiographical implications and its indications of a Rousseauesque sentimentality the author was never completely to abandon.

The guileless Sophie Mortimer has spurned Lord Henry Bedford because she is unwittingly in love with her tutor, comte de Sainville. (It takes the countess to reveal the girl's true feelings to herself.) The count's "secret feelings" for his ward come to light when Sophie finds a flower-garlanded bust of herself in a pavilion he has forbidden her to enter. The countess blames her own chilly exterior for creating the false impression that she is indifferent (a foreshadowing of Matilde in *Delphine* and Lucile in *Corinne*) and offers to put herself conveniently out of the way so that her husband and Sophie may be happy together. But Sophie has already left dejectedly for England, where she receives the count's message that duty and reason must conquer passion. In this doomed triangle, it is not difficult to recognize the impassioned daughter, who imagines that her father returns her love in kind, and the cold-hearted mother, who gets to keep him in the end. No other denouement is possible than that he remain dutifully with the "other woman" while the heroine, rejecting all men (in particular, William Pitt), has no recourse but to pine away. The author, of course, did no such thing. Following the cathartic expression of her own "secret feelings," she accepted marriage with a man she did not love and found other outlets for her intrepid imagination.

The heroine of Staël's historical verse-play *Jane Gray* (1787) is of the same age, sensitivity, and literary predilections as the author. Contrary to the record, Staël's Jane Gray is deliriously happy with her husband, Guilfort Northumberland. Political, religious, and historical considerations are all secondary to this depiction of love-in-marriage. To prevent Jane Gray from assuming the crown, Mary has sent an army against her under General Pembroke, Jane's jilted suitor. When the latter discovers that Jane has no wish to reign, his repressed love bursts forth, and he arranges to spirit her out of prison. After persuading him to save her husband in her place—by delivering the false news that she has escaped to France—Jane faces death with equanimity and the exhilaration of self-sacrifice for love. At the end, having discovered her ruse, Guilfort joins her on the scaffold. Jane is content to die at the height of love, before old age has dimmed their passion—an idea Staël will repeat in *Delphine*. "Epître au malheur, ou Adèle et Edouard" ("Epistle to sorrow, or Adele and Edward," 1795) also depicts a pair of star-crossed lovers dying together—this time, under the guillotine. Again, it is the woman who deliberately courts death for the man she loves.

Staël wrote three unpublished historical tragedies during the same period (1789–90): *Rosamonde*, revolving around Henri II and Eleanor of Aquitaine; *Montmorency*, situated under Louis XIII, probably influenced by the hero's stated resemblance to her father[2]; and *Thamar*, which takes place in a fictional Persia resembling the France of 1789, with a wise minister (like Necker) to counsel the king. Before she was 20, she had already composed three short stories—*Mirza*, *Adélaïde et Théodore*, and *Histoire de Pauline*—which were not published until 1795. Staël attached scant importance to these "fluffy productions" ("Notice," liv), which are suffused with the same doleful sensibility as *Sophie*. Experiments in fiction writing, attempts to contest certain social strictures, and disguised autobiography, these brief pieces lay the groundwork for the author's later full-scale novels.

Subtitled *Letter from a (Male) Traveler, Mirza*[3] subscribes to the eighteenth-century story-within-a-story convention, intended to guarantee authenticity. The initial narrator tells of visiting a Negro plantation in Senegal—a government experiment to suppress slavery by encouraging native agriculture. This naive resolution of the slave trade reflects Staël's lifelong abolitionist stand. The African hero Ximéo, a strikingly handsome native with "none of the defects of men of his color" (*OC*, 2:223), a perfect knowledge of French, and a disconsolate attitude, is really a preromantic Frenchman in blackface, who recounts the following (improbable) story to his visitor.

While affianced to his cousin Ourika (now his wife), he became infatuated with Mirza, a woman he heard singing in the mountains about her love of liberty. (Educated in French language and philosophy, this embryonic Corinne is a perfect partner for the Europeanized hero.) They fall in love and live together happily until Ximéo is called away to war. On his return, his family pressures him to marry Ourika. Mirza is brokenhearted. Wounded in battle, Ximéo is about to be sold into slavery when Mirza offers herself in his place (in a variation of the Jane Gray—Adèle sacrifices for love). The deeply affected governor frees them both. Mirza refuses Ximéo's renewed love as too little, too late. "Passionate souls only recognize extremes," she tells him (*OC*, 2:242), as she pierces her heart with an arrow. Ximéo lives on in perpetual sorrow. The punishment for male infidelity is everlasting repentance.

This early fictional piece has no proper plot, character development, or suspense. Its stick figures play out a sentimentalized version of the lovesick heroine who—like Delphine, Sappho, and Corinne—is superior in all respects to the man who deserts her and yet without whom she cannot live. Set in the kind of exotic locale made fashionable by Montesquieu, Voltaire, and Bernardin de Saint-Pierre, the story makes a brief for human dignity, regardless of race (but with a French tinge).

Adélaïde et Théodore (Adelaide and Theodore) perpetuates the theme of suicide for love. Orphaned at a young age, Adélaïde[4] is a composite of the modest propriety inculcated by her aunt, Mme d'Orfeuil, and the hedonism of her profligate uncle, baron d'Orville,[5] who marries her off at 15 to an elderly husband. After the latter fortuitously dies, Adélaïde takes refuge with her aunt in the country, where she meets and falls in love with the proud but sensitive comte Théodore de Rostain. (It is precisely his hypsersensitivity—like that of Léonce in *Delphine* and Oswald in *Corinne*—that will prove the heroine's undoing.) When he is sure of Adélaïde's affection, Théodore warns her that he will die if she ever loves him a shade less. They marry in secret, against his mother's wishes, and briefly savor the kind of wedded bliss their creator had dreamed of for herself. But their joy is short-lived, sapped by social demands and Théodore's intransigent jealousy. Having returned to Paris at her uncle's request,[6] Adélaïde enjoys the attention accorded an attractive, eligible young widow. As Théodore sulks in silence, the rift between them widens. To help a friend, Adélaïde invites the woman's lover to her house. In his willful misapprehension (like Léonce in *Delphine*), Théodore believes that Adélaïde loves this man. Without a word, he leaves to join his regiment before she has a chance to tell him she is pregnant.

Back in the country, Adélaïde learns from her aunt of Théodore's suicidal intentions. Her distress convinces Mme d'Orfeuil that her love is "worthy" of Théodore's—an idea Staël stresses (*OC*, 2:274). Discovering that her husband is at his mother's home, ill, Adélaïde hides on the Rostain grounds to see him (a spying scene repeated in *Delphine* and *Corinne* but as old as *La Princesse de Clèves*). Théodore is so changed that she cries out and faints, giving herself away. He collapses in turn when Adélaïde tells him she is carrying his child. On his deathbed, Théodore confesses that he wronged her by disbelieving her love. Adélaïde lays him to rest in the grove where they first met, waits until her child is born, and then takes opium and dies. The two older women, joined in contrition, bring up the child, "fruit . . . of love and sorrow" (287).

These two mother symbols of reprobation—incarnations of Mme Necker—will be further fleshed out in the chorus of disapproving women that people *Delphine* and *Corinne*. They get their comeuppance, as does the imperfect hero. Again, a virtuous and loving woman is destroyed by a man's jealous sensitivity. Théodore is too weak, stubborn, and self-centered to air his imagined grievances. The illness and death he brings on himself are fitting chastisements for his failings. Adélaïde's flightiness results from an upbringing beyond her control. Despite her enjoyment of social pleasures—a transgression for which she is made to pay in unjust measure—it is she, not Théodore, who keeps their promise to live for each other. He dies because he has failed to keep faith. She dies because she cannot live without him.

Histoire de Pauline (Story of Pauline) is the most interesting and ambitious of these three novellas. Again, perfect love is marred by (male) misunderstanding, and a joyful marriage sours through miscommunication. This time, the hand of fate is manipulated by a dissolute villain, who

causes the heroine's ruination. As in *Mirza*, the tale is set in a slave country (Santo Domingo) against whose "barbaric trade and profit" Staël
inveighs (*OC*, 2:291). Another young orphan, Pauline de Gercourt,[7] was
married at 12 or 13[8] to a rich and greedy slave merchant. Her husband's
depraved friend, M. de Meltin, having failed to seduce her himself, introduces her to his cousin (another Théodore), who enraptures Pauline. Her
capitulation soon follows, after which Meltin persuades Théodore to
decamp. Society women shun Pauline (as they will Delphine). Alone and
unprotected, she is an easy prey for Meltin's wiles. But when her husband's drowning makes her a rich widow, the villain changes his proposition to a proposal of marriage. A providential circumstance saves the
heroine from perdition. Mme de Verseuil, who once loved Pauline's
father and who nursed Théodore when he fell ill in Le Havre, comes to
rescue the young woman after Théodore dies (stricken by the same fate
as his faithless fictional predecessors). They leave secretly for France,
where Mme de Verseuil gradually inculcates in her young charge an austere morality.

Four years pass. Secluded in the country, Pauline has developed her
mind and grown in beauty. One day, in Le Havre, she attends a martial
demonstration at which comte Edouard de Cerney, colonel of dragoons,
is thrown and trampled as he rides to the rescue of one of his men. The
hero is carried to Mme de Verseuil's house to recover. As she ministers to
Edouard, Pauline's reluctant affection grows. For him, she incarnates an
(impossible) ideal of womanly virtue. Since Mme de Verseuil's dearest
wish is to see the couple married, she tries to dispel Pauline's sense of
unworthiness; she also recounts a modified version of Edouard's statement that he could never be happy with a woman "whose memories are
impure" (*OC*, 2:322). At Mme de Verseuil's instigation, Pauline promises
to conceal her past but feels she must stop seeing Edouard. When he
threatens to throw himself into the sea, she agrees to be his wife. They
are married the next day.

Mme de Verseuil tears up several letters in which Pauline avows her
secret to Edouard. Tormented by scruples, the young wife is not happy
until she bears a son, to Edouard's delight. Staël inserts a paean to
maternity as the blessing of a happy union: "When Providence adds to
this dear bond the full prestige of love, when the child one would cherish as one's own is also the image of the person one loves . . . what
greater happiness can there be?" (*OC*, 2:333). But the past cannot be
suppressed. One evening Edouard returns home livid with rage: he has
challenged to a duel a vile calumniator named Meltin, who was heard to

jest about the promiscuous Pauline de Gercourt. Admitting that the accusations are true, Pauline rejects Edouard's embrace, for she is no longer "worthy" of him (a repeated threnody). After Edouard kills Meltin, she is overcome with remorse. Future happiness is impossible, for she has lost her husband's trust. She turns delirious with grief, then bids Edouard farewell. Abjuring his previous notions, he conjures her to live (in a delicious moment of feminine vindication): "I protest at your feet that Pauline is as perfect and sublime in my eyes as in the happy days we once knew. Time and love have purified your soul; live in order to raise your child; live in order to be adored by the unfortunate man who alone is guilty" (343). Content to know that her image will remain engraved in his heart, Pauline dies. Mme de Verseuil soon follows her to the grave, while Edouard, "devoured by regret" (344), withdraws from society to raise their child. Although the heroine must die, Staël wreaks her revenge on the inadequate lover-husband, whom she destines—like Oswald—to a life of grief and guilt.

In this story of ill-fated love, happiness is once more aborted by a man's stubborn injustice. The heroine is again a beautiful and accomplished young woman, with a single blot on her history, for which her youth, deficient upbringing, and a villain's perfidy are to blame. Meltin represents a devil-figure who lures Pauline to damnation and later destroys her marriage. (Justice prevails, and he is killed in the duel he provokes.) Théodore is Meltin's willing disciple—an irresponsible hedonist who treats women lightly, first enjoying and then abandoning them. He also dies (unaccountably), smitten by remorse. Mme de Verseuil plays a dual part. As a mother-figure (a role reinforced by her former love for Pauline's father), she saves the young woman from Meltin, educates her intellectually and spiritually, and finds her a suitable husband. But she is also the serpent in Eden, responsible for the deception underlying Pauline's marriage; her contrition (Staël tells us) sends her to an early grave. The only major character who survives death is Edouard. A worse fate awaits him. Because he is a narrow-minded perfectionist who clings stubbornly to preconceived principles, fails to recognize the merit of the woman who loves him, and is incapable (like Adélaïde's Théodore) of true communication, he is doomed to a life of misery and repentance. If a blissful marriage between two like-minded lovers is impossible, the fault, as Staël demonstrates, lies with the man.

Staël includes in *Pauline* a feminist outcry against the double standard governing men's and women's conduct—an idea she was to express theoretically in *De l'influence des passions* (*OC*, 3:135) and to illustrate in

Delphine and *Corinne*. Society condones in a man behavior it condemns in a woman: Meltin "was considered a gentleman, because he was only cruel and perfidious toward women" (*OC*, 2:297). Repeatedly, Staël calls for equal treatment of and by both sexes. She is more empathetic and forgiving toward her female than her male characters. Her heroines are stronger, more generous and courageous, than their lily-livered lovers. In spite of the exaggerated sentimentality of these stories, she paints women's social situation as it was. In the light of contemporary mores, a woman had to be better, more virtuous, than a man. And, in Staël's universe, she is.

Zulma (1794) was originally intended as a chapter of *Passions*. The first-person narrator is a white man taken prisoner on the banks of the Orinoco (another exotic setting). The conceit of a Frenchman exposed to foreign customs, with the implicit contrast to European attitudes and mores, had been used to advantage by Montesquieu and Voltaire, among others. (It is also a means for a woman writer to masquerade as a man.) The form is again a story within a story. The nameless narrator has struck up a friendship with a tribal elder, who is to serve as the judge of a crime so heinous that it cannot be pardoned. The old man has misgivings about sending someone to death: "How will my broken heart know whether it is abusing man's right over his fellow man and arrogating divine vengeance unto itself?" By implication, this "savage" is more humane than the perpetrators of the French Reign of Terror; so are his tribal customs, which require judges to ponder the death sentence in solitary appeal to their "eternal conscience" (*OC*, 2:350).

The accused murderer turns out to be a beautiful young woman, Zulma. First apologizing to the grief-stricken mother, she admits to killing the handsome victim, Fernand, but swears before God she is not guilty. Her tale begins with a panegyric of the deceased. Taken prisoner as a child by a Spanish general, he learned martial arts[9] but, chafing under European laws, he returned to his people and became their leader. Fernand taught Zulma everything he knew, developing her mind and her oratorical talent. (In a twist of the Pygmalion story, Galatea is not merely a passive instrument of pleasure but turns against her "creator" when he proves untrue to his creation.) Zulma exacted one promise: that he kill her before ever abandoning her. Devoting herself to his service, she performed "innumerable acts that . . . would [have] formed a sacred bond between two friends, two brothers-in-arms" (*OC*, 2:360). Love and friendship are equated in Staël's mind with acts of generosity and selflessness; she also yearns for the same reciprocity of feeling between man and woman as between military comrades. Zulma saved Fernand's mother from drowning, rescued him from a death sentence, nurtured him for a year in the desert, and when he was reported missing in action, found him lying wounded by a fatal poison amid the carnage of combat; by sucking out the venom, she saved his life at the peril of her own.

After he recovered, Fernand was absent for several days without arousing Zulma's suspicions because, like her creator, she believed in the enchaining power of love: "It seemed to me that . . . a man so passionately loved could not feel himself free" (*OC*, 2:367–38). When Fernand failed to return as promised, Zulma combed the forest and found him at young Mirza's feet.[10] Without thinking, she drew an arrow and killed him. No one, she says, has a greater right to avenge Fernand than she. Her love is beyond the power of any human tribunal: "It is the truth, the flame, the pure element, the primal idea of the moral world" (369). As a murmur arises in Zulma's favor, the judges pardon her. Rather than permit the people to crown her, she pierces her heart with an arrow (like Mirza) and expires on her lover's body, saying: "Did you think . . . I would let Fernand's assassin live? Could I have existed without him, his infidelity would have been justifiable" (371).

Once again, a woman of superior constancy, courage, and love is betrayed by a man who, though outwardly brave, is essentially weak and unfaithful. Again, the man dies in expiation. Staël stresses the power of passion, which makes it impossible for a woman who loves truly and deeply to survive her beloved. By delineating Zulma's acts of devotion— she saves Fernand's life not once but three times—Staël emphasizes her generosity and his unworthiness. Zulma is a learned and eloquent pre-Corinne (who yet refuses a crown); her name recalls Guibert's hyperbolic description of Staël as Zulmé. As the author's alter ego, she epitomizes the exclusivity of love, moves an audience with her oratory, and performs the ultimate self-sacrifice (merely threatened by Staël) as an act of moral superiority to the man she loves. Although the unhappy outcome of all these novellas attests to the author's pessimistic view—not of love, but of men's inadequate response—*Zulma* is more than any other piece a foreshadowing of *Corinne*.

During her first pregnancy (1786–87), Staël read *Emile* (1762), *Du contrat social* (The Social contract, 1762), and *Lettres écrites de la montagne* (Letters written from the mountain, 1764) in preparation for her first important work, *Lettres sur les écrits et le caractère de J. J. Rousseau* (Letters on the works and character of J. J. Rousseau, 1788). Although it appeared anonymously, the social elite knew the author's identity. The work met with immediate popularity. A second edition came out in 1789, as did an English translation. In addition to voicing her personal reactions (her subjectivity would color all her writings), Staël evaluates Rousseau as a person and a writer, while touching on fertile fields for subsequent discussion: the nature of fiction, the bases for good government, woman's role in society, education, music, nature, suicide, and morality. As Sainte-Beuve puts it: "All Mme de Staël's future writings in various genres, fiction, morality, politics, are prefigured in this rapid and harmonious praise of Rousseau's works, much as the entire concept of a great musical opus is contained in its overture" (Bersaucourt, 108). Staël's piece is essentially a hymn to Jacques Necker.

Anticipating the reproach that she lacked the maturity to treat her subject, Staël contends in her preface of 1788 that youth is the best time to appreciate Rousseau, who wrote with the enthusiasm of the young. She asserts in a much later preface (1814) that, although *Rousseau* was published against her will,[11] this happenstance sparked her literary career.[12] But she has no regrets, for mental stimulation has rerouted the course of her life from the usual "decline" that is "woman's destiny" (*OC*, 1:5). In opposition to Rousseau, this second preface makes a brief for the education of women. Reasoning that cultured women make better wives, Staël asserts that "marriage cannot attain its ultimate fulfillment unless it is founded on reciprocal admiration" (8). This statement—reiterating a form of equality endorsed in *Littérature* and *Allemagne*—strikes a revolutionary note in an era when many men still treated their wives like chattel. Nonetheless, Staël refrains from pushing her arguments beyond tolerable acceptability. While advocating intellectual accomplishments for women, she voices the hope that education will not inspire them to be writers, "to divert them from their natural duties so that they enter into rivalry with men, whom they are meant merely to encourage and console" (9). Although Staël was a well-established writer by this time, the words she wrote in 1814 curiously echo her *Journal de jeunesse* of almost 30 years before. The hostility she has incurred by competing on masculine turf is not a fate she recommends unreservedly to her sisters.[13]

She frames her discussion of Rousseau's life and works in six letters. The first deals with his two *Discours* (1750, 1755), the second with *La Nouvelle Héloïse* (1761), the third with *Emile*, the fourth with his political writings, the fifth with his taste in music and botany, and the last with his character. Staël's emphases reflect her own predilections even more than they describe her subject.

When Rousseau began writing at age 40, the first question he tackled was the utility of the arts and sciences. Staël disagrees with his linking art with science and his contention that scientific progress caused the decline of empires (an idea she will contradict in *Passions*). A latent regret for primitive life, translated into an abhorrence of social institutions, permeates Rousseau's second discourse, *Discours sur l'origine et les fondements de l'inégalité parmi les hommes*, on the bases of human inequality. Staël admires his finesse in tracing the progress of ideas, his intellectual imagination, hatred of vice, and love of virtue (all characteristics she shared). Rousseau's writing is inflamed by passion: "When his soul is affected, his writings contain . . . a natural harmony, an emotional accent, a melody precisely attuned to the words he expresses" (*OC*, 1:18). Staël seems to be defining her own emotional rhetoric.

While claiming to admire the persuasive logic of the *Lettre à d'Alembert sur les spectacles* (Letter to d'Alembert on spectacles, 1758)—a puritanical condemnation of plays and actors—she takes issue with Rousseau for denying women a role in public affairs. She also denounces the idea that women are incapable of depicting passion with verve and accuracy. To the contrary, women express feelings with greater sincerity than men, "and the sublime sacrifice, the rueful sorrow, the all-powerful sentiments by which they live and die, may affect readers more deeply than raptures born of exaggerated poetic fancies" (23).

Staël does not conceal her admiration for *La Nouvelle Héloïse*, the pivotal novel of its day. She divides fiction into three categories (which she will expand on and alter in her *Essai sur les fictions* [1795]): a novel can depict contemporary mores, recount gripping events, or bring a moral precept to life. *Héloïse* is in the last category, since its purpose is to encourage women culpable of Julie's "fault" to repent through her commendable example. The moral aim of literature is a repeated theme for Staël. In this work, Rousseau portrays a woman married against her wishes who, though carrying within her heart the memory and love of another man, finds contentment in performing her duty. To excuse Julie for consenting to a loveless union, Staël underscores the difficulty of resisting a father's wishes.

She faces a dilemma in discussing *Emile*. On the one hand, Staël appreciates Rousseau's disregard of conventional education in favor of cultivating individual aptitudes (a method she would apply to her own offspring). She agrees with him that women should tend their infants themselves and not hand them over to servants. Her difficulty lies with Rousseau's plan for Sophie, whose inferior education Staël finds degrading to women.[14] In sharp contradistinction to the tenor of the times, she urges that both sexes be educated on an equivalent level:[15] "If women, overcoming their destiny, dared lay claim to the same education as men; if they were able to say what men must do, if they had the same awareness of their actions, what a noble fate would await them!" (*OC*, 1:47). Again, Staël suggests that women would make better wives (the ultimate criterion) if they could freely choose the man with whom they were expected to spend their future and share their body: "[Women] need great spiritual strength, for their feelings conflict with their fate in a country . . . where—more to be pitied than those pious girls who consecrate themselves to God—they must grant all the rights of love and forbid themselves all the pleasures of loving" (57). As often as she can, Staël nibbles away at the foundations of patriarchal dominion.

Her fourth letter praises the *Contrat social* for expressing certain inalienable political ideals: the general good cannot be subordinated to private interest; a nation cannot obey laws contrary to its well-being; no government can be instituted or maintained without the consent of the people. Nonetheless, above Rousseau's speculative ideas she places the practical wisdom of a statesman "who is less an artist tracing the blueprint of a proper edifice than a man skilled at repairing one already constructed" (*OC*, 1:69). Jacques Necker's experience sets him notches above the unseasoned theorist. By the same token, Rousseau's "Profession de foi du vicaire savoyard" (Creed of a priest of Savoy) in *Emile* is merely the precursor to Necker's epoch-making *De l'importance des opinions religieuses* (The Importance of religious opinions, 1788).

A brief letter on Rousseau's taste in music and botany alludes to his writings on music, his talent for composing simple, evocative melodies, and his predilection for "melodramas," in which music supplements words. Staël expresses the similar conviction that music stirs the soul, awakens memory, and expresses the heart's deepest feelings. Throughout her work, especially in *Corinne* and *Allemagne*, music plays a key role in affecting mood and ennobling character.

She relies on Rousseau's *Confessions* (1781, 1788) to depict his appearance and character, in letter 6. She excuses him for abandoning his children on the grounds that an abominable wife made his life miserable. To allegations that he was a hypocrite, Staël retorts that "exaltation is the delirium of genius" (*OC*, 1:86)—a preromantic notion. She finds

Rousseau eloquent, enthusiastic, and sincere, if at times exaggerated (her own failings). Her explanation for his death (which she ascribes to suicide) is simple: he died because he did not feel loved. Having shed tears on his tomb, Staël deems it imperative that some other person of genius (herself?) pay homage to Rousseau. In a vision worthy of Baudelaire, she imagines a lineage of superior men (and women?) defending their predecessors and setting an example for their successors: "The monument they erect will some day serve as the pedestal of their own statue" (104).

Staël possesses a conscious affinity of temperament with Rousseau—sensibility, enthusiasm, eloquence, a visceral reaction to music, a penchant toward melancholia, and, yes, genius. These characteristics will later be identified with the romantic protagonist. She shares his belief in the superiority of natural instinct over a civilized veneer; because human beings are intrinsically good, emotion is an infallible guide. This cult of feeling nurtures her basic optimism about the indefinite perfectibility of the human species, on which she will expatiate in *Littérature*.

According to Georges Poulet, Staël was the first French critic to adopt a new approach that presupposes the reader's attempt to internalize the thoughts and experiences of the writer. Her critical method—initiated here and infiltrating her other works—is "none other than the participation of the critic's genius in the genial essence of the other."[16] Although Poulet calls the critical aspect of *Rousseau* an act of admiration composed of knowledge bolstered by emotion, Staël is far from being reverentially in accord with Rousseau, as we have shown. What makes her venture unique is her very temerity—as a young woman—in standing up to and challenging the master, particularly in the domain of women.

In 1790 Staël penned a tribute to an old friend who had died in May. *Eloge de M. de Guibert* (In Praise of Guibert) is more a political manifesto than a eulogy. After distilling the essence of the subject's life, Staël praises his early treatise on military tactics, which predicted the present revolution with extraordinary prescience. While admiring his courage in calling for a permanent national assembly, a citizens' militia, and a peace-abiding government, she concurs with Guibert's insistence on maintaining a standing army, enforcing discipline, and upholding military morale. She also lauds his unpublished tragedies and proposed constitutional project. Although Staël claims she wrote this encomium to shield Guibert's memory from hatred and misunderstanding, her underlying purpose seems rather to atone for the injustice meted out to Necker, praise of whom is inserted in the text at every opportune moment.

Her next, fragmentary piece—an anonymous pamphlet, dated 10 May 1791, entitled "Simple extrait du livre de M. Necker sur son administration" (Simple extract of Monsieur Necker's book on his administration)—is a frank panegyric of her father's written apology for his ministry. Although destined for publication in Adrien Duquesnoy's newspaper *L'Ami des patriotes* (The Patriots' friend), Staël's piece never appeared in print. It consists of selected passages from Necker's apology for his administration, linked by comments extolling the book's qualities and goals.[17] Posing as a male writer pained by the ingratitude shown Necker, the author proclaims: "I know of no one who possesses as many virtues as M. Necker; I esteem him with all my soul and have no doubt that if this is the expressed opinion of a few, it is the conviction of all" ("Ouvrage inconnu," 27).

Necker's contributions to the Revolution are enumerated: (1) convening the Estates General; (2) doubling the Third Estate; (3) staving off bankruptcy; (4) preserving France from famine; (5) saving the country from civil war by preventing the king's departure in October; and (6) persuading the king to swear allegiance to the constitution. In spite of the "atrocious indifference" with which these services were met, the author cites passages of Necker's book that show "with what a gentle but proud spirit this man of angelic disposition requites the offenses he received" ("Ouvrage inconnu," 27). Emphasizing the incorruptible morality and honor underlying his actions, the writer admires Necker's courage in defending a policy of moderation and prudence. "He" regrets not being able to quote Necker's book in its entirety: "Ah! I find in this work ideas and sentiments I believe to be the true and unique source of public prosperity; but less courageous than M. Necker, intimidated by the tenor of the times, I am like many weak and honest men, who might discover their strength if only they dared come forward" (42).

In this incomplete work, unknown to the public, Staël attempts to communicate her admiration for, and parry criticism of, Necker's conduct of affairs of state by dwelling on his upright character and achievements. In so doing, she tumbled headlong into the kind of political controversy that it might have been unseemly for a woman to engage in publicly. Her insistence on anonymity (and her final decision not to publish this fragment at all) stemmed less from the timidity she cites in the text as from the realization that championship by his daughter—a blood relative and a woman, to boot—could damage, not enhance, public acceptance of Necker's book.

In her earliest writings, Staël tried her hand at confessional literature, which she soon gave up (perhaps as being too revelatory). She composed poetry (with dismal results), verse-plays, and short stories—genres traditionally practiced by women. It was not until she turned to literary criticism and political manifestos that she found herself on terrain traditionally barred to women. Her next works, theoretical in nature, ambitious in scope, constitute an advance in her thinking and an exploration of new areas by a woman writer.

Chapter 3

A Passion for Politics

The events of the Revolution left Germaine de Staël palpitating to act, to shape the course of history in some oblique way. Despite her experiments with imaginative writing, her preponderant interest was always political.[1] Combining historical analogies, psychological generalities, and moral convictions with impassioned pleas for tolerance, restraint, and generosity, her political works stand in a class by themselves. For convenience, we may divide them into two categories. The first were written in the pressing heat of circumstance, as Staël used a persuasive amalgamation of rational and emotional appeal to influence events or effect needful change. The second type of political work—to be discussed in chapter 9—was a ruminative rethinking of the events in question in order to polish the author's (and her father's) image.

Her first political piece appeared in April 1792 in *Les Indépendants*, a newspaper published by her friends Jean-Baptiste Suard and Jean-Charles de Lacretelle. The title asks the question, "A Quels signes peut-on reconnaître quelle est l'opinion de la majorité de la nation?" (What signs indicate the majority opinion in the nation?). Without offering a definitive answer, Staël suggests that public opinion is irresolute and inconclusive during revolutionary times. Although the majority may favor equality and freedom, they also want the stability that legitimate monarchy alone can guarantee. As she would continue to do, Staël preaches moderation—an intermediate position between aristocrats and Jacobins—favoring liberty combined with limited monarchy. This brief article is a diatribe against both political extremes, especially Jacobin-fostered terror and other obstacles to freedom; it also offers a persuasive argument for an English-style regime.

Staël's second incursion into political writing was an energetic defense of Marie-Antoinette titled *Réflexions sur le procès de la reine, par une femme* (Reflections on the queen's trial, by a woman, September 1793),[2] which appeared almost simultaneously in England, thanks to Talleyrand. Staël's authorship was no secret to anyone.[3] To pen such a petition at the full height of the Terror was an act of almost reckless courage, although the pamphlet is less a legal brief than an emotional plea that prefigures the

basic elements of Staël's stylistic method. Accumulating evidence to but-
tress her arguments, she poses questions to which she provides immediate, indisputable answers. She echoes her adversaries' arguments, only to
refute them with overriding counterarguments. Combining fact and fervor, she tries to convince the mind while entreating the heart. As she
often does, Staël poses as a political neutral whose goal is to unify opposing factions. She calls on republicans, constitutionals, and aristocrats
alike to unite and save the queen, whom she portrays as an innocent and
benevolent sovereign, the target of derisive slander that vilifies women in
general: "Men ignobly deny the respect due the queen through the kind
of calumny that stigmatizes all women" (*OC*, 2:16). While refuting
Marie-Antoinette's intention to reclaim the throne, she warns against
awakening Austrian vengeance by martyring the queen. She confesses
sympathy for her sovereign's misfortune—not out of love for royalty, but
because sorrow for her is a "sacred cult" (29). Guilty or not, the queen
has been punished enough. At the end, having exhausted her eloquence
on judges and adversaries, Staël exhorts the women of France to rally to
their queen and rescue her child. The author's humanitarian appeal is
nonpartisan, predicated on the rights and dignity of womanhood.

Her next two political pieces, also anonymous, represent Staël's first
involvement in foreign policy. The twin *Réflexions sur la paix* hold England
up as the model for a French constitutional monarchy and call on the
nations of Europe to foster international peace. In advance of her return to
Paris, Staël had the first—*Réflexions sur la paix, addressées à M. Pitt et aux
Français* (Reflections on peace, addressed to Mr. Pitt and to the French)—
secretly printed in Switzerland in 1794 and openly in Paris, 1795. Rightly
adjudging England the nexus of the allied coalition, she adjures the bellicose Prime Minister Pitt to desist from war and promote a united peace.
Concurrently, she makes a brief for the constitution of the year 3 (1795),
on which many of her friends were working. As usual, the preface
announces the structure of Staël's argument in advance: the chapters of
the first part will deal with France's present political and military power,
the conduct of the allied forces, and the advantages of peace for Europe;
the second part will consider whether peace is in France's national interest.

Because the French are now the mightiest force in Europe, an allied
coalition is doomed. While allaying European fears that the victorious
French might reinstate a terrorist regime, Staël urges that freedom
be restored to all nations: "A person must . . . advance with his century and
not exhaust himself in a retrograde struggle against the irresistible progress
of enlightenment and reason" (*OC*, 2:52). The concept of progress and

perfectibility is a continuing leitmotiv. Enumerating European errors in
dealing with the French, she blames their misguidance on émigré aristocrats and makes a strong plea for La Fayette's release from imprisonment.[4] She also advances philosophical and pragmatic reasons why
peace is in Europe's best interest and, as is her wont, responds to possible refutations. For example, to appease anxiety over continued French
hostilities, she cites demobilization, domestic interests, depleted
resources, and the unlikely revival of fanaticism as reliable safeguards.
She assures her readers that the French themselves—the dominant moderates, that is—would welcome peace provided the allied powers recognize the republic and guarantee the integrity of French territory.

The second part of Staël's treatise, directed to the French, argues that
peace is to their country's advantage, for "only through peace can the
people's independence be ensured" (OC, 2:79). Against a picture of
phased demobilization, agricultural and commercial prosperity, and the
implementation of a moderate constitution, Staël sketches the centuries-
long disaster that would befall France and Europe should the present
war continue. Venting her hatred of Robespierre, "that colossus from
hell," she pays tribute to her ideological friends, who will furnish France
with "a just, free, and enduring constitution" (86). Peace alone can protect the freedom for which the Revolution was fought.

This brochure highlights Staël's self-appointed mission as a negotiator
between two opposing factions. On a more ambitious level than reconciling royalists and republicans in her salon, she has constituted herself as
a moderator between England and France. Without naming her, Pitt's
adversary Fox cited her recommendations (especially two chapters from
part 1) in a major speech before Parliament on 24 March 1795, in which
he attacked Pitt and the war against France.[5]

In spite of Pierre-Louis Roederer's laudatory review in the *Journal de
Paris* in early June, two months later Deputy Legendre denounced Staël
on the floor of the National Assembly, obliging her to take refuge outside Paris. While staying with Mathieu de Montmorency, she corrected
the proofs of a brief work scheduled to appear in October (Vendémiaire),
a political piece that François de Pange warned her not to publish.
Réflexions sur la paix intérieure (Reflections on domestic peace), pendant to
Réflexions sur la paix, did not appear until 1821, four years after the
author's demise. Although it exerted no effect on contemporaries, it is a
noteworthy index to Staël's political theories.

Until the execution of Louis XVI, she had remained faithful to her
father's ideal of a constitutional monarchy on the English model. By

1794 the press of circumstances and the influence of Benjamin Constant
had persuaded her to accept the notion of a republic, provided it could
maintain order, defend property, and guarantee liberty. Composed while
Staël was eagerly following every meeting of the Convention, *Paix
intérieure* denotes her concern with the constitutional question (to be
more fully explicated in *Circonstances*). It contains the radical proposal
that constitutional monarchists and conservative republicans combine to
form a strong, moderate, republican party. Staël reiterates her hatred of
Robespierre and distrust of the common people, who gullibly followed
this contemptible leader. Above all, she insists that freedom be preserved.

The first part purports to persuade "royalist friends of freedom" to
renounce monarchy and embrace republicanism. Delineating the abuses
of absolute monarchy and a hereditary aristocracy, Staël enumerates the
difficulties in finding a king acceptable to all parties. She makes specific
constitutional pronouncements. The executive should have the power to
initiate and, like the American president, veto legislation. Government
should be in the hands of a propertied class, "a small number designated
by the hazard of birth or the power of choice" (*OC,* 2:128). After fending
off objections to a republic, she recommends that advocates and oppo-
nents cooperate in good faith to ensure its success.

The second part addresses "republican friends of order," whom Staël
urges to join forces with constitutional royalists in supporting the modified constitution now being elaborated. The first chapter demonstrates
that both groups seek the same objectives: a bicameral legislative body,
an independent executive branch, and the precondition of property for
holding office. The second chapter describes the kind of recruits who can
best serve the republic's needs (i.e., the constitutionalists): "The first step
toward freedom can only come from the class which is most distinguished by its virtues, talents, and consistent opinions" (*OC,* 2:163).
While corruption and compromise sullied France under the Terror, Staël
bemoans the loss of enthusiasm, "the sole celestial pleasure left on this
sad earth" (161). (She was to devote the concluding chapters of
Allemagne to enthusiasm, the ultimate quality of the sensitive and creative person.) Pleading again for La Fayette's release, she touts a republic
as the government most favorable to nurturing talent, republicans as the
most upstanding of men, and a republican constitution as the most
advantageous for the nation.

Containing a clarion call for conciliation, this brochure is written with
proselytizing zeal. Staël is persuaded of the need to unite the moderates

of each party in a concerted effort to found a republic on high-minded principles of virtue and justice. She leans toward an American-style constitution, with a bicameral legislature and executive veto. In the republic she envisions, to be established and governed by men resembling her constitutionalist friends, property is a prerequisite. She betrays an elitist view of the masses, whom she holds responsible for Robespierre's rise; ignorant and easily deceived, they are swayed by passion rather than reason. She stipulates that an equitable government can only be formed by men who did not participate in the Terror. Above all, the republic must be built on a bedrock of freedom.

Whatever influence this work might have had on Staël's contemporaries was voided by its suppression. Only a few later critics even mention its existence or—like Gautier and Balayé—bother to summarize its content. As usual, Staël finds an admiring advocate in Albertine Necker de Saussure: "If it is possible to read these writings objectively, to assess the circumstances of the period and what they required of a writer, the reader will be astonished by the persuasive power displayed, the respect for various interests and opinions, the candor, and not only the intelligence—that goes without saying—but the solid, logical reasoning" ("Notice," lxvii). Sainte-Beuve has nothing but praise for the two *Réflexions sur la paix*, especially the second, in whose ringing exhortation to join rival factions in a common cause he detects a combination of compassion and justice: "Great political sagacity and understanding of the true situation are to be found in the mature advice that escapes beneath that passionate accent" (Bersaucourt, 111).

If scholars and biographers paid scant attention to *Paix intérieure*, they spilled even less ink over the program outlined in *Des Circonstances actuelles qui peuvent terminer la Révolution et des principes qui doivent fonder la république en France* (On present circumstances that can end the Revolution and on principles that must underlie a republic in France), written in 1798, two years after *Passions*. Like *Paix intérieure*, this "veritable treatise of political science"[6] never came to light during its author's lifetime.[7] From textual indices, Omacini situates its composition between 23 June and 27–28 October 1798, at Saint-Ouen (*Circonstances*, xxv). It is unknown when or why Staël gave up the prospect of publication. *Circonstances* has been neglected by most scholars and biographers,[8] whereas in point of fact it marks a significant step in the progression of Staël's political beliefs. Although several critics[9] affirm that the book helped prepare Bonaparte's coup of 18 Brumaire, nothing could have been further from the author's mind than an abrogation of revolutionary gains, a return to hereditary empire, and the curtailment of freedom. To the contrary, Staël is so concerned by the repressive measures following upon the 18 Fructidor coup (mentioned 19 times in the text) that she advances a bold and controversial (if unpublished) program to ensure free elections. Although many of her ideas derive from Montesquieu, Rousseau, and the ideologues Georges Cabanis and Antoine Destutt de Tracy, it is less the originality of her theses than their compelling logic and cohesiveness that merit attention. What Staël proposes is nothing less than a new constitution for France, for which she has pondered every detail, from the relationship between legislative and executive powers to the role of the judiciary, the place of religion in the state, freedom of the press, the role of writers and intellectuals, and so forth. We can only marvel at the lucid combination of theory, pragmatism, and persuasiveness with which she has informed this work. (We may add that no woman had heretofore addressed political issues in such detail nor written a polemical work of such depth and complexity.)

As she does in *Paix intérieure*, Staël calls for appeasement and unification among antagonistic parties. As in *Littérature*, she professes a woman's objectivity, with no political axe to grind: "I believe one should not put forth a theory without prescribing its application; she whose womanly existence is certain to inspire no umbrage nor suspicion of personal ambition may possess the merit of speaking the truth" (*Circonstances*, 4). Announcing the structure and argument of her book, she proceeds from an abstract contemplation of republican theories to suggestions for their practical implementation.

Instead of a hereditary aristocracy, Staël advocates a "natural" aristocracy of intellectual and ethical distinction. "Every man possessing the necessary conditions of citizenship[10] has the right to participate in shaping the laws that govern him," she asserts in the introduction (*Circonstances*, 13). The only viable possibility is representative government, which upholds "the interests of the nation, not of the individuals who compose it" (17). The articles of constitution must be self-evident, like the laws of morality, and palatable to the people. In the spirit of moderation and relativism that will permeate *Littérature*, Staël predicates the form of government that is best suited to national character. She also foreshadows a theme of *Littérature* by proposing to apply mathematics to politics: "A legislator can calculate a nation's passions like its births, deaths, and marriages; the application of mathematics to all branches of morality marks the ultimate degree of intellectual perfectibility" (27). To explain the phenomenon of the Terror without inculpating the

Revolution itself, Staël asserts that the public was insufficiently educated to accept a republic.

The first part (how to hasten the end of the Revolution) deals in successive chapters with royalists, republicans, public opinion, newspapers, the uses of power, and revolutionary laws. The second part (how to establish a free and happy republic) covers the constitution, religion, political virtues and crimes, and writers. The conclusion emphasizes the power of reason in contemporary France.

Addressing herself first to the royalists, Staël alleges that the Revolution has made a limited monarchy unfeasible, for equality is incompatible with hereditary privilege. Because she cannot countenance reinstating an aristocracy in France, she faults the Constituent Assembly for creating a single legislative chamber, a counterpart to the English House of Lords. She would often sustain the distinction that in England the peerage is accessible to anyone of merit and accomplishment. Stressing that there is no longer an alternative to a republic, she implores the royalists to accept this type of government and avert needless suffering. Energetic in defending freedom, the republicans are unified by an unwavering partisan spirit: "Their morality resembles the physical laws of nature; it allows enlightened men to choose the path but will not compromise over the goal" (*Circonstances*, 74). Despite her admiration, she censures the republicans' "absurd distrust" of intellectuals (95), their natural allies in fighting prejudice.

While championing freedom of the press, "the greatest agency for stemming oppression and propagating knowledge" (*Circonstances*, 113), Staël differentiates between newspapers and books. Journals that hawk news in the streets do not disseminate ideas; they are scandal sheets that besmirch women (like herself) and ruin the reputations of great men (like her father). She clamors for a law to decree that "printing a newspaper is a public act, whereas writing a book is the exercise of a sacred right" (115–16). She is especially strident in blaming the press for slandering women, who have no means of rebuttal. "Men will say, we only attack women if they intrude in political affairs; to accuse them of doing so is precisely the aspersion" (119). Unlike a man in the public eye, a woman is the subject of chimerical innuendos against which she is defenseless; she is "feared like a man, useless as a woman, unable to find refuge because imaginary suspicions follow her everywhere!" (120). Staël also decries press power to smear a fine statesman (like Necker) so that in retirement "the great man will see his glory grow dim before his eyes, without a single action or word having clouded its luster" (122). Perhaps it is only natural that Staël, the butt of so much hostile criticism from a vindictive press, should advocate curbing the yellow journalism that flowed unchecked in the Paris streets. Nonetheless, as the voice of opposition to oppression and a self-styled champion of liberty, she is surprisingly subjective in her endeavor to muzzle the press.

In ruminating about the "uses of power," she urges that the government, after achieving the goal of abolishing hereditary privilege, arrest the course of the Revolution. "As soon as men believe they are strong enough to stop fearing and hating, they will govern successfully and rebuild what they have overthrown" (*Circonstances*, 129). Staël makes specific recommendations to the administration: appeal to public opinion, protect commerce, acknowledge the public debt, select educated men, repatriate innocent émigrés, and make concessions that do not impinge on the republic's welfare. She condemns revolutionary laws aimed at expurgating enemies of the republic and seizing their property, for such acts sow seeds of revenge for centuries to come. Instead of further expropriations, the government should hasten to sell all remaining nationalized assets, discontinue unjust confiscation, close the roster of émigrés, and "terminate . . . the revolutionary movement, in order to instill national confidence in the present order" (151).

The second part begins by considering the constitution, which must contain three fundamental provisions: division of executive power; the people's right to elect the Council of Five Hundred (crux of the representative system); and nonheredity of power. Staël also broaches measures to safeguard property and prevent legislative turnover, including lifelong tenure for the Council of Ancients. She insists that a "natural aristocracy" of merit and talent, in contradistinction to an artificial aristocracy of birth, guarantees government by the best minds of the nation. Power is necessarily concentrated in the hands of a few: "What Rousseau said can be proved like a mathematical truth: there is no democracy in representative government" (*Circonstances*, 170). To prevent repetition of the 18 Fructidor coup, Staël recommends certain constitutional changes: the executive must not be required to enforce legislation of which it disapproves; the Directory must be powerless to invalidate the people's choice of elected officials; no one may obtain a government post without first having occupied an inferior one; to ensure an independent judiciary, judges must be free from popular favor and executive power. She espouses greater electoral freedom and favors abolishing age and marital restrictions for office, again citing her absence from the political scene as a guarantee of objectivity.

Religion is essential for maintaining ethical standards in a republic. While obliquely inveighing against Catholic dogma as incompatible with rationality, Staël is fair enough to decry the terrible persecutions perpetrated against the priesthood. She proffers reasons for nominating Protestantism as the new state religion: its venerability and impressive ritual; the absence of hierarchy among its ministers, who as husbands and citizens can further public education and morality; its ability to counteract Catholic influence.

Staël undertakes to prove by a process of reductio ad absurdum that, even for the sake of 30 million people, "injustice has never benefited a nation" (*Circonstances*, 245). Enemies of the state must be tried according to the same laws that apply to all citizens. She denounces fanaticism—source and scourge of the Terror—as the most deadly human emotion (an idea she expounded at length in *Passions*). Reiterating her conviction that "the greatest misfortune in establishing the Republic derives from its having preceded by ten years the writings that would have prepared it" (275), Staël descries a special role for writers in educating the public. Voicing the concept of continuing perfectibility that will underlie *Littérature*, she dates human progress from the discovery of printing, which placed a wealth of knowledge within everyone's grasp: "Perfectibility of the human mind is . . . not purely a metaphysical speculation. . . . Thanks to printing . . . we possess a fixed chain of ideas and can progress from one to the other—a slow but sure process whose limit is necessarily indefinite" (280).

Eloquence remains a powerful instrument that "transforms the convictions of reason and the analysis of duty into electrical impulses"[11] (*Circonstances*, 285) inspiring courage, virtue, and self-sacrifice. Creative works can also serve the national interest if they become closely attuned to human nature. Emphasizing emotion over reason and the lives of common folk over the history of kings and queens, the new literature will redefine taste. Staël expresses the entirely modern notion that the deterioration of language entails a degradation of the human spirit, and vice versa:[12] "The reign of crime gave rise to all the coarse and barbaric expressions that still soil our language. Vulgar speech . . . deprives man of his dignity, his respect for others and for himself" (287–88). The ability to expand the sphere of reason is a positive moral force. Despots always fear independent thinking (a prescient remark): "Kings encourage poets, sages, generals, and men of talent and uncommon knowledge, but they do not want thinkers. Thought is a judge who threatens the crown" (292). By eliminating fanaticism through reason, citizens of every nation and party can form a philosophical fellowship and renew mutual esteem regardless of political convictions.[13]

Repeating her belief in the mathematical certainty of moral right, Staël concludes with a paean to the "power of reason." As before, she preaches conciliation and compromise. At this juncture, the moderates must form a coalition with the republicans, whose excesses they can curb but whose lapses they must overlook in pursuing a common goal. Constitutional changes are needed in order to preserve the republic, recapture public opinion, and thwart factional strife. Staël ends by asserting the supremacy of life over the dubious heroism of dying on the scaffold or battlefield. "Life is of far greater worth to the person who cherishes thought, affection, imagination, and enthusiasm than to the one who knows only the material aspects of existence. . . . There is nothing of value except for the man who loves and prizes life" (*Circonstances*, 346).

Staël's political, social, religious, and philosophical ideas are all predicated on faith in fundamental human goodness. Buoyant optimism leads her to the ingenuous conviction that she can persuade warring factions to unite in pursuit of equity and justice. She places strong reliance on morality and virtue as the bases for good government and human well-being. By the same token, she deems it "impossible for the free choice of the people, that is, public opinion, not to seek out knowledge and virtue" (*Circonstances*, 12). When all men are free to compete for political office, the people will naturally elect the most honest, enlightened, and meritorious candidates. She presupposes that democratic ideas will be propagated in other countries through reason and example: "France's fortune and the writings of her philosophers will necessarily bring about political change in the rest of Europe" (5).

A profound love of liberty explains her altered political ideals. Staël was enough of a pragmatist to bend with the winds of change. Where she had formerly supported a constitutional monarchy, she now advocated a republican government as the best means of preserving freedom and, above all, of preventing a relapse into anarchy and oppression. Eminently practical, she defended a flexible approach to altered circumstances. Different methods may be utilized to attain the same goal of freedom. As she put it in *Paix intérieure*: "What sailor . . . would always perform the same maneuvers, whatever the wind?" (*OC* 2:120). *Circonstances* defines Staël's republicanism in clear and conclusive terms. She was still sufficiently conservative to insist on a well-to-do electorate with a vested interest in retaining property and possessions. She was enough of an intellectual to assign a role in government to a well-educated elite. Although she favored a strong executive branch, to which she would assign limited legislative powers, she was a partisan of near-equal balance among the branches of government.

Certain ideas hark back to other writings. Denunciation of fanaticism, the hope of political conciliation, an immoderate faith in reason and morality, and a fierce love of liberty are carryovers from *Paix intérieure* and *Passions*. The concept of continuing human progress—a theme of *Passions* to be continued in *Littérature*—is enunciated repeatedly. Its corollary is confidence in the scientific method. Adopting Condorcet's and the ideologues' approach, Staël tends increasingly to apply mathematics to morality.[14] "No one states that a triangle is square, but people permit themselves misconstructions as invalid in politics as in morality. . . . The mathematical proof of morality is experience" (*Circonstances*, 245). To endow moral phenomena with the validity of empirically proven fact, she proposes evaluating them objectively and scientifically. "Moral forces are calculated according to laws as positive as [those governing] physical forces. If they were completely known to us, we could foresee every happening in life by a chain of cause and effect, just as Newton measured the movement of the earth" (305).

Circonstances was intended to (a) posit the bases for a new constitution, (b) unite royalists and republicans, and (c) lay fanaticism to rest. Inspired by the explosion of illegitimacy set off by the 18 Fructidor coup, its possible usefulness was nullified by the coup of 18 Brumaire, which, installing Bonaparte on the first rungs of power, would temporarily silence Staël's political pronouncements.

Without entering the debatable realm of Freudian psychocriticism, we can suggest that Staël's motivations for writing political treatises were twofold. On the one hand, she was vying with (and outstripping) her mother, whose writing efforts—stunted by Necker—remained stalled in the area of didactic moralism. On the other hand, she was following her father's example and doing so on his home turf, so to speak. Although she could never, as a woman, wield the political power he had enjoyed, she could ply the pen he had taken up when he lost that power. And by emphasizing the role of an intellectual elite in government, by stressing the superiority of literature over journalism, by entering the masculine mainstream of political writing, Staël could hope to carve out for herself a place in the political process.

Chapter 4
Elaboration of a Theory

Interwoven with Staël's political treatises were other forms of writing—experiments in literary criticism, psychological analysis, and the correlation of culture and climate. Concurrently with her political concerns, she was absorbed in elaborating various theories—of fiction, of the "passions," of literature. But woven more or less perceptibly into each of these works is the thread—no, the fabric—of her political persuasion. All of Staël's writing, including her later fiction, is to some extent hortatory. Invariably she has a thesis to propound, a proposition to prove.

The anthology of novellas she published in April 1795 contained the *Essai sur les fictions* (Essay on fiction)[1]—a daring, if roundabout, apology for the novel, which was traditionally considered an inferior genre suited to women readers and writers.[2] Not only does Staël place fiction on the same plane as the classically approved genres, but she posits its superiority to history, philosophy, allegory, and tragedy. Her aim is to authenticate a field in which women have written successfully. At the same time, she sets herself apart from other women writers by composing a theoretical work, *not* a novel. Her most cogent argument is fiction's uplifting effect on morality. (Staël is still measuring by her mother's yardstick.) Classifying fiction as "marvelous" or allegorical, historical, or realistic,[3] she dispenses quickly with the first two categories in order to concentrate on the third, "where nothing is true but everything is true-to-life" (*OC*, 2:178).

Blaming Greek and Roman mythology for permitting supernatural intervention in human affairs, Staël stipulates the necessity for re-creating reality: "Whatever is invented must be credible" (*OC*, 2:182). Allegory is even less valid than myth, for it substitutes images for ideas. Her criteria are universality and timelessness: "A work of fiction . . . is effective only when its elements can touch all readers in all ages" (191). Scathing toward historical fiction, which fails to separate fact from invention, she discounts philosophical novels that violate verisimilitude; thus, she prefers Richardson and Fielding to Voltaire.

Although she decries the plethora of tasteless works in a genre where "perfection requires genius . . . but mediocrity lies within everyone's grasp"

(*OC*, 2:199), Staël praises fiction in definite and defiant terms: "In its highest conception, a novel . . . is one of the most beautiful products of the human mind and one of the most powerful influences on individual morality, which is the foundation of public virtue" (200). To achieve its deserved prestige, fiction must escape from its current preoccupation with love and reach out to encompass a gamut of emotions, including ambition, pride, avarice, and vanity. (She seems to be ruminating on the subject of her next book, which will analyze these and other passions.)

To bolster the preeminence she accords fiction, Staël contends that novels like Samuel Richardson's *Clarissa* (1747–48) and *Sir Charles Grandison* (1753) are more persuasive than philosophical tracts in inculcating a sense of duty. As exemplary "masterpieces" she specifies Marie-Madeleine de La Fayette's *La Princesse de Clèves* (1662), Bernardin de Saint-Pierre's *Paul et Virginie* (1787),[4] Fanny Burney's *Cecilia* (1782), Claudine-Alexandrine de Tencin's *Mémoirs du comte de Comminges* (1735), Marie-Jeanne Riccoboni's novels,[5] *Caliste* (1787) by Isabella de Charrière,[6] *Camille* (1785),[7] and, above all, Rousseau's *La Nouvelle Héloïse*. Staël's preference for works that portray the miseries of an adulterous passion seems to undercut her injunction against focusing on love.

Her essay champions fiction as a genre in its own right, no less valid and even more effective than philosophy, poetry, and drama. Its arguments are predicated on the moral goal of literature. Fiction's primacy over other forms is twofold: it is more closely related to reality; by affecting the emotions, it is a more compelling means of moral persuasion. *Fictions* also marks a step in the development of Staël's methodology. Dividing her subject into categories would be a frequent device. Underscoring moral values would be a reverberating refrain. Analyzing specific types of fiction prefigured the form of her next two works—one, dissecting the causes and effects of various "passions," and the other, evaluating the "literature" of different nations.

As Balayé observes, Staël was the only woman of her day to theorize about literary art. *Fictions* points to the novel as the literary genre of the future, the only area in which creative imagination has full rein (Balayé, 51–52). Hogsett calls *Fictions* a direct response to Rousseau's *Lettre sur les spectacles*, with its misogynistic attitude toward women in general and women writers in particular. Staël counters this position indirectly in her book, which claims the utility of fiction and, by its very existence, contradicts Rousseau's denial of women's ability to write (Hogsett, 42–43). Staël goes one step further. While making a stand for the supremacy of fiction, she illustrates a woman's ability to write something other than fiction.

She worked on *De l'influence des passions sur le bonheur des individus et des nations* (The Influence of passions on the happiness of individuals and nations) from approximately 1792 to 1795.[8] She felt it necessary—as in *Fictions*—to substantiate her credentials as a serious writer and extend the subject of her work beyond the female-dominated field of love. In its general outline, *Passions* is a meditation on the violent emotions unleashed under the Terror and on other passions that can undermine individual happiness and national welfare. Battered in her personal life by Narbonne's increasing coldness and Ribbing's indifference, Staël's firsthand experience of suffering infuses her book. While advocating the wisdom of dominating emotions and retreating from worldly affairs (like Necker), she is too young, ambitious, and high-strung to follow her own advice—hence the mixed messages of *Passions*, published in September (or early October) 1796.

The "Avant-Propos" is the kind of self-denigrating apology with which Staël often prefaced her works, as if attempting to propitiate her critics in advance. She excuses her unseemly haste in publishing a half-finished work by alleging the wish to be judged for her writing, not for irrelevant reasons, and justifies the ensuing discussion as offering a solution to pressing problems of individual and political well-being. As announced in the introduction, the book was originally to consist of two symmetrical parts, the first focusing on the individual, the second on the social framework. The latter (unwritten) section was to have elaborated Staël's recommendations for a republic based on freedom and equality, to be shaped by an intellectual and ethical elite. The discovery that individuals and nations share the same traits, albeit on a different scale, is a crucial concept that permits the author to generalize about Nordic and southern peoples in *Littérature*, Teutonic nations in *Allemagne*, Italians in *Corinne*, and Russians in *Dix années*.

The first volume (all we have) of *Passions* is divided into three sections: (1) the influence of specific passions on human happiness; (2) the relationship between emotions and reason; and (3) inner resources that can help combat passion. Section 1, "On Passions," covers (on a scale of decreasing desirability) love of glory, ambition, vanity, love, gambling (including avarice and intoxication), envy and vengeance, factionalism, and crime, with emphasis on the disadvantages inherent in each. In spite of her psychological penetration, Staël accepts the contemporary tendency to define personality in terms of a single trait or motivation, without recognizing the complex interplay of "passions" in each person's makeup.

She considers "love of glory" to be the most creditable of human desires. After picturing the intoxicating pleasure of inspiring men, commanding events, and receiving the plaudits of the masses (an achievement she, as a woman, can never hope to realize), the author enumerates obstacles to achieving glory in a present-day republic, where the mob can withhold its spontaneous enthusiasm without reason. Although individual glory may fade, "the human race benefits from the legacy of genius, and the truly great men are those who have rendered their peers less necessary to subsequent generations" (*OC*, 3:56). Naturally, Necker figures in this pantheon. Unlike love of glory, which seeks permanent renown, "ambition" thirsts for power and possessions; it exacts a heavy price in dissimulation, uncertainty, unremitting effort, and hypocrisy: "No one has ever occupied a high position in peace" (80). The passion for glory settles for nothing less, whereas ambition snatches at every stage and degree of power.

To illustrate her contention that "vanity" is concerned with trivial perquisites, Staël invents "characters" reminiscent of La Bruyère, whose pretentious boasting masks the underlying unhappiness of egocentrism. Women are particularly prone to vanity, for the same efforts that reward men with glory and power bring women only momentary commendation. Even if exceptionally gifted, they face solitude and suffering: "Palms of glory may crown the rare souls driven by talent or character to diverge from the common rule, but they will not escape the misfortune that adheres inevitably to their lot" (*OC*, 3:103). Most women are—and should be—content with developing their intellects for the sake of the man they love. Those few who nurture more grandiose hopes are doomed to lovelessness—an unnatural and, for Staël, unwanted fate. As expressed in the desire for oratorical brilliance and acclaim, she counts vanity as one cause of the Revolution.

The writer anticipates criticism of her chapter on "love" because "everyone believes he has known love, and almost everyone is wrong in this belief" (*OC*, 3:115). Rejecting classical ideals in favor of the more sensitive and subjective concept of love evinced in Voltaire's tragedies, Rousseau's *Nouvelle Héloïse*, Goethe's *Werther* (1774), German tragedy and English poetry (models the romanticists would emulate), Staël views love as the complete immersion of one self in another; it is the closest earthly experience of heaven, for which marriage is the crown and consummation. The loss of love, on the other hand, can cause such despair that suicide is the only release.[9] Staël's acknowledgment of women's inferior status is a tacit denunciation of patriarchal standards: "Nature and society have disinherited half the human race; strength, courage, genius, independence, all belong to men, and if they pay homage to us in our youth, it is only to amuse themselves by overthrowing a throne" (134). She decries the double behavioral expectations of men and women. Accounted honest and estimable even when they betray feminine trust, men are subject to a different moral code.[10] Women who surrender to seduction are undone, while men "command armies, govern empires, and barely recall the name of those whose destiny they destroyed" (140). Because of this dual ethic, Staël advises women to embrace virtue as their sole protection; otherwise, "men will ruin your life for a few moments of their own" (141).

She lumps together passions like "gambling," "avarice," and "intoxication" as vulgar, degrading, and compulsive. Men hurl themselves into a drunken frenzy to blot out reality; they crave excitement at the gaming table or on the battlefield. The miser is an egotist who loves money not as a means but as an end in itself. Nourished by resentment, "envy" feeds endlessly on itself. Other people's good fortune is odious to the envious person, who would prefer "the equality of hell to gradations in paradise" (*OC*, 3:152). These passions create a slavish dependency that annuls the self-control necessary for inner peace.

The desire for "revenge" that has followed upon the Revolution derives from a warped sense of justice. "Do unto others the evil done unto you" is a disastrous maxim. Revolution ceases only when vengeance is laid to rest and people regard their enemies as human beings, like themselves. Like revenge, "partisanship" ferments during periods of unrest, joining men in a common, uncompromising hatred that can lead to persecution and war. Citing Robespierre's tyranny as an abhorrent example, Staël claims that the human mind cannot realize its full potential unless it achieves a necessary, impartial distantiation from prejudice. Love of "crime," a passion fired by internal rage, impels the criminal to act blindly, like a frenzied animal that has tasted blood. The true criminal cannot be rehabilitated but is condemned eternally to repeat his crimes, like the mythological torments of Sisyphus and Tantalus.

Staël next considers "sentiments intermediate between passions and resources within the self" (*OC*, 3:196): friendship, familial affection, and religion. Posing as an impartial moralist, she cautions the reader not to discount her advice just because she has failed to follow it herself. She finds most women incapable of "friendship"—an exigent affection demanding requital; vying with their sisters to please men, they practice "an art which is not falsehood, but a certain arrangement of the truth" (204). The inequality inherent in "filial, paternal, and conjugal affection" precludes reciprocity in kind or degree. Marital ties can afford the same contentment as love or friendship, but not all marriages are happy: "Self-control, strength, and sacrifice are needed to maintain peace in this union, which more closely approximates the pleasures of virtue than the raptures of passion" (217–18). "Religion" offers a moral code to govern behavior and affords the soul a calm if unexciting sense of well-being. Religious faith is a gift, like beauty or genius, which cannot be acquired by striving. Piety, however, is not necessarily a sign of goodness. A child of the Enlightenment, Staël considered personal morality a better guide than religious dogma (a thesis she would illustrate in *Delphine*).

Before invoking inner resources that can counteract passion, she addresses the youthful tendency of denial. Young persons cannot conceive of sorrow; only at age 25[11] do they begin to realize that unhappiness is an inevitable consequence of passion. To these sensitive souls, she offers the consolation of "philosophy," which can effect a serene transition from youth to age. While demanding concentrated spiritual powers, philosophy affords the satisfaction of self-possession. Intellectual stimulation and "study" can also prove enriching. Science demonstrates the accidental nature of our existence, while historical awareness puts present-day ills in perspective. Life, happiness, and passion follow the natural stages of birth, growth, and death, but thought, progressing indefinitely, provides an intimation of immortality. "Benevolence," which encompasses all altruistic acts, derives pleasure from giving without hope of recompense. It provides the only satisfaction that can fill the void left by passion. To exemplify her point, Staël conjures up Almont (another "character"), who incarnates dedication to others.

The conclusion prescribes seeking interests that are gratifying in themselves and exempt from passion's sway, like public service, a literary career, or a loving relationship. She will have accomplished her purpose, Staël maintains, if she has brought peace to tormented souls by understanding and alleviating their pain. She has also been self-motivated: "I have written in order to discover myself . . . to achieve a measure of detachment so that I may observe my own sorrow . . . and generalize from my own experience" (*OC*, 3:284). Exalting mercy, especially in revolutionary times, she ends by summoning the victorious French forces, with no enemies to fear and no further battles to win, to extend their generosity to the vanquished.

A guide to behavior, a moral treatise, a diatribe against revolutionary excesses, a paean to Necker, and an oblique denunciation of the status of women, *Passions* is one of the first "psychological" analyses in literature. In a preromantic spirit, Staël's empathy extends to the unfortunate, supersensitive, love-stricken victims of discouragement and sorrow. She considered this her most important work, as she wrote the publicist Pierre-Louis Roederer, to whom she sent a copy on 1 October 1796: "It is my mind's testament; I hope to finish it before I am 30, so that I may die at that age, known and regretted" (Jasinski, 3, 1 pt. 2:247). Sainte-Beuve waxed ecstatic over *Passions*: "A kind of sentimental inspiration [and] a mysterious reflection issuing from the heart's depths, illuminate the entire book . . . and cast over it an indefinable charm which, for certain melancholy characters, and at a particular time of life, no other reading can match" (Bersaucourt, 118).

Staël published nothing between *Passions* (1796) and *De la Littérature considérée dans ses rapports avec les institutions sociales* (The Influence of literature upon society, 1800). Envisioning literature as a cause and consequence of national differences, the second book develops two principal ideas: the concept of human perfectibility and the contrast between Nordic and Latin cultures. Again, the author's perspective is political. To explain the horrors of the recent Reign of Terror, she submits that anarchy is not a gratuitous evil but a necessary precondition for social and political amelioration. *Littérature* is carefully and thoroughly structured, its ideas classified under headings and subheadings. The first part, dealing with "literature among the ancients and moderns," is divided into 20 chapters progressing from Greek tragedy, comedy, philosophy, and oratory through "Northern" literature to present-day France. The second part, titled "The Present state of enlightenment in France and its future progress," addresses the postrevolutionary period. Purporting to analyze all national literatures since classical times, with tangential digressions, Staël's is a breathtaking endeavor. Primary among her concerns are questions of French culture, the Revolution, women's place, literary taste and style, and the moral underpinnings of literature.

While her book is chockablock with new ideas, Staël continues the lineage of Montesquieu, Rousseau, Voltaire, and the encyclopedists. Even more vigorously than Diderot, she links reason and sensibility. Rejecting eighteenth-century atheistic attitudes, however, she deems Christian morality fundamental to literature. Prefiguring *Corinne* and *Allemagne*, she introduces to the French reading public the literary output of England, Germany, and—to a lesser degree—Italy. In confronting the literatures of North and South—each influenced by climate, mores, and government—Staël leans unhesitatingly toward the melancholy inspiration of the Germanic North. In advising the French to renew inspiration by delving into their past rather than imitating the classics, she rehabilitates chivalry and the Middle Ages as fecund literary sources.

The "preliminary discourse" projects the book's overall plan and the author's intention of examining the reciprocal influence on literature of religion, mores, and laws. As in *Fictions*, she emphasizes literature's moral impact, which can be applied in turn to the political arena. Wary of a vulgar, uneducated populace, Staël advocates government by an intellectual elite. In assigning a dominant role in the state to intellectuals and writers, she forecasts the political commitment of the romantic movement.

In her reiterated view, observation and experience confirm the uninterrupted progress of humankind, even in history's darkest periods. In line with this theory, she must somehow discredit the literary supremacy of the ancients—a feat Staël accomplishes in several ways. Unable to denigrate their artistic excellence, she makes a curious distinction between poetry and other genres. Inspired directly by beauty, the poet transmits his impression to others. There is no gradation in this experience, no possibility of improving on the immediate, initial sensation; hence, poetry is not perfectible. Secondly, the ancients are subordinate to the moderns in their childlike wonder, primitive religious orientation, and inability to recognize love and the importance of women. Lastly, Staël separates imaginative from philosophical works. The arts are not infinitely perfectible, because the brilliance of original inspiration can never be duplicated. Powers of reason, on the other hand, continually develop and expand. One generation begins where the previous generation left off, "and across the ages, philosophical thinkers form a chain of ideas unbroken by death" (*OC*, 4:74). This concept of passing the intellectual torch from one generation to the next, already expressed in *Rousseau*, would become part of the romantic credo.

Staël starts out by tracing intellectual progress under the early Greek bards and philosophers. While admiring Homeric imagery, she attributes deficiencies in the Greeks' emotional constructs to the exclusivity of male friendships and inadequate appreciation of women. As an implicit lesson for contemporary France, she ascribes the rapid development of Greek literary genres to governmental encouragement of talented men. She finds drama propitious for conveying national customs, religion, and laws but faults Greek tragedy for its supernatural elements. Comedy played the same role for the Athenians as newspapers for the present-day French, bringing about a "democratic levelling process" (*OC*, 4:117). Dismissing Aristophanes as commonplace and vulgar, she furnishes two reasons for the unrestrained coarseness of Greek comedy: it catered to an amoral populace, and it excluded women.

While distinguishing three successive periods of Roman literature— before, during, and after the reign of Augustus—Staël naturally favors the republican era, when talented men called to public service excelled at oratory, history, and philosophy; with Augustus, as under Louis XIV, literature became servile, flattering, and pretentious. During the totalitarian era after Augustus, few men dared pursue literary and philosophic studies. Staël proposes the following reasons for the fall of Rome: uncurbed crime, slavery, inadequate mass education, conflicting ideologies about right and wrong, and indifference toward death and cruelty. The degeneracy of the South prepared the triumph of the North.

In contradistinction to prevailing opinion, she professes that the Middle Ages marked a cultural advance, not a retrogression. The northern invasion stimulated a cultural interchange between assailants and victims while Christianity, binding the peoples of North and South in a common belief, helped abolish slavery, raised the status of women, and inculcated the concept of charity. Theological study encouraged abstract reasoning, which generated the rebirth of letters and science. The Renaissance proved that the so-called barbaric centuries had actually been a civilizing force. Bacon, Machiavelli, Montaigne, and Galileo far outdistanced their Greek and Latin precursors. In according preeminence to individual writers, the Renaissance spurred them on to perfect language, revitalize philosophy, and create new scientific methodologies.

Much of the modern era's uninterrupted advance is due to the influence of women, whom Christianity elevated to a position of (spiritual) equality. Women are responsible for the sensitivity and psychological awareness that enhance modern masterpieces. Although Staël acknowledges that women have not composed outstanding works in their own right, she asserts that they have contributed enormously to cultural progress by revealing nuances of character and emotion that revolutionized literature: "Every book written since the Renaissance contains ideas that did not exist before women were granted a measure of civil equality" (*OC*, 4:218).

With the exception of Ariosto and Tasso, Italian literature is by and large a disappointment to Staël. She dislikes Petrarch's affectation and Boccaccio's indecency. Dante's innumerable defects reflect the inadequa-

cies of his era. Italian comedy aims to amuse, not to reform what it
ridicules. Except for Machiavelli's lucid political analysis and Italy's
major scientific contributions, Italian works possess no utilitarian value.
On the whole, Staël has little but contempt for Italian mores and character (an attitude that would change with closer acquaintance): "The
Italians . . . relish exaggeration in all things, and feel sincerely about
nothing. They are both vindictive and servile. They are slaves to women,
and yet strangers to any deep and lasting feeling. They are miserably
superstitious in practising Catholicism, but do not believe in the inseparable union of morality and religion" (*OC*, 4:234–35). By joining northern with southern imagination, knightly grandeur with oriental
splendor, Spain should have produced a more noteworthy literature. But
royal despotism and the Inquisition combined to stifle independent
thinking. A few scattered examples—*El Cid* and the comedies of Pedro
Calderón and Lope de Vega—reveal the heights that Spanish literature
might have attained.

Steeped in the gloom of a misty climate, northern poetry constitutes
the outpouring of an indomitable people for whom servitude is unbearable. Staël admits to favoring this kind of literature, which is permeated
with the desire to "escape the confines that circumscribe the imagination" (*OC*, 4:263) and whose sensibility stems from traditional Germanic
respect for women. While disagreeing with French allegations that
northern literature is tasteless, Staël will not yet concede that taste is a
relative concept. "People seek pleasurable impressions in creative works.
Taste is knowing and anticipating what can produce these feelings"
(272). By this criterion, she objects to frightening scenes, convoluted
plots, obscure terminology, and improbable developments.

In her enthusiastic embrace of Shakespeare, Staël plants herself firmly
on the side of romanticism *avant la lettre*. Instead of imitating the
ancients, he originated a new kind of literature imbued with the spirit of
northern poetry, gave fresh impulsion to the theater, and portrayed
moral anguish to an incomparable degree. The English have no comic
author like Molière, nor would they appreciate his subtlety if they did.
They require a more robust and roughshod humor as an outlet for their
monotonous home life, stern religious practices, serious occupations, and
unrelenting climate.

As she does in discussing the ancients, Staël divides English politics
into three eras: before, during, and after the English Revolution, when
the stable constitution of 1688 guaranteed peace and freedom. Whereas
English writers like Thomas Hobbes, Adam Ferguson, John Locke,

Adam Smith, David Hume, and the Earl of Shaftsbury treat politics as a purely intellectual science, French writers like Montesquieu enliven their analyses with emotional appeal. Because a free government emables them to implement their ideas, the English evince an interest in children's education, charity, political economy, criminal legislation, science, morality, and metaphysics.

A note prefacing the discussion of Germany reiterates Staël's purpose of relating literature to religion, customs, and government. Her intent is not to evaluate individual writers and works but to illustrate her thesis with relevant examples. For this reason, she has omitted many fine German works as unnecessary to prove her point. This contestation was a reproof to critics who had attacked her limited knowledge of German literature.

Inhabiting a divided country with no central intellectual capital, the Germans have not yet formulated taste or standardized language; new words proliferate confusingly. Shunted to the political sidelines, men of letters turn to self-scrutiny and the contemplation of nature. Nowhere have the depths of passion, suffering, and philosophic consolation been expressed with greater feeling. Mirroring the German character, Goethe's masterpiece *Werther* represents society's effect on a sensitive individual and portrays a sickness of soul that makes life unbearable. "Only Rousseau and Goethe[12] have been able to depict reflective passion—passion that knows and judges but cannot conquer itself" (*OC*, 4:346). Unfortunately, German exaltation invites inferior imitation that vitiates taste. Writers like Christoph Martin Wieland tend to mix philosophy and fiction—a blending of forms against which Staël inveighs in *Fictions*. Conversely, German writers banter in their serious works and patronize their readers: "One must not descend to the level of the majority, but aspire to the highest possible limit of perfection; the public's judgment is always, in the end, that of the nation's most distinguished men" (357). This elitist view of literary appreciation echoes Staël's political prescriptions.

She ascribes the courtly elegance and refinement of French literature to the need for currying favor under the monarchy. While absolutism limited intellectual horizons, it encouraged scorn of studious exertion and preoccupation with social pleasures. Leisure honed conversational wit, at which women excelled. Although fear of ridicule may have impeded originality, it stimulated the perspicacity of a Molière: "Men beguiled by vanity, deceived by self-interest, or deceitful out of pride—this multitude enslaved by and living only for other people's opinion—

have never been portrayed better than by the French" (*OC*, 4:374–75). The masterpieces of the period are models of stylistic purity in keeping with aristocratic inclinations to delicacy and finesse. Style represents the manner, accent, and gesture with which a writer addresses his readers. Under no circumstances can vulgarity increase the power of ideas—an admonition the republicans should heed. (Staël admits that she coined the term *vulgarity*[13] and promises in the second section to consider reasonable rules to permit neologisms.) Where it had been an instrument of amusement, literature became a weapon after Louis XIV. In analyzing the contributions of Voltaire, Montesquieu, and Rousseau, Staël ascertains the first effects of political freedom on literature and concludes that prose is a better medium of communication than poetry because it is not constrained by the rules that govern verse.

The second part begins with a recapitulation of part 1 and a general overview of postrevolutionary conditions. Instead of marking a new era of intellectual progress, the Revolution has resulted in a temporary literary and cultural decline. Stung by uncouth republican speech and manners, Staël pleads for retaining aristocratic refinement shorn of affectation. Indicative of self-respect and regard for others, good taste can be a political asset: "The taste required in . . . republican literature is not a separate skill but the perfection of all talents; instead of opposing deep feeling and energetic expression, the natural simplicity it prescribes is the only adornment compatible with vigor" (*OC*, 4:431). Politeness is also of literary and political importance; it inspires affection, preserves status, and marks the consideration a person deserves. During the past ten years, ignoble and ignorant men of revolting arrogance have been in power. To the contrary, government leaders must possess a balanced combination of moral qualities (like Necker, of course). Instead of encouraging specialists, the republic should offer a broad-based education so that it may be enriched by diversified endeavors. Staël endorses her father's view of an aristocracy of merit: "The necessary condition for a republic founded on political equality is to establish distinctions among men according to talent and virtue" (459).

In the capital chapter on "women who cultivate letters," she projects a leading role for women in the new republic, provided cultural attitudes are altered. Voicing the hope that progressive legislators will pay serious attention to their education and civil protection, Staël harks back to the image of women as slaves, held in an untenable social and political situation: "If they wish to rise, they are accused of aspiring to power which the law has not granted; if they remain enslaved, their lives are oppressed" (*OC*, 4:464). She draws a parallel between women's condition and the government under which they live. In a monarchy, women writers are ridiculed; in a republic, they are hated. The distinction is negligible. If it wishes to promote enlightenment, the republic must encourage women to develop their minds. Since the Revolution, however, men have found it politically and morally expedient to reduce women to a state of mediocrity and thus to quell expansion of their reasoning powers. To remedy this situation in the ideal republic, Staël urges that women not be relegated to an "insipid" or "frivolous" state but instead prompted to foster ideals of humanity, generosity, and delicacy. By virtue of their innate sensitivity and enforced isolation from public affairs, they can be objective in singling out injustice and ignoble acts. More emphatically than in *Rousseau*, she urges again that women receive the same education as men. "To enlighten, instruct, and perfect women like men[14] and nations like individuals, is still the best secret for achieving . . . all those social and political relationships whose durability one hopes to establish" (472). This radical idea would not bear fruit for another century.

As if intimidated by her own temerity, Staël repeats her warning about the fearsome consequences awaiting the exceptional woman, "whom nature would consign to the torment of an importunate superiority" (*OC*, 4:473). The entire social order takes up arms against a woman who aspires to masculine achievement. Subject to slander and vilification, she is prevented from fighting calumny with truth. Obviously (and rightly) regarding herself as a prime victim of misunderstanding and malevolence, Staël cautions any woman who would like to emulate her example to entertain realistic expectations. What is the testimony of such a woman's life? "Some private virtues, obscure services, hidden feelings . . . and a few written works that will make her known in countries she does not inhabit at a time when she is no longer alive" (476).

Next, Staël considers the kinds of literature suitable to a republic. Once France achieves a free constitution, comedy will no longer mock social institutions but will concentrate on universal human foibles. Quoting the German observation that "beautiful tragedies should make the soul stronger after tearing it apart" (*OC*, 4:494), Staël presupposes that political equality will alter the nature of tragedy. Taking Shakespeare as a model and eschewing classical rules, she proposes radical dramatic innovation: "Writers must learn to compose verse so simple and natural that its poetic beauties do not detract from the profound emotion that should supersede every other consideration" (502). All imaginative writing must transcribe real feelings. Staël recommends what we might term "psychological" awareness of hidden motivations: "The purpose of poetic style should be to arouse . . . interest in people's instinctive ideas and feelings; like everything else akin to thought, poetry must follow the philosophical progress of the century" (505).

In the belief that political solutions will someday be as self-evident as algebraic ones, she proposes applying scientific methods to the social sciences. Patterning her reasoning on Condorcet's work on the calculation of probabilities, she suggests that by taking the mean number of deaths, births, divorces, and assassinations over a ten-year period, one can predict the statistical probability of divorces in Berne, murders in Rome, and so forth. Similar calculations can determine the best political institution for a given population, she concludes, envisioning the day when all moral problems can be submitted to mathematical proof.[15] She stipulates one premise, however: calculations incompatible with morality are ipso facto false. Refuting motives of self-interest, she claims that love of virtue is an innate quality, anterior to reason, which arises simultaneously with the instinct for self-preservation.

To counteract stylistic changes introduced by the Revolution (a false emphasis on brevity, the sterile creation of new words),[16] Staël equates stylistic beauty with moral rectitude. Style is not a matter of form but of content. Good writing requires three ingredients: images, feelings, and ideas. As a corollary to her argument in *Fictions*, she considers philosophical works ineffective unless they involve imagination and emotions. Furthermore, style attests to character; it is not an acquired skill but the imprint of the self. By appealing to public opinion and reviving moral values, Necker was a paragon of stylistic authenticity.

Staël arrogates to oratory a sovereign role in directing the popular will, which in turn determines the political destiny of a free nation. Since the Revolution, oratory has degenerated into scandalmongering and specious reasoning in a climate of cupidity, self-interest, and vice. But the author's innate optimism comes to the fore. What is intrinsically good is bound to prevail. Human nature will respond to burning sincerity. "Since eloquence requires spiritual impetus, it addresses men's emotions, and the emotions of the masses invariably incline to virtue" (*OC*, 4:581). In spite of her frequent distrust of the people, Staël expresses a Rousseau-like confidence in the primal goodness of humanity.

People who have no use for intellectual pursuits beyond their practical application find human perfectibility a mockery, she says in conclusion. Some even belie learning as harmful to human welfare. To the contrary, she believes that morality and knowledge are interdependent and inseparable. The propagation of ideas can only be repressed through terrible and fruitless measures, which she describes in detail. Unsettled by criticism, Staël admits to hesitation in setting her convictions on paper. She has decided nonetheless to publish the present work. Echoing her discouragement of would-be women writers, she voices regret at having embarked on a literary career, with the publicity and frightful solitude of success. Like the 19-year-old who penned her *Journal de jeunesse*, she rues especially lost possibilities for love.

In spite of its title, the book is not a mere literary treatise. It is a moral disquisition, political dissertation, handbook of psychology, and meditation on philosophy and religion, as well as an overview of Western literature from ancient times to the present. Amid her many subjects of discussion and the tangential ideas they generate, Staël never fails to include references to the horrors of the French Revolution, the recurrence of which she thereby hopes to avert. Her overriding concern is to prepare literature and culture in the formative republic—hence her repeated emphasis on the moral aim and value of art, corroborated by scientific demonstration. Her praise of England and Necker is designed to provide two ready-made models of national and individual excellence. In politics as in literature, she places leadership in the hands of an intellectual cadre. She also carves out for women a determinant role in orienting society toward a gentler, more uplifting and charitable outlook. Her thesis of continuing perfectibility is intended to prove the natural evolution of an enlightened republic that can incarnate her dream of national freedom.

Littérature set off violent controversy when it appeared. Reactions ranged from the ecstatic to the contemptuous. Staël's partisans praised her acuity, perceptiveness, breadth of knowledge, and deductive ability. No one mentioned her call for women's education. Detractors found her boring, prolix, ill-informed, contentious. Among the derogatory articles that reviled the book and author, two pieces by Louis de Fontanes in the *Mercure de France* were the most venomous in deriding Staël's person as well as her writings—a common male stratagem for devaluating women's creativity. Hurt by these jibes, she justified herself six months later in a preface to the second edition, claiming that her main purpose was to demonstrate a relationship between literature and social institutions within each century and country—an endeavor never before attempted. Careful to exempt imaginative works from her criteria of perfectibility, she asserts not that the moderns have greater intellectual ability than the ancients but that the cumulative mass of ideas has increased over time. To support her position, she cites authorities like Talleyrand,

Turgot, and Condorcet in France, Ferguson in Great Britain, and Kant in Germany. She is merely the first to have applied the concept of perfectibility to literature.

Chateaubriand's criticism was devastating:

My mania is to see Jesus Christ in all things, just as Mme de Staël sees perfectibility. . . . Had I the honor of her acquaintance I should say to the authoress, "You are without doubt a woman of superior intellect. Your capabilities are great, and your ideas are often seductive. Nevertheless your book is far from being what it might have been. Its style is monotonous, and laden with metaphysical expressions. The sophistry of its ideas is repellent, the learning is insufficient, the heart is often sacrificed to the opinions. Your talent is only partially unfolded, and is smothered in philosophy . . . [which] will never fill the void in your days, for who has ever been able to fertilize the desert without water?" (Blennerhassett, 2:399–400)

Constant was sufficiently incensed to repay Chateaubriand in kind:

To take my mind off other follies, ... I read Chateaubriand. It is difficult not to succeed in finding some felicitous words and resounding phrases in the space of five volumes, but for the most part, it is pure gibberish; a measure of poor taste in the finest passages betrays the absence of both sensitivity and good faith. His ideas on allegory, descriptive poetry, and the sensibility of the ancients are plundered from the book *De la Littérature*, with this difference: what the author of the latter work attributes to Perfectibility, he ascribes to the Christian religion.[17]

Sainte-Beuve notes that *Littérature* proposed an ideal of republican literature that was no longer applicable after Bonaparte's coup d'état of 18 Brumaire. Nonetheless, the book became the prospectus for a romantic movement that would not come to fruition until many years later: "Mme de Staël's book was a bit like Janus: it looked no less toward the future than toward the past" (Sainte-Beuve, 68). In partial explanation of the wealth of ideas permeating the book (which Sainte-Beuve cannot believe are original with a woman of the world), he quotes Charles-Julien de Chênedollé, who resided at Coppet during 1798, while Staël was composing *Littérature*: "She wrote a chapter every morning. At dinner or in the salon during the evening, she set forth the subject of the chapter she planned to treat and, inciting you to discuss the text, she *spoke* it herself in a rapid improvisation; and the next morning the chapter was written. . . . Her improvisations were far more brilliant than her written chapters" (69–70).

Although a goodly portion of the criticism directed toward Staël attacked her as much on the ground of gender as ideas, *Littérature* marked a pivotal moment in French literary history. Appearing at a time when classicism was being revived, it pointed in the direction romanticism would take with its (1) introduction of English and Germanic literatures to France; (2) emphasis on sensibility and melancholy; (3) advocation of creativity over imitation, national inspiration over classical perfection; and (4) rehabilitation of the Middle Ages—thus of France's national past—as a profitable source of literary inspiration. Many ideas that germinate in *Littérature* will be developed, altered, or expanded upon in *Allemagne* and, peripherally, in the novel *Corinne*.

Chapter 5
Forays into Fiction: *Delphine*

Staël's two principal novels were to earn her spectacular success. Her first full-length work of fiction, and her only experiment with the epistolary form,[1] was the hugely popular *Delphine*. Recapitulating themes touched on in her short stories, *Delphine* has a well-developed if convoluted plot, presents a number of sharply defined characters, exemplifies social criticism at its most daring, and marks Staël's emergence as a best-selling writer. The book's conception dates from April 1800. Staël began writing that summer, as she apprised Adélaïde de Pastoret on 9 June 1800: "I am writing a novel . . . and preparing for a literary career. Contrary to the usual sequence, I started with generalities and have now embarked on a work of the imagination. We shall see what happens" (Solovieff, 176). By September, she informed Pastoret that she was focusing on women's condition: "I am continuing my *novel*, which has become the story of women's destiny presented under various guises" (181).

Delphine appeared in December 1802. By the following May, it was in its fourth edition; two translations had come out in London and three in Germany. Although Staël specified that political polemics would have no part in her novel, she situated the action during the last years of the Revolution. This time gap facilitated treating such tinderbox questions as divorce and monastic vows, which are germane to the plot.[2] The book's dedication—a quotation from Mme Necker's posthumous *Mélanges*—sums up the fictional dilemma: "A man must be able to challenge public opinion, a woman to submit." The tragedy of *Delphine* arises from the reversal of these sex-related roles; the hero is incapable of defying society, while the heroine is incapable of yielding.

The preface to the first edition, summarizing the history of fiction in a single paragraph, is like a précis of the *Essai sur les fictions*. Although writing fiction may appear easy (witness the slew of mediocre novels), in effect it requires uncommon imagination and sensitivity. Like Henry Fielding's *Tom Jones* (1749), *Clarissa*, *La Nouvelle Héloïse*, and *Werther* (titles already mentioned in *Fictions*), the novel must probe hidden feelings and inculcate moral lessons. While explaining the tenor of knightly romance and granting nodding recognition to Marie-Madeleine de La

Fayette, Staël places fictional mastery firmly in eighteenth-century England. Overlooking Chateaubriand's devastating critique of *Littérature*, she lauds his "original, extraordinary, overwhelming imagination" (*OC*, 5:xlv) in the *Génie du christianisme* (The Genius of Christianity, 1802) while at the same time specifying that creative inspiration is antithetical to religious dictates.

The first part of *Delphine*, which begins in April 1790, initiates a confrontation between two rivals for the same man and highlights their personality clashes. With the generosity that will be her downfall, Delphine d'Albémar offers a gift of land to facilitate marriage between her cousin-in-law Matilde de Vernon and Léonce de Mondoville. (This is the first of many ironical twists of plot, for it is Matilde's eventual marriage to Léonce, accomplished by duplicity when he and Delphine are already in love, that will doom the heroine to suffering and death.) The contrast between the two women is a product of character and upbringing. Raised in the Catholic church, Matilde is a cold, self-righteous religious bigot, whose conformity to convention provides a counterpoint to Delphine's candor and spontaneity. The latter's moral character has been formed, not by church dogma, but by her late husband. (Like Adélaïde and Pauline, she was married young to a much older man[3] but was genuinely fond of her husband, who was more like a father than a spouse.)[4] Delphine echoes her husband's (and Staël's) humanistic creed: "He believed in God and trusted in the soul's immortality; virtue based on goodness constituted his cult toward the supreme Being" (*OC*, 5:17). Staël's valuation of natural goodness over ritual (and of Protestantism over Catholicism)[5] is concretized by Delphine's later serving as lay confessor to Matilde's dying mother and as moral mentor to Léonce. Functioning as Delphine's confidante and surrogate mother, her sister-in-law Louise d'Albémar warns against the unscrupulous ambition of Sophie de Vernon, Matilde's mother and Delphine's close friend. Ugly and deformed,[6] Louise has buried herself in the country because her physical defects have eradicated any hope of love or marriage.

Léonce de Mondoville's composite background—half Spanish, half French[7]—supposedly accounts for his hypersensitivity and prickly code of honor. He explains (prophetically) to his preceptor Barton why he has not yet fallen in love: "I was afraid to love a woman who might not agree with me about the importance I attach to people's opinion, and whose charm would ensnare me while her way of thinking made me suffer" (*OC*, 5:104). The stage is set for an impasse between the impulsive, unconventional heroine and the tradition-bound hero. While recognizing the disparity between Léonce's character and her own, Delphine is smitten by pity when she sees him pale and in pain. Among Staël's heroines, sympathy for a suffering hero is an invariable prelude to love.

Staël inserts vignettes of the duc de Mendoce, a "flatterer," Mme du Marset, a busybody, and M. d'Ervins, a man consumed by self-interest. These social "types," like those traced in *Passions*, create the background of conventional attitudes against which Delphine's story will be played out. Societal pressures are exemplified in the famous incident when Delphine, accompanying Sophie de Vernon and Léonce to the Tuileries to see the queen, defies the assembled society by befriending Mme de R., who has been collectively snubbed.[8]

Delphine's guileless generosity precipitates her disgrace and Léonce's desertion. In a weak moment, she agrees to lend her home for a tryst between her friend Thérèse d'Ervins and M. de Serbellane, Thérèse's lover. When the irate husband discovers the couple, he challenges Serbellane to a duel and is killed. Delphine confesses her part in this event to her presumed friend Sophie who, while promising to exonerate her to Léonce, in actuality persuades him that Serbellane is Delphine's lover and hastens his marriage to Matilde. Delphine attends the church ceremony, hidden behind a pillar, where Léonce imagines he sees her reaching out to him.

In the second part, Matilde's absorption in religious duties prompts Léonce to describe the void of his marriage, in terms that reflect Staël's own marital deception: "Side by side we will proceed along the path that leads to the grave—a road we ought to travel together; the journey will be as silent and somber as its destination" (*OC*, 5:256). Matilde's bigotry extends to a cousin who has divorced and remarried, whom the more open-minded Delphine visits and whose story she learns. After a miserable first marriage, Elise fell in love with Henri de Lebensei. Although his strength of character and complete indifference to other people's opinion have provided a bulwark against the world's disfavor, she has been obliged to withdraw from the society she defied for the sake of love.

At a performance of *Tancrède* (a play Staël repeatedly favored), Delphine spies Léonce hidden in a cloak, shaking with sobs as the hero expresses his love for Aménaïde and despair at her infidelity. Realizing that she has been maligned, Delphine determines to regain Léonce's esteem. Thérèse decides meanwhile to become a nun and entrust her daughter Isore to Delphine's care. When Léonce learns from the child that Serbellane was courting her mother and not Delphine, he implores the latter to tell him the truth, but she refuses to exculpate herself for fear of angering him against his mother-in-law.

Summoned suddenly to Sophie's deathbed, Delphine is handed a confessional letter tracing the steps that led the older woman from a tormented childhood to a perverted, amoral, self-centered adulthood.[9]
Orphaned at age three, she was brought up by an unprincipled tutor
and then forced to marry a man she detested lest she be confined to a
convent forever; her only recourse was hypocrisy and deception.
Although she led a life of pleasure, she gave her daughter a strict
Catholic education. Afraid of losing an inheritance when d'Albémar
married Delphine, she studied the young woman's character carefully: "I
soon realized that you were governed by your good qualities—kindness,
generosity, confidence—as others are controlled by passion, and that it
was almost as difficult for you to resist your virtues, however unpremed-
itated, as for others to withstand their vices" (*OC,* 5:459). Because she
resented Delphine for endangering Matilde's marriage, she did not intercede with Léonce after d'Ervins's death, as she had promised. Ironically,
a child (Isore) uncovered her duplicity. Now that she is dying, she can
speak the truth. Delphine is the only person she ever loved, who sometimes made her doubt her heartless calculations. Countermanding
Matilde's order to send for a priest, Sophie asks Delphine to hear her
prayers. In replacing the traditional clergyman, the heroine plays the
role of confessor whose saintly ministrations rehabilitate the sinner and
whose religious morality, untainted by dogma or prejudice, supersedes
the arid rigidity of Matilde's creed. After the emotional turmoil of
Léonce's unexpected arrival, his furious denunciation of his mother-in-
law's treachery and deceit, and Sophie's death, Delphine falls dangerous-
ly ill.

In the third part, Léonce—disregarding his customary subservience to
social pressure, and with no qualms about the risk to Delphine's reputation—begs her to live with him as man and wife. When she refuses to
see him again, Léonce first threatens to inform Matilde of their love,
then contrives to change Delphine's mind with the prospect of reform-
ing him spiritually as she had Sophie. In confirmation of Staël's assertion
in *Passions* that true love means merging one's self with the beloved,
Delphine tells Léonce: "At present I am merely a creature who lives for
the man she loves and exists only for the interest and glory of the object
she has chosen" (*OC,* 6:50–51). Léonce announces his presentiment that
he will die young, happy to perish in the full ardor of love, before age
makes the heart grow cold (another Staëlian notion).

Like Théodore before him, Léonce grows jealous of Delphine's social
success as the center of attention in every salon, where men and women
stand three deep to hear her. Wanting her all to himself, he asks to spend

the winter together at her country house of Bellerive—again inducing Delphine to flaunt convention. While there, he admires her unsuspected housewifely skills,[10] and they visit the Belmont ménage, which exemplifies marital happiness. Mme de Belmont gave up a fortune to marry a blind man, whom she loves and nurtures. With their two children, they form a picture of self-contained domestic bliss, as Belmont describes it: "Life offers no greater joy than the union of marriage and the affection of children, which is only perfect when one cherishes their mother. . . . No relationship outside marriage is permanent. External events or natural disinclinations shatter once-solid bonds. Opinion pursues you . . . and poisons your happiness" (*OC*, 6:116). For Staël, love in marriage is still the ultimate utopia.

Uneasy about the imminent arrival in Paris of a man named Valorbe (who will play the villain's role assigned to Meltin in *Pauline*), Delphine asks Louise to dissuade him from visiting her. A royalist, Léonce is pained by Delphine's prorevolutionary sentiments. Like her creator, she claims to detest factionalism and to cherish liberty. Before entering the cloister, Thérèse begs Léonce not to damn her by making Delphine "guilty." In the furious belief that Delphine is conspiring to leave him, he insists she prove her love by swearing, at the very altar where he took his marriage vow, that she will be his; if not, he will kill himself on the spot. Praying heaven to protect her, Delphine falls in a faint.[11]

In the fourth part, Delphine's rash generosity once again incurs society's stigma. Having unwisely granted Valorbe political asylum for the night, thereby provoking an altercation between him and Léonce, she is maligned for giving an assignation to two men in one night. Léonce cannot avenge the affront to Delphine's honor because, as Lebensei explains, "we can only protect the bonds that society sanctions—a wife, a sister, a daughter—but never the one who is linked to us by love alone " (*OC*, 6:312–13). Lebensei also furnishes philosophical and moral arguments in favor of divorce (which the Constituent Assembly is about to ratify): society encourages marriages of convenience without permitting a means of escape (including adultery); a bad, irreversible marriage makes for a hopeless old age; youthful inexperience can entail a lifetime of misery; children are adversely affected by "the eternal circle of suffering formed by an ill-assorted and indissoluble union" (327). This liberal position—a courageous stand for women's rights and a refutation of Mme Necker's posthumous work opposing divorce—was to cost the author dearly in social and critical disapproval. Although at one point she considered divorcing her husband and marrying Narbonne,[12] Staël eventually gave up the idea, as she has Delphine reject it. The latter returns to society in a futile attempt to silence wagging tongues. Ostracized at a social gathering, she flees in humiliation (a reversal of the incident when she alone befriended Mme de R.). Having learned that Matilde is carrying Léonce's child, she departs incognito for Switzerland with Isore.

The fifth part begins on 7 December 1791, as Delphine crosses the border. The bleak weather and bare trees remind her of death. In a rare allusion to the harmony between nature and mood, a storm on the lake mirrors her agitation.[13] She flees to Zurich on learning that Valorbe, who has vowed to stop at nothing either to win or to punish her, is in Lausanne. When she takes up residence in a convent run by Mme de Ternan, Léonce's aunt, Delphine is warned by a new friend, Henriette de Cerlebe, against the abbess's authoritarian and self-centered character. Afraid that the new divorce law will encourage Léonce to abandon Matilde for Delphine, Mme de Mondoville asks her sister, the abbess, to do everything in her power to separate the two. Mme de Ternan resolves to make Delphine a nun. At the latter's behest, Lebensei tries to dissuade Léonce from joining the émigré forces to fight against France. His arguments against civil war and party prejudices repeat ideas contained in *Passions.* Like Staël, Lebensei voices the patriotic duty not to tolerate foreign armies in the land and declaims that "liberty . . . is the prime happiness and sole glory of the social order; history is adorned by the virtues of free peoples" (*OC*, 7:84). This type of liberal dissertation, upholding freedom and revolutionary ideals, particularly irked Bonaparte.

Henriette de Cerlebe tries to persuade Delphine to accept Valorbe; not believing in romantic love, she lauds filial and maternal affections instead. She recounts her life story: at her father's urging, she retired to the country to raise her children herself; she has learned to enjoy domestic duties and the calm contemplation of nature in company with a sensitive, intelligent, and indulgent father (with whom she enjoys the creator's fantasized relationship with the widowed Necker). Delphine spurns Henriette's suggestion; death is preferable to a mismatched marriage. Indignant at her rejection, Valorbe vows to pursue and possess her.

Yielding unwisely to pity when he is arrested for debt, Delphine travels to nearby Zell to bail him out. The ingrate locks her up in his house; if she will not marry him, he will dishonor her by publicizing the fact that they spent the night together. Upon Delphine's return to the convent next morning, Mme de Ternan threatens to expel her unless she takes the veil. After learning that Valorbe has threatened to carry her off by force and Matilde has borne a child, Delphine tearfully accedes.

When he finds out what she has done, Valorbe clears her name, then kills himself. Henriette points up the ironic twist: "A week after pronouncing her vows, she learned that the terrible sacrifice she had made was for nought" (*OC*, 7:179).

When the sixth part opens, Matilde and her newborn son have died; her last wish was that Léonce marry Delphine. Lebensei is dispatched to find the hero, who has left for Switzerland. Having heard of a nameless woman resembling Delphine in Paradise Abbey, Léonce is ecstatic at the prospect of seeing her. But when she appears, veiled in black, he shakes the grill in anguish. "Matilde is dead," he cries. "Delphine, can you be mine?" "No," she replies, "but I can die!" (*OC*, 7:223). To save the two, Lebensei proposes that Delphine return to France, where monastic vows can be broken by law, and there live with Léonce in defiance of "absurd prejudices" (229). Always the voice of rational judgment, Lebensei urges Léonce to disregard social convention, citing reasons why Delphine's impetuous act should not bind her eternally. Although Léonce ostensibly agrees, Delphine worries about his underlying conviction. For health reasons, she receives permission to spend two months at Baden with him.

In the original ending, Delphine realizes that Léonce is still troubled by other people's opinion when a crowd murmurs against her in public and he complains that life without honor is unbearable. Aware that they cannot be happy together, she swears that she will never be his wife; Léonce swears in turn that he will not survive without her. He writes to announce his intention of joining the émigré army: the only way he can reconcile the conflict between his character and his love is to sacrifice his life.

With Serbellane's help, Delphine finds Léonce in a Verdun prison, where he is about to be judged and shot. He tells Delphine that the proximity of death has made him understand life's priorities; if she obtains his pardon, they can be happy together. At her insistence, Léonce prays to God for the first time in his life. By dint of eloquent supplication, Delphine prevails on the judge to release him,[14] but a commissioner from Paris rescinds the order. Serbellane arrives with a reprieve, provided Léonce declares he did not intend to bear arms against France, but he refuses lest people think he signed falsely; at the point of death, he still bows to public opinion. (This last-minute pardon, with an untenable alternative to execution, echoes *Jane Gray*).

After swallowing poison in "a moment of convulsion and despair" (*OC*, 7:346), Delphine accompanies Léonce to his execution so that she may serve him (as she did Sophie) in lieu of a priest. In the tumbrel, she prays for and with him; their love will endure forever: "Those who succumb slowly beneath the weight of time can believe in destruction, for they have experienced it in advance; but we who approach the grave full of life attest to immortality!" (350–51). Just as Léonce tells the firing squad to dispense with a blindfold and aim at his heart, Delphine collapses and dies. The deeply affected soldiers are ready to spare the prisoner, but he hurls insults until one of them fires and kills him. After burying the lovers in the same grave, Serbellane muses: "Léonce should have defied opinion . . . when happiness and love made it his duty to do so; Delphine, to the contrary, over-confident of her heart's purity, was never able to respect the power of opinion to which women must submit; but do nature and conscience teach the same moral lesson as society, which imposes contrary rules on men and women? and did my unfortunate friends have to suffer so much for such pardonable errors?" (357).

This ending, consonant with the tenor of the story and the character of the protagonists, makes Delphine a suicide-for-love and Léonce a misguided hero to the last. It reenacts with greater pathos the execution scenes sketched in *Jane Gray* and "L'Epître au malheur." The conclusion echoes Staël's youthful credo that it is better to die at the height of love than to witness its decline. Serbellane's final reflection emphasizes the antithetical roles of hero and heroine: if Léonce had disregarded convention (as a man may) and Delphine had observed it (as a woman must), their tragedy would have been averted.

Because Staël herself was caught between Scylla and Charybdis— between braving and submitting to public opinion—her personal dilemma reflects that of her heroine. Long after *Delphine* appeared, its author took certain criticism to heart and, unlike her heroine, ceded to public outcry. Not only did she write a preface defending her moral intentions, but she even penned an alternative, nonsuicidal ending in order to appease her detractors. It was her son Auguste, rummaging among his mother's papers after her death, who discovered this alternative denouement as well as the apologetic "Quelques réflexions sur le but moral de *Delphine*" (Thoughts on the moral goal of *Delphine*), which he published with her collected works.

In the new ending, Léonce solemnly confirms his promise to marry Delphine by placing a ring on her finger in the presence of the rising sun. Back in Mondoville, near the royalist enclave of the Vendée region, it is soon rumored that the young lord is about to dishonor himself by wedding a nun. An old soldier of his father's accuses Léonce of disgracing the family name; when Delphine overhears him explain that he cannot abandon a woman who has sacrificed everything for him, these

words take a mortal toll. Dying, she writes Léonce to explain the basic
discord between her sensitivity and society. Weary of suffering, she is
content to die before love palls. Sophie de Vernon was right: the differences in their characters would have prevented their being happy, even if
there had been no obstacle to their union. She asks to have music played
during her last night (like Mme Necker) and dies at dawn. At her
request, Léonce entrusts Isore to Louise d'Albémar, then departs for the
Vendée, where he is killed in his first encounter.

In this second ending, Léonce's liaison with Delphine is legitimized in
a ring ceremony under the aegis of nature, if not of the church; Delphine
manages to die for love without committing suicide; there is no religious
conversion by Léonce and no priestly ministrations by Delphine. If the
situation is artificial and lackluster, the underlying message is twisted to
hold Delphine, not society, responsible for her tragedy. We may dismiss
this alternative as an inauthentic compromise with the very conventions
that Staël's novel seeks to undermine.

Despite the mediocrity of this new denouement, "Le but moral de
Delphine" is a significant critical and feminist text. Insisting that her
novel stands on its own merits, without apology, Staël states that a literary work is vindicated by "the imposing impartiality of time" (*OC*, 5:v).
Because society as a collective personality tries to maintain the status
quo and ensure that outward conventions are observed, it feels threatened by extraordinary individuals—especially women—and judges them
harshly. Delphine's difficulties arise out of her character; Staël never
intended to present her as a model to emulate—the epigraph blames
both Léonce and Delphine. She considers her novel useful because it
stresses goodness in a postrevolutionary period when sympathy toward
misfortune is imperative. It teaches women not to trust their good qualities but to respect opinion, else it will crush them. The author also feels
that *Delphine* admonishes society to deal kindly with those of exceptional mind and spirit; otherwise it commits a disproportionate injustice that
may ruin a promising career.

In balancing a graceless Matilde against a superior Delphine, Staël
claims to have demonstrated the overriding force of morality, for, in spite
of her cold religiosity, Matilde's honesty outweighs all Delphine's qualities and charm. Although men may sometimes escape punishment, "the
social order makes it impossible for women to avoid the unhappiness
that results from wrongdoing" (*OC*, 5:xix). Once a man has obtained a
woman's affection—unless their bond is sanctified by marriage—his
ardor cools first: "[Men's] lot is too independent, their lives too dynamic,

their future too certain, for them to experience the secret terror of loneli-
ness that ceaselessly pursues even those women whose destiny is most
brilliant" (xxiv). *Delphine* can help those who are victimized by their feelings (as another way of instilling the lesson of *Passions*). "We do not sufficiently realize the dire combination, for our happiness, of being endowed
with a mind that judges and with a heart that suffers from the truths the
mind reveals" (xxvii). Mirza was also meant to illustrate the dichotomy
of reason and emotion.

Staël professes that she changed the ending for various reasons, but
not because some readers objected to Delphine's suicide.[15] A writer does
not express a personal opinion when characters act in a certain way. Nor
can an argument be found for or against suicide in the example of a
woman who lacks the strength to endure life after the man she loves has
gone to the scaffold. Moral severity must be tempered with sympathy
and understanding (attributes Staël claimed for herself in *Passions*): "One
must have suffered in order to be heard by those who suffer and . . . to
have tried a dagger on one's own heart before asserting it does not hurt"
(*OC*, 5:xxxvi).

According to her stated intention, Staël populated *Delphine* with an
assortment of women whose lives represent the various possibilities open
to their sex, none of which is satisfactory. In spite of a loving heart and
sensitive nature, Louise d'Albémar is condemned to spinsterhood for no
reason other than her physical unattractiveness. Thérèse d'Ervins, like
Elise de Lebensei and countless others, is married against her will to a
despicable husband. Her attempt to find happiness in adulterous love is
doomed; not only is she ostracized by society, but she is forced to bury
herself in a convent, that is, to embrace a living death. Elise de Lebensei
depicts the woman shamed by divorce who, in embracing love, must
retreat from society. Furthermore, her decision requires collaboration by a
man strong enough and willing to support her in her isolation. Mme de
Belmont epitomizes the fulfillment of perfect love in marriage; however,
it must be noted that her husband, being blind, depends on her like a
child.[16] Henriette de Cerlebe celebrates the joys of maternity and domestic tranquillity in a rural setting, where she rears her children herself—
but with the help and emotional support of a loving father. Mme de
Ternan's story exemplifies women's destiny: while young and beautiful,
she turned men's heads; when her beauty faded, life lost its meaning. In
her latter years, she had no option but the cloister. Sophie de Vernon illustrates the depravity to which an inadequate or uncaring upbringing can
lead. However selfish and deceitful she has been, however deeply she has

wronged Delphine, her "confession" explains her character defects according to woman's obligatory status. As a youngster, Sophie's feelings and intellect were repressed. She was forced to marry a man she loathed because the alternative was life imprisonment in a convent (a centuries-old way of coercing women into wedlock). While deploring her stunted character, Staël is careful to show that circumstance forced her to become what she was. She also has Sophie properly repent before she dies.

Although fictional characters are often composites of people the author may have known, critics over the centuries have enjoyed the game of designating Staël's probable models. In this respect, *Delphine* has been a fertile field for treasure seekers. The title character shares a number of her creator's traits. Clever, kind, and impetuous, she is an impassioned lover, faithful friend, and champion of freedom. Ambivalent about social conventions, she flaunts them while acknowledging their abusive power. Delphine is also pictured as beautiful—an attribute her creator sadly believed she lacked.[17] Some contemporaries and present-day critics take Sophie de Vernon to be the portrait of Talleyrand in skirts.[18] Because she is married to an older man and is one of the most seductive beauties of her time, Thérèse d'Ervins has been likened to Juliette Récamier (Levaillant, 37). Louise d'Albémar resembles Suzanne Necker to some extent, although she is more sympathetic than Staël ever believed her mother to be. Gutwirth calls Matilde "Mme Necker's grossly caricatured surrogate" (112) because, while pious and prudish, she is also critical of and a rival to Delphine. Léonce is supposedly a combination of Narbonne and Ribbing, with greater emphasis on the first.

Contrary to Staël's naive assumption, *Delphine* did not win the approbation of the first consul. Quite the opposite. A number of elements in the book were almost guaranteed to arouse Bonaparte's ire. To begin with, Staël's bold dedication "to silent and enlightened France" was a backhanded slap in the face. Her defense of divorce and denigration of Catholic ritual in favor of a humanistic Protestantism appeared soon after Napoleon signed a concordat with the pope. Her running indictment of society and arranged marriages was regarded as a criticism of the status quo, as were the liberal views she expressed via Lebensei. Her profeminist attitudes were also anathema to a man who felt that women were good for only one thing—child-rearing.

Bonaparte was all the more incensed when *Delphine*'s appearance in December 1802 became an epochal event. To counteract its popularity, he instigated a virulent press campaign. The *Journal des Débats* of December 1802 attacked Staël's immorality in denying divine revelation and advocating divorce. Bonaparte criticized both book and author: "I do not like women who try to be men any more than I like men who are effeminate. . . . I cannot abide that woman" (Diesbach, 260). In May 1803 one Emmanuel Dupaty staged a parody entitled *Delphine, ou l'Opinion* (Delphine, or, Opinion), satirizing both Staël and one of her detractors, Félicité de Genlis, but a coalition of Staël's friends ensured the play's swift demise. Charles de Villers was ecstatic about Staël's novel; he wrote her on 4 May 1803: "Your work sparkles with beauties of detail, observations, perspicacious and profound views, and passages of eloquence, purity, grace, and breath of feeling. . . . You have feminized Rousseau's pen" (Jasinski, 4:627 n. 4).

Delphine may retain the prolix and sentimentalized excesses of its period, the epistolary form (also symptomatic of its age) may be artificial and confining, and the proliferation of plot and subplot may tax the patience of today's reader; nevertheless, the novel has much to recommend it. The characters, especially the gallery of female portraits, are lifelike and appealing. When not enraging, the love story is engaging. The heroine is not a two-dimensional stereotype but a woman of multiple facets and accomplishments. Her early, isolated education, like Emile's, fostered the very spontaneity and impulsive generosity that bring her into conflict with the severe social arbiters among whom she is thrust. Her suicide at the end is as much a gesture of defiance as despair.

From a feminist point of view, as Noreen Swallow aptly points out in her excellent analysis of *Delphine* (65–76), Staël's heroine is the victim of a patriarchal society whose dictates are reinforced by the very women it represses. Church and society collaborate in maintaining women within a circumscribed role wherein their primary function is to marry and bear children. The laws, customs, and attitudes sanctioned by society contribute to the subjugation of women while perpetuating the pleasure and security of men: "Anticipating modern feminist literature by over one hundred and fifty years, Mme de Staël sets to work to expose these deeply ingrained, chauvinistic values, showing how they operate, often below the level of consciousness, to obstruct the development and fulfillment of women, to undermine relations between the sexes, and to poison the moral outlook of society" (66).

In the course of the novel, Delphine's inveterate kindness and affection are consistently disparaged by a Greek chorus of minor characters, many of them women. It is Delphine's mischance to fall in love with a man who lives by the patriarchal code she challenges. Léonce does not merely represent a contrasting attitude toward societal traditions. He embodies masculine freedom from the values that govern women's lives. He can marry as he chooses, leave his pregnant wife to woo another woman, and scuttle back and forth between the two without a hint of disapprobation. He is selfish enough to try to force Delphine into the kind of behavior he excoriates—and although her "virtue" remains intact, her reputation is tattered: "Through the arrogant imposition of Léonce's will both Matilde and Delphine are devalued as individuals" (Swallow, 72). The book reinforces Staël's contention that society accepts in a man behavior it finds contemptible in a woman.

Staël's criticism of patriarchal society repeatedly calls into question the double standard governing men's and women's lives. The same frustration in the face of convention, the same struggle between love and independence, the same destruction of woman's potential by man's selfish privilege, pervades Staël's fictional masterpiece *Corinne*, which carries woman's fight for love and self-fulfillment onto a higher and more complex plane.

Chapter 6
A Mythical Double: *Corinne*

Much as George Sand has been identified with her creature Lélia, Germaine de Staël is represented in the popular imagination by her fictional double, Corinne.[1] The protagonist's personality, cultural background, familial influences, career, and love interest are so "Staëlian" that the identities of character and creator merge.[2] Staël was increasingly associated with her heroine,[3] as were those women who emulated her example. Ralph Waldo Emerson dubbed Margaret Fuller the "Yankee Corinna"[4]; similarly, Kate Chopin was known as the Corinne of St. Louis.[5]

Corinne germinated in Staël's mind as a twofold conception. It was to be a novel—a love story illustrating her frequent lament that social mores prevent even the most exceptional woman from reconciling love with a career. Inspired by the author's trip to Italy,[6] it was also to be a travelogue[7]—the Italian equivalent of the book on Germany she had temporarily shelved. This second purpose accounts for the disquisitions on Italian landscape, customs, monuments, artworks, sculpture, and music that are injected more or less harmoniously into the text. Many of Staël's experiences—her perilous winter crossing of the Mont-Cenis, ascent of Vesuvius, coronation by the Arcadian Academy—are transposed directly into the novel. The title—*Corinne, ou l'Italie* (Corinne, or Italy)—underscores the book's dual emphasis.[8]

The first mention of her project occurs in a letter of 8 August 1805 to the poet Vincenzo Monti, who had introduced Staël to the beauties of Italian verse: "I have read the beginning of my Italian novel to my friends; they think it better than anything I have written hitherto" (Blennerhassett, 3:152). On her return from Italy, she set aside the notes for *Allemagne* and began writing *Corinne* at fever pitch. The novel appeared on 1 May 1807 and was an overnight sensation.[9] Written in the narrative third person, it is divided into 20 "books" that alternate more or less erratically between plot development and travel guide. The titles approximate the contents.

"Oswald" (book 1) begins with a handsome and sensitive hero, a heartfelt sorrow, and a departure. Grieving over the recent death of his father,[10] Oswald, Lord Nelvil, leaves the gloom of his native Scotland for sunlit Italy, where he will meet Corinne. As in *Delphine*, the setting is in place for an inevitable rift between the traditional hero and the free-spirited heroine, products of their conflicting cultures. En route, Nelvil meets an ebullient Frenchman, comte d'Erfeuil, whose outrageous chauvinism is counterbalanced by his innate kindness. Like Léonce, Nelvil proves his heroic mettle, singlehandedly saving the town of Ancône from a fiery conflagration; later, he will rescue an old man from drowning.

In book 2, "Corinne at the Capitol," Oswald learns of preparations to crown the most famous woman in Italy. Not only is Corinne an outstanding poet and *improvisatrice*,[11] but she is also a superb actress and dancer, a brilliant conversationalist, and a skilled artist. Her background is a mystery, her surname and birthplace unknown. Arriving at the Capitol in a chariot drawn by four white horses (like the winged victory favored in French republican representations), Corinne is dressed in white like Domenichino's sibyl, with a blue ribbon accentuating her bosom and an Indian shawl wound round her head: "Her arms were strikingly beautiful, and her figure was large, a bit heavy, like a Greek statue" (*OC*, 8:42).[12] Improvising verses while strumming her lyre, she celebrates the architects of Italy's past glory—Dante, Tasso, Petrarch, Ariosto, Michelangelo, Raphael, and Galileo—and rhapsodizes over the country's natural beauties. Noting Oswald's doleful expression, she extols the sweetness of grief in a land filled with memories of the illustrious dead. When she thanks him in English for retrieving the crown that has slipped from her head (a symbolic omen), her native accent startles him.

In book 3, Corinne receives d'Erfeuil and Oswald in her tastefully decorated home. Their admiration of her English elicits a refusal to discuss her past. She explains improvisation in terms of supernatural, sibylline inspiration:[13] "I feel myself a poet, not only when a felicitous choice of rhymes and melodic syllables or a happy combination of images dazzles my listeners, but when my spirit is uplifted and gazes with disdain on selfishness and infamy. . . . Then it is that my verses are better" (*OC*, 8:94). Art still has a moral purpose for Staël.

Book 4, "Rome," traces a romantic itinerary through the Eternal City, with Corinne acting as Oswald's spiritual and intellectual mentor. In spite of the prophetic warning of her friend Prince Castel-Forte, she cannot help falling in love with Oswald. For his part, Oswald is fearful of contravening the wishes of his dead father, who had intended that his son marry his best friend's daughter, Lucile Edgermond. The tour continues, in book 5, among "Tombs, Churches, and Palaces," which

Oswald finds appropriate to his melancholy disposition. "In your happy country, clear skies make somber thoughts vanish; but sorrow that has bored to the bottom of our soul disrupts our life forever" (*OC*, 8:161). Staël demonstrates fictionally her theories of climate and character; beyond the incompatibilities that divide the protagonists of *Delphine*, she adds national characteristics that cannot be overcome.

A controversy between Oswald and Corinne is Staël's pretext for describing "Italian Habits and Character" in book 6. Jealous of the success of Corinne's sensational Neapolitan dance,[14] Oswald criticizes Italian flightiness and infidelity, then writes Corinne a letter denigrating Italian men; her reply vindicates Italian military, republican, and artistic renown, which cannot be sustained under current political conditions. Vigorously defending Corinne against a compatriot's unsavory innuendos, Oswald wants to protect her against calumny by wedding her. But first, he must resolve the mystery of her past.

In one of the liveliest scenes of the novel, a coterie of intellectuals discuss the relative merits of English, French, and "Italian Literature" in book 7. Oswald favors Shakespeare and his native drama, d'Erfeuil strongly supports French tragedy, Corinne (the only female voice) champions Italian spontaneity and imagination, while Castel-Forte moderates among them. Stressing Italian contributions to comedy, defending the energy of the Italian character, and deploring the effects on literature of Italy's lost independence, Corinne is the author's mouthpiece for reviving contemporary Italian literature. Countering d'Erfeuil's chauvinism, she insists that other nations should not pattern themselves on the French, for imitation leads to sterility: "Genius is essentially creative; it bears the mark of the individual who possesses it. . . . Imitation is a kind of death" (*OC*, 8:238–39). Castel-Forte offers the conciliating opinion (also Staël's) that the literature of one nation can provide important insights for another. He proposes that Corinne display her talents as tragedian in her own translation of Shakespeare's *Romeo and Juliet*. During her magnificent portrayal of Juliet, Corinne addresses to Oswald the speeches meant for Romeo. Experiencing twinges of pleasure and jealousy, he would have preferred that Corinne, like a reserved Englishwoman, perform for him alone.

Resuming her role as cicerone in book 8, Corinne conducts Oswald on an art-appreciation tour of "Statues and Paintings" that enables Staël to confront two contrasting attitudes. Curiously, she has Corinne represent the classical and Oswald the preromantic position. Perceiving art from a moralistic point of view, Corinne regards sculpture as pagan and paint-

ing as Christian: "Painting indicates the mysteries of contemplation and
resignation and, by its ephemeral colors, gives voice to the immortal
soul" (OC, 8:310).[15] They visit Corinne's house in Tivoli, appropriately
situated near the temple of the sibyl: "What place could be more suitable as Corinne's dwelling, in Italy, than the abode consecrated to the
sibyl, to the memory of a woman animated by divine inspiration!" (323).
Corinne exhibits her gallery of historical, religious, and literary paintings. When she sings Scottish ballads in front of an Ossianic landscape,
Oswald breaks down and asks her to become his wife; he insists, however, that she hide nothing from him. Corinne promises to tell all after the
approaching religious holiday.

In book 9, "A Popular Festival and Music," they return to Rome for
carnival, which Staël describes in its colorful riotousness. D'Erfeuil warns
Nelvil about compromising Corinne; flighty though the Frenchman may
appear, he claims he would never flout social conventions. To prepare for
"Holy Week" (book 10), Corinne retreats to a convent. Oswald spies her
on Good Friday in the Sistine Chapel, transported by the solemn
Miserere into a prayerful state of meditation. Afterward, she contrasts
her religious credo, embracing art, poetry, and joy, with the moral aus-
terity of Oswald's Protestantism, urging him to blend "love, religion,
genius, the sun, perfume, music, and poetry; the only atheism is coldness, egotism, and baseness" (OC, 8:391).

Hero and heroine visit sites of historical and literary interest near
"Naples and the Hermitage of Saint-Salvador" (book 11). For Staël, the
South truly begins in the Neapolitan region, with its orange-scented aro-
mas and prolific vegetation—a palpable contrast to the bleak northern
clime.[16] A cloud covering the moon seems to Corinne to bode ill for
their love. During a simple but moving service that takes place aboard
an English warship and confirms British values of sobriety and discipline,
Oswald is pleased to see Corinne seated among the English wives, who
are too timid and constrained to speak. This misinterpretation of her
character is a prelude to disaster.

An excursion to Pompeii impresses the travelers with a distressing
sense of time's passage, life's brevity, and the abrupt transition from life
to death. As they ascend Vesuvius, passing from the fertile plain to a
scene of ashes and death, Oswald tells "Lord Nelvil's Story" (book 12).
Raised by a beloved father, he left at age 21 for France, where the con-
niving Mme d'Arbigny gulled him into remaining against his father's
wishes by falsely claiming to be carrying his child. Her cynical and ego-
tistical confederate M. de Maltigues revealed the truth after Oswald

spared his life in a duel. Berating himself for causing his father's death, young Nelvil returned to England and swore on his father's grave never to marry anyone of whom the elder Nelvil might have disapproved. He now has Corinne read his father's advice on honoring parents (passages significantly lifted from Necker's *Cours de morale religieuse* [Course in religious morality, 1800]).

In book 13, "Vesuvius and the Naples Landscape," the lava creeping down the mountain and flames crackling in the crater seem a dread portent to Corinne. Before recounting her past, she requests a week's reprieve in order to arrange a party for Oswald at Cape Misenum, with a visit to the temple of the Cumaean Sibyl.[17] Hoping to sparkle once more for the man she loves, Corinne performs a second improvisation on her lyre. Singing of nature, poetry, and history on this sacrosanct site of the *Aeneid*, she compares volcanic forces with human passions and grieves for Pliny, Cicero, and Scipio, who died here. In a premonitory allusion, she empathizes with the women of this region—Cornelia, Agrippina, Brutus's wife Portia—who lost and mourned the men they loved. On their return to Naples, Oswald offers her the ring his father gave his mother and promises not to marry anyone else until or unless she sends it back.

"Corinne's Story" (book 14) apprises Oswald that she is Lord Edgermond's daughter by his first marriage, to a Roman woman; Lucile Edgermond is her half-sister. Raised in Italy, Corinne lost her mother when she was ten. At 15 she was brought to England, where her gentle three-year-old sister was her sole comfort. Her father's cold and self-righteous second wife reproached Corinne for initiating conversation at table and quoting Italian love poetry. Forced to cultivate her talents in secret, she loathed the monotonous existence of English women who, taciturn and withdrawn, would sit for hours after dinner waiting for the men: "When it was time to leave, they went off with their husbands, ready next day to resume a life which differed from that of the preceding day only by the date on the calendar and by the trace the years etched on these women's faces" (*OC,* 9:138). Attempting to impress the elder Lord Nelvil with her dancing, singing, and improvisation, she was judged too "vivacious" to marry his son Oswald. When she became financially independent on her father's death, she departed precipitously on an Italian ship. Assuming the name Corinne after a Greek woman poet,[18] she has spent the last six years in Rome, while Lady Edgermond spread the rumor that she had died at sea. Now that Oswald knows her story, she offers him his freedom.

In "Farewell to Rome and the Voyage to Venice" (book 15), Oswald is overwhelmed by this confession and feels he must return home to find out why his father opposed their marriage. After Corinne recovers from a plague that is decimating Rome, she and Oswald pursue their travels across the Apennines, along the Adriatic coast, through Bologna, Ferrara, and on to Venice (duplicating Staël's own itinerary). As they glide over the Venetian waters, a cannon blast signals that a nun has taken the veil, and Corinne shivers with foreboding at this "solemn warning given by a resigned woman to others who still struggle against destiny" (*OC*, 9:224).

"Departure and Separation" (book 16) begins with admirers importuning Corinne to act in a comedy—a pendant to her performance in *Romeo and Juliet*. Staël underscores the ironic contrast between the heroine's brilliant comic improvisation and the sad fate that awaits her: "Ah! who would not have pitied this sight, had he foreseen that such trusting gaiety would call down a thunderbolt and that such triumphant joy would soon turn to bitter grief" (*OC*, 9:244). When Oswald announces his departure the same night, a violent storm accentuates their tearful leavetaking. Once back in his homeland, he recognizes the superiority of robust English values. In the hope of persuading Lady Edgermond to acknowledge Corinne, he visits Northumberland, where he meets the beautiful, angelic Lucile. Nettled by Oswald's defense of Corinne, Lady Edgermond informs him of a letter proving his father's inexorable opposition to this marriage and his wish that Oswald choose the younger sister.

With incisive poignancy, Staël describes Corinne's solitary despair in "Corinne in Scotland" (book 17). Her life has come to resemble the monotonous English existence she once deplored: "She kept looking at her watch, hoping that an hour had gone by, and yet not knowing why she wanted time to pass because it brought nothing but a sleepless night, followed by an even more anguished day" (*OC*, 9:307). Unable to endure her torment, and yet realizing her folly, she determines to travel to Scotland to see Oswald. The latter is prey meanwhile to conflicting emotions. Duty precludes his marrying Corinne; convention forbids his living with her. As usual, he postpones making a decision. In England (where at first she falls ill), Corinne attends a theatrical performance where every eye, including Oswald's, is trained on a blonde beauty in Lady Edgermond's box. Aware that she cannot compete with "this innocent image of the springtime of life" (318), Corinne conceals herself in a corner of her loge (like Delphine at Léonce's marriage). She hides again in her carriage, draped in a black shawl, when Oswald takes Lucile for a gallop in Hyde Park. Noticing a dark, lurking figure (as Léonce imagined he saw Delphine in church), Oswald dismisses his supposition as a mistake. Half-crazed with sorrow, Corinne wraps Oswald's ring in a note saying, "You are free." Following him to Scotland (and falling ill again), she stops to visit her father's grave and finds a ball in progress at her ancestral manor. Lucile, wandering through the grounds, glimpses a white-swathed figure who resembles her long-dead sister and swoons. When she comes to, she kneels at their father's tomb, where Corinne overhears her praying to be Oswald's wife. Sacrificing her happiness to the child she once held in her arms, Corinne hands her note for Nelvil to a blind man, then falls in a faint.

In "The Sojourn in Florence" (book 18), it is d'Erfeuil, ironically, who finds and nurses Corinne back to health: "The frivolous man tended her, and the sensitive man broke her heart" (*OC*, 9:357). After seeing a newspaper announcement of Oswald's impending marriage to Lucile, she returns to Italy. Ill, feeble, and wasted, she chooses to live in isolation in Florence rather than return to the site of her former triumphs and Oswald's presence. Like the preromantic hero, Corinne suffers more intensely than ordinary people: "I am an exception to the universal rule. . . . There is happiness for everyone else; the terrible capacity for suffering, which is killing me, is a way of feeling unique to myself" (369–70). Unable to write, she pens meaningless words conceived in delirium. Although Staël believed, like the later romanticists, that genuine feeling is a sine qua non of poetic expression, the writer must achieve the equilibrium of distance, otherwise a too-present agony will produce "a somber agitation which harps ceaselessly on the same thoughts" (378). The loyal Prince Castel-Forte comes to stay with Corinne. As her health deteriorates, she can no longer hide her despair: "Unhappy love quenches all other feelings. . . . For this reason, duty commands women, and especially men, to respect and fear the love they inspire, for this passion can forever devastate both mind and heart" (389—90). The recurring threat of dementia as Corinne's anguish increases echoes the early "follies" Staël wrote and reflects the author's repeated fear of losing her mind over unrequited love.[19]

Peeved that Corinne has sent back his ring, Oswald has been easily maneuvered by Lady Edgermond into marrying Lucile at the outset of "Oswald's Return to Italy" (book 19). When he learns from d'Erfeuil the full story of Corinne's visit, he is devastated: "No one would ever love him as she had, and . . . he would be punished in some way for his cruelty toward her" (*OC*, 9:408). Though tempted, he cannot leave for Italy because Rome and Florence are already occupied by the French. While he is away at war, Lucile bears a daughter and learns of his relationship with Corinne. When he returns four years later, Oswald finds little Juliette to be a replica of Corinne.[20] Grown sick from nursing his mother-in-law, who has died after a lingering malady, he calls out deliriously for Corinne and the sunny South. When he recuperates, he is surprised that Lucile has arranged a trip to Italy. Setting out in December, they encounter a raging blizzard on the Mont-Cenis (like Staël herself). The weather is cold and dreary, and snow falls outside Milan. They visit a church in Parma where Lucile, cradling Juliette, looks exactly like Correggio's *Madonna della Scala*. Anxious inquiries about Corinne reveal that, living in retirement in Florence, she has written nothing and seen no one for years. In Bologna, Oswald is entranced by Domenichino's painting of the Sibyl. Lucile asks him timidly if he prefers this picture to Correggio's *Madonna*. Comprehending her intimation, he replies: "No longer does the Sibyl deliver oracles; her genius and talent have departed. But Correggio's celestial figure has lost none of her charms, and the wretched man who mistreated the one will never betray the other" (446).

In the Conclusion (book 20), Oswald is beset by memories as they cross into Tuscany. Ingrained reserve and timidity prevent him from communicating with Lucile, and vice versa. He learns from Castel-Forte that Corinne is seriously ill. In spite of his plea, she refuses to see him, for he has hurt her too deeply. Mouthing Staël's refutation of a double standard for men and women, Castel-Forte tells Oswald that he is at fault: "A man may wrong a woman without detriment in the world's opinion; these fragile idols, adored today, may be broken tomorrow, without anyone's coming to their defense. . . . A dagger's thrust is punished by law, while the cleaving of a sensitive heart is the subject of jest; it would be better to permit the dagger" (*OC*, 9:452–53). Miserable at the anguish he has caused, Oswald writes Corinne to explain that he would never have left her had he known she was in England, although he doubts they could have been happy together: "Uncertain as I am, could I choose one fate, however wonderful, without regretting another?"[21] He begs to see her, but Corinne again refuses, on the grounds that his presence might endanger the religious peace she has finally attained. She agrees, however, to give Juliette daily lessons. She also undertakes to brighten her sister's marriage by teaching Lucile to resemble the woman Oswald most loved. Her last wish before she dies is that Oswald find traces of her in Lucile and Juliette, "and that he never have a joyful feeling without remembering Corinne" (473).

No longer able to improvise, she arranges for a last performance of her written poetry so that "the ingrate who had deserted her would again realize that he had dealt a death blow to the woman of her era who was best able to love and to think" (*OC*, 9:474). An immense crowd gathers at the Florentine Academy, as a cold wind batters the windows (in nature's harmony with human grief). Dressed in black, Corinne totters to her seat; a young girl in white chants her verses, which Oswald hears through his sobs. Corinne's swan song is a solemn farewell to life, to Rome, to her talent, and to her love. Greeting death calmly if bitterly, she regrets not having devoted her talents to religion and the celebration of God: "Of all the spiritual faculties with which nature endowed me, suffering is the only one I exercised fully" (482). When the program is over, Corinne is carried home where, pointing to the same cloud that covered the moon in Naples, she expires, with Lucile and Oswald at her feet.

What happened to Oswald? the author asks. At first in so desperate a state that his life and reason were in danger, he sequestered himself at Tivoli until duty at last brought him back to family and England. "But did he forgive himself for his former conduct? did the world's approval console him? was he content with a common lot, after what he had lost? I know not; I do not wish, in this regard, to blame or absolve him" (*OC*, 9:486). The author's arch pretense of ignorance does not obviate the implicit conclusion that once again the aberrant hero is punished for his dereliction. Oswald is doomed to a life of remorse—a fitting chastisement for the annihilation of genius. From beyond the grave, Corinne exacts an exquisite vengeance. Not only does she fashion Oswald's wife and daughter in her image. She enters his marriage as an invisible third party responsible for whatever pleasure he may know. Although she denies resentment in the name of newfound religious peace, Corinne's revenge is sweet indeed.

Nowhere in literature can we find anything like the triumphal procession celebrating female achievement that Staël offers in *Corinne*. Whereas the heroine is borne through the streets like a conquering general, her victory—as Staël expressly points out—is that of genius, not military might (a not very subtle repudiation of Napoleon and of all martial values). Corinne is crowned at the Capitol with the conquering hero's laurel wreath in the presence of the highest dignitaries of the land. No apotheosis could be more gratifying.

In some ways, *Corinne* is a reworking of *Delphine* on a higher moral and intellectual scale, with greater values at stake. The impossible relationship between two mismatched lovers extends beyond conflicting attitudes toward society and convention to encompass questions of female creativity and fulfillment. Whereas Delphine was also beautiful, intelligent, and sensitive, her defiance was dictated by generosity and confined to social conduct; it was not based on an innate talent she wished or needed to express. Nor did she shake the foundations of patriarchy by aspiring to literary glory, like a man.

Just as Corinne is a more ambitious and talented Delphine, Oswald is a more enlightened version of Léonce. Equally weak and indecisive, he rejects love out of respect for his father's wishes (for Staël, a primordial value) rather than from some ingrained but questionable allegiance to convention. Although Oswald also bows to tradition, he evinces a greater breadth of cultural interest, a surer understanding of art, a more deep-seated religious conviction, than anything Léonce is capable of feeling. Both heroes are physically brave and morally deficient. Their inability to withstand social pressure for the sake of the women they love condemns them to a position of inferiority vis-à-vis those very women, whose generosity and strength of character far exceed theirs. Although Staël has attempted in each case to construct a male prototype on a par with her female protagonist (if only to justify the latter's love), she fails to draw him with the same compassion or to endow him with the breath of life that vitalizes her women characters.

The time warp between *Delphine* and *Corinne* is less pronounced than their spatial differentiation. *Delphine* is situated during the Revolution, which impinges only marginally on the story. The action of *Corinne* begins during the winter of 1794–95—prior to Napoleon's Italian campaign of 1796—and resumes four years later. The locale in *Delphine* scarcely exceeds the boundaries of salon life, until Delphine enters a Swiss convent; external decor is minimized. *Corinne*, to the contrary, is saturated with "local color." In fact, it is one of the first European novels to present a dazzling background of changing scenery. The careful detail with which Staël presents rumbling Vesuvius, the Neapolitan *lazzaroni*, or the hurly-burly of Roman carnival corroborates data gleaned from personal experience. The author takes pains to create a realistic setting for her highly romanticized tale. Critics rarely credit Staël's quest for exactitude—a concern that prompted assiduous research for *Allemagne* and inspired her latter-day plan to visit the Orient in order to secure material for "Richard the Lion-Hearted," a work she did not even commence in the absence of on-the-spot documentation.

In addition to writing the love story of a woman of genius, Staël's second, equally important purpose was to dissect the cultural life of a foreign people for French consumption—an embryonic project she would bring to fruition in *Allemagne*. Although the interspersed travelogue may stall the plot's progress, Staël's disquisitions on geography, art, music, religion, architecture, and local customs are intended as a form of sociological instruction. *Corinne* repeats or revises themes already present in *Littérature*. The North-South duality acquires significance and poignancy as it shapes the character and affects the destiny of the two protagonists. The insuperable difference that separates them betrays a fatal irresistibility. Superficially, Oswald embodies the conservative, home- and hearth-oriented, bleak and foggy North, while Corinne represents the sunny, impulsive, generous, and carefree South. The dualism is more complicated, however, than the contrast between hero and heroine.

Corinne herself is an amalgam of both England and Italy. She bears within her personality the warring modalities of two alien cultures. Through the father—the patriarchal society that prevails in the end— she belongs to a tradition of male supremacy and female subservience amid a climate that is described as dreary, sad, and stultifying. Through her earth-mother, she is a child of sun-drenched Italy, whose fecund vegetation is mirrored in its prolific classical culture and tonic recognition of female achievement and independence. Within her Italian identity, Corinne is Janus-faced. Her improvisation at the Capitol looks to past and future alike; after lauding the bygone splendor of her adopted land, Corinne envisions the glories that lie ahead. As Castel-Forte remarks, Corinne is "an admirable product of our climate and fine arts, like a scion of the past and an augury of the future" (*OC*, 8:51).

Other theories of national difference predicated on climate resonate throughout the novel in digressive observations and discussions. Intellectual indolence, for example, is attributed to the ease of obtaining sustenance; the Italians have no more need to cultivate their minds than to till their soil. Nonetheless, cultural knowledge and appreciation are broadly disseminated among the populace: "The common people of Rome are familiar with the arts and reason tastefully about sculpture; paintings, monuments, antiquities, and literary distinction are of national interest to them" (*OC*, 8:38). Italy offers the advantage of being less strict about social decorum, more tolerant of behavioral lapses, than northern lands. Therefore it provides a perfect retreat for Corinne from the narrow conventionality of English opinion.

Staël establishes a geographical counterpart to each stage in the development and decline of Corinne's passion. Rome (her mother's city in more ways than one) is the site of her initial triumph; the coronation at the Capitol marks the *summa* of her career. Rome also provides a romantic background for Corinne's burgeoning love, which reaches heights of abandon with Roman carnival, as she risks her reputation for her lover's sake. Pompeii and Vesuvius, linked with death and destruction, are harbingers of sorrow. The insalubrious atmosphere of Rome in July marks the onset of Corinne's physical decline. With its coffinlike gondolas, lugubrious Venice is the scene of separation. In England, Corinne falls ill. In Scotland, she renounces love. In Florence, she dies.

Corinne contains in germ a number of preromantic notions. With Baudelairean intuition, Staël detects "correspondences" among sensory perceptions, equating songs and fragrances, sounds and colors. The scent of orange trees affects the mind like a musical melody (*OC*, 9:5); nightingales warbling in the rosebushes mingle "the purest songs . . . with the most delicate perfumes" (9:7). Plastic art resembles music: "The felicitous combination of colors and chiaroscuro produces . . . a musical effect in painting" (8:314). The arts are interconnected and interchangeable. Music and painting, dance and sculpture, borrow elements from each other in fertile cross-pollination. In addition to (and excusing) its erotic implications, Corinne's famous shawl dance[22] partakes of all the arts: "While dancing, Corinne transmitted her feelings to her audience, as if she were improvising or playing the lyre or sketching; everything was a form of language for her: watching her, the musicians were encouraged to partake of the spirit of their art; and I know not what passionate joy and imaginative sensitivity electrified the witnesses of this magical dance, transporting them into an ideal existence where one dreams of happiness which is not of this world" (8:193–94). Corinne's dance is part painting, part sculpture, part poetry; above all, it is a form of direct communication and inspiration—coaxing the musicians to greater heights of performance and the audience to dreams of an idyllic otherworld.

Of all the arts, Staël was most sensitive to the transcendental qualities of music, which stirs the soul with bittersweet longing. While it can offer serenity and consolation, music's greatest power is evoking memory: "Nothing brings back the past like music. . . . At its summons, the past reappears, like the shades of our loved ones, wearing a mysterious and melancholy veil" (*OC*, 9:163). Staël is enamored of the musicality of the Italian language, whose harmonies are perfectly suited to poetry: "Italian has a musical charm that affords pleasure in the sound of words, almost independently of ideas. . . . One is aware that this melodious and colorful language was formed among the arts, beneath a sunny sky"

(8:90). The soft sounds of Italian captivate the listener: "Our gentle words exert a charm . . . like the murmur of water or a palette of colors" (8:234). One sound evokes another—a dance, a brook or waterfall, a tempest or a battle—and conjures up color in another kind of "correspondence." Although Staël assigns the arts a capital role in *Corinne,* she herself prefers sentiments to statues, as she wrote Monti on 30 March 1805: "To represent a secret of the soul, a manner of suffering less and of being loved more, affects me a thousand times more than those beautiful feet and hands people keep talking about" (Solovieff, 305).

A preromantic strain of melancholy, with a strong filiation to Werther and René, takes a morbid pleasure in contemplating ruins of past splendor and comparing the grand impassivity of nature with the insignificance of humankind. The vegetation sprouting among the tombs of Rome suggest that "this earth . . . cherishes its dead, covering them lovingly with useless flowers and plants that spread along the ground and never grow tall enough to be separated from the ashes they seem to caress" (*OC,* 8:165). The ocean's thundering waves, their "aimless movement . . . eternally renewed without our comprehending its cause" (9:6), evoke an awed awareness of infinity. Sometimes nature echoes human feelings, like the violent storm that erupts when Oswald takes leave of Corinne (9:261); sometimes it seems cruelly oblivious to human needs, as Corinne's sorrow contrasts with the radiant countryside she and Oswald cross: "Ah! . . . ought nature to offer so many signs of happiness to friends who are parting!" (9:218).

Preceding Victor Hugo and Honoré de Balzac, Staël expresses the preromantic notion that the man (or woman) of genius is a superior being whose talents place him or her above the common need to conform. Normal family ties and societal obligations are suspended for such an individual. Belonging to a separate category from ordinary mortals, the artist is subject to different criteria: "Corinne had to be judged as a poet, an artist, in order to be forgiven for sacrificing her rank, family, country, and her name to the enthusiasm of talent and art" (*OC,* 9:96–97).

Although the person of genius may enjoy special prerogatives (as Balzac was to insist), he or she is hounded by a malevolent destiny. The fatal image of genius, doomed to sorrow and defeat, is another preromantic concept: "Does fate not pursue exalted souls, poets whose imagination is sparked by the power of love and suffering? . . . I do not know what involuntary force plunges genius into misfortune: he hears the music of the spheres which mortal ears cannot capture; he fathoms mysteries of feeling concealed from other men, and his soul harbors a God it cannot hold!" (*OC*, 9:114–15). A concomitant idea, which romantic poets like Hugo and Alfred de Vigny were to stress, stipulates that the person of genius is more impressionable, more alive to sensation, than other people: "When a person of genius is truly sensitive, this faculty alone magnifies his woes; he makes discoveries within his own suffering . . . and, since the heart's sorrow is inexhaustible, the more ideas he has, the more acutely he feels" (9:220). The solitude of genius, embodied in Vigny's "Moïse" (1822) has affinities with *Corinne*, which Vigny was reading at the time he composed his poem (Pellegrini, 62). Romantic love as a fatal passion that victimizes an elite and elected creature is a corollary theme. Corinne's pain is aggravated by her inordinate sensitivity and overworked imagination. The person of genius loves more deeply, climbs higher, falls farther, than the mediocre majority.

There is one problem. None of Corinne's accomplishments attests to her supposed genius. Although we are told that she has written several books, the accomplishments we witness consist of improvisations, a shawl dance, two theatrical performances—ephemeral art forms, at best; at worst, mere entertainment. Corinne seems never to be inspired by the unquenchable spark of genius, never impelled by an irresistible creative force. Her talent is meant to attract, impress, beguile, or—at the end— move Oswald to remorse. While improvisation bears a resemblance to the conversational art at which Staël excelled, the improvisations she "records" are disappointingly commonplace. They do not glow with an inward fire. Corinne's superiority remains suspect.

The breath of religious tolerance infusing *Corinne* marks a distinct evolution since *Delphine*. The petty bigotry and rigidity of a Matilde become, in Corinne's brand of Catholicism, a spiritual vehicle for self-perfection. Staël has moved from the humanistic religiosity of *Delphine*, with its acerbic attitude toward Catholic dogma and ritual, toward a position of compassion and acceptance.[23] When Catholic Corinne faces death, like Protestant Delphine, Staël glosses over ritual to emphasize the spiritual peace and salvation that genuine faith can bring. On the other hand, the moving Protestant service aboard a British man-of-war provides a counterpart to Catholic pomp: "Nothing speaks to the soul like divine service on a ship, where the noble simplicity of the Reform cult seems particularly adapted to one's feelings" (*OC*, 9:22). Staël has reached the point of reconciling religious differences in the ecumenical credo that all approaches to God are valid.

On 25 May 1807, three weeks after the book appeared, Suard wrote that of all Staël's works, *Corinne* enjoyed the most immediate and flattering triumph.[24] It was read avidly, not only in France but in Switzerland, Italy, Germany, and England.[25] Like *Delphine*, *Corinne* was meant to propitiate the emperor but had the opposite effect. While supposedly apolitical, both books were in fact subversive acts undermining the status quo. Napoleon was incensed, for *Corinne* made no mention of his Italian conquests; it apotheosized the British navy after the French defeat at Trafalgar; in comte d'Erfeuil and Mme d'Arbigny, it caricatured the worst aspects of French character; its hero was an Englishman, ergo an enemy of France, who represented the British political system at its most orderly and reliable; reminding the Italian people of their former greatness, Corinne urged them on to unity and independence; and the book held up an image of uncommon female achievement.

Corinne made a deep and lasting impression on the author's contemporaries. Her ever-admiring cousin Albertine Necker de Saussure considered it Staël's masterpiece, her political writings excepted ("Notice," cxxii). For Constant, the book heralded a new era in literature (Bornecque, 254). After enthusiastically reading *Corinne* in 1809, Alphonse de Lamartine said he felt "transported into another world, ideal, natural, and poetic" (Pellegrini, 68). Alexandre Guiraud, one of the founders in 1823 of the *Muse Française*, proclaimed in an article titled "Our Doctrines" that *Corinne* was "a monument raised to the literary glory of the nineteenth century" (40). Lord Byron wrote in a copy of *Corinne* belonging to his love, Countess Guiccioli, on 23 August 1819: "I knew Madame de Staël well—better than she knew Italy. . . . She is sometimes right, and often wrong, about Italy and England; but almost always true in delineating the heart, which is of but one nation, and of no country—or rather, of all."[26] Sainte-Beuve was enthusiastic in his praise: "[A]s art, as poetry, the novel *Corinne* by itself would represent an immortal monument" (Bersaucourt, 99).

The chorus of acclaim was far from unanimous. In a May 1810 letter to his sister Pauline, Stendhal called *Corinne* "excellent when its hyperbole and inflated sentimentality are not detestable."[27] His journal of 9 March 1811 contains further allusions to the novel's pretentiousness; moreover, the plethora of "trite ideas and patently overblown feelings" make him ill.[28] Writing in 1820, three years after Staël's death, Charles Nodier called *Corinne* "less the interesting narration of a series of realistic adventures than a framework for inserting descriptions and scenes."[29]

Furthermore, he found the heroine too high-flown to appeal to men: "She is a woman whom only a woman could invent" (388).

Prosper de Barante, divining that Oswald was patterned on himself, was quick to take umbrage; he wrote Staël on 6 June 1807: "You reproach me cruelly, and you have shut me up in this Oswald where I cannot defend myself. Ah! if one day he could describe what he felt, people would know how he has suffered" (Solovieff, 342). In actuality, like all of Staël's heroes, Oswald is a composite of various men she loved at the time. The moonlight promenades in Rome are a nostalgic re-creation of her nocturnal perambulations with don Pedro de Souza,[30] whom she had met at the Arcadian Academy (as Corinne met Oswald at the Capitol). Maurice O'Donnell, whom Staël first encountered in Venice and pursued for years, doubtless lent his charm to Oswald's character. The hero's puritanical principles may reflect the moral convictions of Mathieu de Montmorency, whose faithful friendship is mirrored in Castel-Forte. As noted above, Oswald contains traits of Benjamin Constant. He also represents aspects of the author herself, as Necker de Saussure was the first to note: "Corinne and Oswald are enthusiasm and sorrow, and both are herself" ("Notice,"cxxiii).[31]

In the final instance, *Corinne* is an insurgent, if muted, outcry against woman's subservience to patriarchal ideals. The narrow domesticity prescribed for (and accepted by) the British paradigm is a constraint against which Staël has her heroine exultantly revolt. Corinne's personal fortune and quasi-orphaned state afford her a financial independence lacking to most women, then and now. Moreover, she is endowed with talents for which she must find an outlet. In Italy, she enjoys the incomparable good fortune of having her gifts crowned with the highest imaginable honors.

Corinne's ultimate downfall illustrates the contention, already expressed in *Littérature*, that an outstanding woman is doomed by her very uniqueness. Love is as vital to her as breathing, but she cannot tolerate the role tradition designates for a woman. There is no way in which Corinne can remain true to herself, in the full integrity of her being, and retain Oswald's love. In contradistinction to her own life choice,[32] Staël has her heroine give up all—talent, beauty, independence, life itself—for love. This self-immolation is perhaps the single factor that makes the story improbable, even unpalatable, for today's readers. We must recognize that any other denouement—either Corinne's living happily ever after "in sin" or, like a man, renouncing love in order to further her career—would have been unthinkable in 1807.

Chapter 7

Discovering Germany

Although at first she shared her compatriots' misapprehensions, Staël developed an early interest in Germany. To Jacob Meister's invitation to meet Christoph Wieland, she replied on 18 March 1796: "I know everything the Germans have to say, and everything they will say fifty years hence. I like their talent but not their wit, and in conversation, wit is all that counts" (Pauline de Pange, 13). When Goethe sent her a superbly bound copy of his *Wilhelm Meister* in April 1797, she could merely admire the covers. Two years later, she remedied this deficiency with German lessons that would stand her in good stead when it came to reading and translating German writers for French consumption.

An army of French émigré friends (Narbonne and Suard, Camille Jordan and Joseph-Marie de Gerando) brought a whiff of German culture back to Coppet from their exile abroad. After learning that his articles had molded a chapter of *Littérature*, Charles de Villers, editor of an émigré newspaper in Hamburg, began a lengthy correspondence with Staël, who apprised him on 1 August 1802 that she was studying German diligently: "I am sure that only there will I find new thoughts and deep feelings. . . . It is the country numbering the most remarkable philosophers and men of letters in the world today" (Jasinski, 4:541).

Her departure precipitated by Napoleon's harassment, Staël set out for Germany in November 1803. The damp, chilly weather seemed a daunting omen, but her triumphant reception in Weimar caused a change of heart. Germany could not be so benighted if it feted her accomplishments even more spiritedly than the sophisticated French. When her trip was broken off by her father's death, she tabled the plan to write a book reflecting her experiences.[1] The first spasm of grief was superseded by work on Necker's papers, a tour of Italy, and the hasty composition of *Corinne*. Staël did not resume her German project until the summer of 1808, following a second trip to Vienna and southern Germany. Because Napoleon had banned publication, *De l'Allemagne* (On Germany) first appeared in England in June 1813; the French edition came out after Napoleon's eclipse the following year.

Staël's purpose was to introduce Germany to her compatriots, as she had introduced Italy in *Corinne*. But this was to be a far more intensive and ambitious study than a fictional work could possibly encompass. As in *Littérature* and *Passions*, the subject is bewilderingly vast—in this case, nothing more nor less than an exhaustive overview of German history, climate, and national character as these impinge on its literature, philosophy, religion, and moral attitudes. As before, Staël offers a didactic lesson to the French. Her book abounds in philosophical maxims, literary precepts, and doctrinal positions. Through interspersed accolades of the British system, she appeals for a united coalition against the tyrant, Napoleon. Once again, the subtext is political. The book treats all literary genres, including drama, epic and lyric poetry, the novel, the short story, history, criticism, even philosophical, moral, and religious writings. No one before had ever analyzed German culture in such abundant and rhapsodic detail. Staël was both wise and daring to couch her observations in nonfictional form. Wise, because otherwise her book might have been received as another woman's story, like *Corinne*, but its message would have been overlooked. Daring, because once again she was treading terrain traditionally considered a male preserve.

Part 1, "Germany and Its Customs," begins with an overview of the German countryside and character, then differentiates the southern area (Austria and Vienna) from the North (Saxony, Weimar, Prussia, Berlin) in terms of society, conversation, language, and educational institutions. Part 2, "Literature and the Arts," provides a cursory history of German literature that serves as a springboard for examining individual authors—Wieland, Friedrich Klopstock, Gotthold Lessing, Johann Winckelmann, Goethe, and Schiller. A chapter on style and versification introduces a discussion of poetry in general and Staël's famous distinction between classical and romantic poetry. A chapter on taste precedes general observations about dramatic art, with analyses of plays by Lessing, Schiller, Goethe, and a number of lesser playwrights. Staël devotes a chapter each to comedy, acting, and fiction, two chapters to history, and another to literary criticism, and ends with a discussion of the fine arts in Germany. Part 3 rounds out the book with comparisons of English, French, and German philosophies. Staël confutes the immorality and cynicism of the Locke-Condillac school with an in-depth inquiry into Kant, then analyzes the effect of a new school of philosophy on German intellectual development, literature, art, science, and character. A discussion of morality includes an exploration of German sensibility, love and marriage, and the relationship between ignorance and frivolity on the one hand and morality on the other. Part 4 centers on religion and enthusiasm. General considerations of German religiosity precede an investigation of Protestantism, the Moravian sect, Catholicism, mysticism, theosophy, sectarianism, and nature. The book concludes with a significant discussion of enthusiasm as it affects learning and happiness.

The above schema indicates the stupendous scope of Staël's effort—a feat never before attempted by any French writer, and certainly not by a woman—to comprehend Germanic culture in its entirety. Critics who carp on lacunae in her knowledge, on small errors of fact or insignificant omissions, fail to recognize the immensity of her vision and the courage of her undertaking. Staël is an intrepid explorer charting new territory. Later maps may supersede the early ones she devised, but the discovery is hers alone.

The pervasive spirit of the book, which combines travelogue, sociological commentary, and moral maxims with literary and philosophical criticism, is one of rare cultural liberalism. Time and again, Staël compares the imaginative if naive creative energy of the Germans with the jaded and overconfident French, whose literary endeavors are fettered by sterile imitation of classicism, an outmoded concept in the contemporary world. She calls insistently for acquaintanceship with the literary products of other nations. In redeeming German culture, she never loses an opportunity to insert oblique praise of the British.

Describing in her preface of 1 October 1813 the sudden and unexpected impounding of her book,[2] Staël repeats Rovigo's insulting explanation: "It seemed to me that the air of this country did not suit you, and we are not yet reduced to seeking models among the countries you admire" (*OC*, 10:7). Submitting her calumniated work to public judgment, she states that since Germany is the geographic heart of Europe, no continental association can attain independence without its support (a prophetic assertion). Acquaintance with the country she calls the "*patrie de la pensée*" (21) can help revitalize French literature, now threatened by sterility (a veiled reference to Napoleon): "People submit to accepted ideas, not as they would to truth but as they bow to power; and thus human reason becomes accustomed to servitude, even in the realms of literature and philosophy" (24).

"Germany and Its Customs" provides a travel documentary larded with sociological commentary and generalizations about German traits. Staël finds that the country's geographical features—broad forests, harsh climate, and vast, uninhabited tracts—produce feelings of sadness and

oppression, which she later relates to the northern penchant for melancholia in literature. As an aristocratic federation, Germany has no cultural or political center; this fragmentation has favored individual
creativity, if it has impeded patriotism and political commitment.

She devotes a prime chapter to women, whom nature and society
have accustomed to suffering. More generous, sensitive, and devoted
than men, their habitual self-abnegation strengthens their inner
resources; while men spend their lives in vulgar pursuits, women cultivate their minds. Conversant with art and poetry, German women are
confident in love because disdain and infidelity are rare—a residue of
German chivalric honor.

Reverting to the climatic theory of *Littérature*, Staël decrees that the
arts flourish best in a cold or hot latitude. Southern Germany, which lies
in a temperate zone, enjoys comfort incompatible with literary effort.
Deploring Austria's intellectual apathy and its ban on foreign books,
Staël recommends the free circulation of ideas as the best guarantee of
stability (a proposal sure to irk Napoleon). *Littérature*, *Corinne*, and
Allemagne all stress retention and cultivation of national traits rather than
reductive and colorless assimilation.

The banality and barbarity of German social customs lead her to
expatiate on the delights of conversation, a pleasure the Germans have
not yet learned to practice or appreciate. Their effusive formality is
inconducive to the brevity and brilliance for which the French are
renowned. A cumbersome language, German is better suited to abstract
theorizing than witty exchanges. "The merit of the Germans is to fill
time well; the talent of the French is to help forget its passage" (*OC*,
10:123). The delicate precision of this epigram illustrates the exquisite
lightning thrust of French, compared to which German is lumbering and
verbose.

In Saxony, birthplace of Protestantism and free inquiry, literature,
music, and art are cultivated freely. Intellectuals work in isolation, their
research divorced from any practical application. Weimar is the seat of
literary and artistic refinement. Dubbed the Athens of Germany, it is the
only place where a common cultural interest links different strata of society. A devotee of French literature to the detriment and exclusion of
German, Frederick II tried to turn Berlin into a second Paris, although
in the author's view he should have developed his country's native
potential instead. Freedom of the press (a continued emphasis and
implicit criticism of Napoleon), a nucleus of educated men, and literary

appreciation have made Berlin the true capital of the new Germany. Unfortunately, women are excluded from scientific and literary activities.

Admiration of the German university system inspires Staël to express her own educational ideology. In line with her brief for cultural interaction, she favors language study over mathematics and science. Diverging from Rousseau's educational precepts, she embraces the Pestalozzi pedagogical approach, which evaluates a child's learning ability and matches educational progress to mental development. Neither reward nor punishment plays a part in this system, which is to be commended for offering education to the working classes.

In treating "Literature and the Arts," Staël explains the French inability to appreciate German poetry by the paucity of French speakers who understand German (another reason for language study). She recommends once more an international cultural exchange of benefit to both nations—especially the French, whom she blames insistently for their preformed bias. German literature is better known among the English, who are more inclined to language study and have a greater affinity with the German mentality. After furnishing a historical overview of German literature from the early troubadours to the present, Staël turns to the critical achievements of Lessing and Winckelmann, the Germanic imagination and sensitivity of Goethe, and the virtuous talent of Schiller, who was imbued with love of freedom, respect for women (a characteristic she is bound to admire), passion for art, and adoration of God.

Next, Staël addresses German style and versification. A superabundance of dialects affords continual linguistic renewal. Although German's archaic grammatical structure is unsuited to the contemporary world, no modern poetry is as striking or varied. She defines poetry as a comprehensive emotional response to beauty in all its guises—landscape, music, the gaze of a loved one, the awareness of God. Conceived within the soul, it shakes the very foundation of being: "Poetry is a momentary possession of everything our heart desires; talent erases the limits of existence and turns vague hopes into brilliant imagery" (*OC*, 10:269). Staël's conception of poetry is, like her appreciation of music, a transcendent experience with religious overtones.

A key chapter, "Classical and Romantic Poetry," defines two contrary literary tendencies and introduces the term "romantic" into French. Whereas "classical" is often synonymous with artistic excellence, Staël confines it to Greco-Roman antiquity, applying the expression "romantic" to literature deriving from the knightly Christian tradition. Refusing to pronounce on their relative merits, she posits a choice, not between classical and romantic poetry, but between imitation of the first and inspiration by the second. Artifically transplanted into modern times, classical literature attracts a small erudite elite; indigenous to national life, rooted in popular appeal, romantic literature alone is capable of growing and flourishing. To illustrate her thesis, Staël analyzes in detail (and excerpts in her own translations) poems by Wieland, Klopstock, Johann Voss, and Goethe, while intercalating artistic precepts and philosophical commentary throughout the text.

Representing the static rigidity of French dramatic conventions, which stifle originality and obstruct theatrical innovation, she urges the French to put aside petty pretensions to superiority and recognize beauties that may be obscured by flaws of literary taste. After discussing Lessing's dramatic theories as exemplified in three of his best-known plays, she enters into minute analyses of Schiller's *Die Räuber* (1781), *Don Carlos* (1787), *Wallenstein* (1800), *Maria Stuart* (1801), *Die Jungfrau von Orleans* (1801), *Die Braut von Messina* (1803), and *Wilhelm Tell* (1804). Dubbing Goethe a versatile "German Racine" (*OC*, 10:498), she finds him passionate in *Werther* and *Egmont* (1788), historically accurate in *Götz von Berlichingen* (1773), tumultuous in *Faust* (1808), and monumental in *Torquato Tasso* (1790), *Die Natürliche Tochter* (1804), and *Iphigenie auf Tauris* (1787): "Goethe . . . is like a force of nature that produces every kind of result; one may prefer his southern to his northern climate, without ignoring those talents which correspond to different regions of the soul" (502). *Faust* for Staël is far more than a sardonic philosophical jest; by making the devil his hero, Goethe has destroyed the moral world and replaced it with hell. Germany's foremost contemporary playwright is Zacharias Werner, author of the popular *Luther* (1807) and *Attila* (1808), among other noted works. Staël's depiction of Attila as the "scourge of God" who fills Europe and Asia with dread and nurtures a religious belief in his own might is too close to Napoleon's image for anyone to mistake her intent. In discussing plays by August von Kotzebue, Heinrich von Gerstenberg, Friedrich von Klinger, Ludwig Tieck, and Heinrich Josef von Collin, she betrays her preference for the romantic mode and reinforces her injunction against imitation: "A contemporary writer will never succeed in composing ancient poetry. It is better for our religion and mores that he create modern poetry, as beautiful in its essence as that of the ancients" (*OC* 11:37).

Glossing over German comedy with some generalized precepts and a few examples, she blurs the line between tragedy and comedy by demanding "burning emotions" in both: "Genuine talent consists in composing in such a way that the same work, the same scene, contain elements which make people laugh or cry and provide thinkers with an inexhaustible subject for meditation" (*OC*, 11:45). The buffoonery and fantasy indigenous to German comedy are illustrated in Carl Friedrich Hensler's popular opera *Die Nymph der Danau* (The Nymph of the Danube, 1803), about a knight who loves a fairy but marries a stolid housewife instead; his life is disrupted by magic until, with his wife's consent, he agrees to spend three days a year with the fairy.[3] The best illustration of allegorical comedy is Goethe's *Der Triumph der Empfindsamkeit* (The Triumph of sensitivity, 1787), in which a pretentious prince falls in love with a mannequin whose silence he interprets as modesty and tacit affection; although she concedes its ingenuity, Staël does not consider this idea a sufficient basis for good comedy.[4]

She takes the next logical step by debating theatrical representation on stage. German and French acting styles differ in the same way as their tragedies: the first is natural and unaffected (though mediocre), the other orotund and precise. Staël acclaims the German ability to play both comic and tragic roles—a versatility displayed by the incomparable actors David Garrick and François-Joseph Talma. A long encomium of the latter[5] analyzes the components of his acting style, which comprise "the charm of music, painting, sculpture, poetry, and especially the language of the soul to inspire in his audience a gamut of generous and terrible passions" (*OC*, 11:72).

Modern authors often try their hand at fiction, which they consider the easiest form of writing. While dismissing the recent flock of German love stories, Staël is ecstatic about Goethe's *Werther*. The elements to which she responds (already limned in *Littérature*) are precisely those that will affect romantic sensibility: suffering caused by love, spiritual disquietude, and this century's "malady of the imagination" (*OC*, 11:86). The philosophical novel is an increasingly popular form, of which Goethe's *Wilhelm Meister* (1795–96) is the finest example. Using morality as a criterion for fiction, as she did in *Fictions*, Staël questions the moral pessimism of *Die Wahlverwandtschaften* (Elective affinities, 1809). After devoting several pages to Tieck and Claudius, she discusses the bizarre originality of J. Paul Richter, who, despite his reputation in Germany, is virtually unknown abroad.

No branch of literature has more practitioners in Germany than criticism. Immanuel Kant, Goethe, and Johannes von Müller wrote critical reviews expounding significant philosophical theories, as did Schiller and

the two Schlegels among the younger group of writers. August Wilhelm
von Schlegel's perception of poetry resembles Winckelmann's method of
describing statues: "The next best thing to genius is the ability to recognize and admire it" (*OC*, 11:139). Although more interested in philosophy, Friedrich von Schlegel wrote a first-rate account of Greek and
Roman culture. Both Schlegels are partial to medieval chivalry. For Staël,
the progress of civilization is based on cumulative knowledge: "Art
should not regress but combine, if possible, the diverse qualities which
the human mind has developed in different periods" (142). She repeats
her view that nations, diverging in climate, environment, language, government, and history, can profit from mutual borrowings: "Every country would do well to welcome foreign ideas; in this case, hospitality
enriches the host" (145).

In light of the book's amplitude, Staël devotes a relatively brief chapter to German art—painting, sculpture, dance, and music. Although
most art in Germany is derivative, the modesty and simplicity of pre-
Reformation painters like Albert Dürer, Lucas Cranach, and Hans
Holbein may have influenced the predecessors of Raphael, Perugino,
Andrea Mantegna, and Leonardo da Vinci. Despite Winckelmann's
appreciation of classical sculpture, Staël warns artists to beware of the
same pitfalls that beset writers who take classical beauty as a model.
Young Ida Brun[6] is a graceful and gifted dancer whose poses represent
poignant poetic and mythological moments: "Her dance is a succession
of ephemeral masterpieces that one would like to arrest forever" (*OC*,
11:156). Although Staël is more responsive to music than to the plastic
arts, she fails to appreciate the great German composers. Dismissing
Christoph Gluck and Mozart in a single paragraph, she finds Haydn too
intellectual and omits Beethoven altogether. All in all, she prefers Italian
to German and vocal to instrumental music, citing as the peak of musical experience hearing the Miserere sung in Rome (as Corinne did).
Being prelinguistic, art appeals more to the emotions than to the mind:
"Artistic . . . language is composed of color, form, and sound. If we could
imagine our soul's impressions before it knew speech, we would better
understand the effects of painting and music" (160).

In "Philosophy and Morality"—the focal point of her book—Staël
sustains the primacy of Kantian philosophy over French materialism and
stresses the importance of enthusiasm in achieving renewal and progress.
First discrediting Hobbes and Locke in England and their French successors—Etienne de Condillac, Helvétius, and baron d'Holbach, she fierce-
ly refutes sensationalist philosophy as negating the moral validity of

human actions and holds it responsible for the worst excesses of the French Revolution. Not only does she point out the error of believing that all ideas derive from sense impressions; she underscores the pernicious consequence of creating individual codes of morality. Staël makes a brief for the mathematical, scientific, and theological writings of Gottfried Leibniz, a man of immense erudition and enthusiasm, whose rejection of Locke's theories of sensory perception preserved a philosophy of moral freedom in Germany. Even more fervid in embracing Kant's antimaterialist philosophy, she outlines the fundamental concepts of his categorical imperatives, stresses his distinction between innate (subjective) ideas and (objective) sensory impressions, and subscribes to his reliance on sentiment as a guide to transcendental truth and his belief that "conscience is the innate principle of our moral being" (*OC*, 11:241). In spite of stylistic obscurities, Staël blames the French for not taking the trouble to study Kant's thorny works, which are appreciated in Germany by patient, persevering readers. Whereas Lessing, François Hemsterhuis (a Dutch philosopher), and Jacobi attacked materialism even before Kant, his successors Johann Fichte and Friedrich von Schelling attempted to simplify his system, the former by submitting idealist philosophy to scientific scrutiny, the latter by striving to elevate matter to the status of the soul.

As is her custom, Staël tries to avert criticism by first voicing it herself. Partisans of the above philosophers will rightly accuse her of treating them superficially, while worldly readers will wonder what earthly purpose philosophy serves. She defines philosophy in terms of a moral aesthetic that attests to human dignity and ministers to the soul. The study of philosophy develops powers of concentration that, combined with observation and perseverance, can lead to astonishing discoveries.

She attempts next to adduce the effect of the new German philosophy on art, literature, science, and national character. Although idealist philosophy is not generally conducive to experimentation, the Germans have made important scientific discoveries, like gunpowder and printing. They tend to proceed from theory to experiment, while the French reverse the process. Most great discoveries at first seemed absurd: "The universe is more like a poem than a machine; if we had to choose between imagination and mathematical reasoning to conceive of it, imagination would more closely approximate the truth" (*OC*, 11:315).

Just as she disavows sensationalist philosophy as spawning a self-centered ethos, Staël is equally vehement in condemning morality based on national interest. Whatever the rationale, governmental injustice is always a crime,[7] for it sacrifices one segment of society to another and corrupts the integrity of future generations. Like mathematics, morality admits of no exceptions: "If two and two do not make four, the most profound algebraic calculations are absurd; if a single theoretical case exists in which man ought not to do his duty, then all philosophic and religious maxims are overturned, and only prudence or hypocrisy remains" (OC, 11:339). Applying this dictum to public life under the Terror, she subscribes to Kantian philosophy because it controverts morality based on individual or national interest and denies temporal happiness as the goal of life. Kant attributes the same primitive force to the notion of duty as to that of time and space; a sense of duty, he asserts, is the necessary condition of our moral being. "Human destiny on earth is not happiness but self-perfection," Staël adds (350).

Expanding the discussion of women's lot in *Littérature* to assess the institution of marriage, she maintains that mutual affection and fidelity are essential preconditions, without which marriage is hell on earth. The recompense for a life of conjugal devotion should be a husband's undeviating fidelity; it is unfair to expect constancy from one partner while condoning promiscuity in the other. To illustrate her point, Staël imagines a man saying to his wife, after his initial ardor cools: "You who usually possess greater imagination and sensitivity than I, who have neither career nor distraction, while the world offers me both; you who live only for me, while I have a thousand other interests, are to be satisfied with the cold, subsidiary, shared affection I choose to give and are to deny yourself every expression of more glorious and tender feelings" (OC, 11:382). Staël's demands for sexual equality are truly revolutionary for her day. With respect to human perfectibility, she rejects the theory that progress and decadence alternate. It would be disheartening to believe that each generation is occupied like Sisyphus in useless labor. Despite her condemnation of the idle French upper class, whose ignorance perpetuates the sterile adoption of unexamined ideas, she discerns a pattern of progress throughout human history.

Part 4, titled "Religion and Enthusiasm," considers these qualities endemic to the Germanic peoples. The Reformation was a natural product of their introspective bent. Luther courageously attacked abuses and dogmas inspired by fanaticism. From being a political force, religion became an instrument of reflection. Staël seconds Lessing's rebuttal of the proposition that it is dangerous to disseminate certain ideas, finding it presumptuous for some people to hide truth from others (by implication, to stand between God and man). The basic premise of

Protestantism is the right to examine what one is expected to believe. To prove that the reform movement is compatible with ascetic contemplation, Staël cites the Moravian sect as equally strict in practice but less demanding than Catholic monasticism: Moravian convents require no vows, have no vested priesthood, permit marriage, and treat men and women alike. More broad-minded than ever before, she accepts denominational differences as mere distinctions of nomenclature. If men like Klopstock, Jacobi, Friedrich Stolberg, and Johann Herder are equally devout, why should they be labeled "Protestant" or "Catholic"? The Christian religion resides in the depths of the heart. Divine service affects us through inner feelings, not outer trappings.

Tending to react emotionally, and probably swayed by her Coppet visitors Krüdener and Werner (whom she does not, however, mention), Staël leans toward mysticism as "a more intimate way of feeling and conceiving of the Christian religion" (*OC*, 11:454), the basic premise of which is resignation to God's will. All cults and dogmas are differentiated forms of the same religious conviction that "the only free human act . . . is the performance of duty" (463). A strong affinity exists between mysticism and genius. "Generally speaking, idealist philosophy, Christian mysticism, and true poetry have the same origins and goals" (472). All seek to substitute intellectual culture for social artifice and turn mediocre men into energetic, sincere, generous, and thoughtful human beings. Men like Jakob Böhme in Germany and Louis Claude de Saint-Martin in France find in Christian revelation the key to understanding creation. Although spiritual and materialist philosophers seek truth by diametrically opposed paths, they do not realize that "the secret of existence lies in the mysterious joining of both" (490).

In a foreshadowing of romanticism, Staël bathes her chapter on the contemplation of nature in a religious aura. Among German nature writers, she singles out Novalis and Christian Schubert. The poetry of Novalis is marked by religious simplicity and introspection; Schubert's consoling concept of "ascending" metempsychosis promises a continual "promotion" from stone to human existence to complete perfection (*OC*, 11:509). When nature does not mirror our moods or raise our spirits, its cycle of decay and rebirth serves as an instructive reminder that life is not chained to the material world but is a prelude to the soul's immortality.

In their reinstatement of enthusiasm, the final chapters form the glorious climax toward which the entire book has been circuitously heading. Vilified in the aftermath of the French Revolution, enthusiasm must be reclaimed as an imperative of artistic endeavor, moral virtue, political potential, and human perfectibility. A quality Staël possesses in abundance, for which she has been scorned, disbelieved, and betrayed, enthusiasm is defined most nobly in the Greek sense as, "God within us," for it combines love of beauty, spiritual idealism, and the joy of devotion (*OC*, 11:520). "The Effect of Enthusiasm on Knowledge" is the crux of her book, according to Staël. Enthusiasm is a German trait propitious for seeking absolute truth. Under its spell, philosophers work patiently, unconcerned with acclaim, and cherish learning for its own sake. She tries to instill this concept in the disabused French, rendered cynical by the Terror. In the final chapter, "The Influence of Enthusiasm on Happiness," she decries the fruitless lives led by people who, content to avoid doing ill, perform no noble acts and nurture no lofty ideas; they are imprisoned within a tenacious mediocrity, without productivity or progress. In contrast, enthusiastic persons commune with nature, delight in art, respond deeply to music, and react pleasurably to fiction, which awakens "passions purified by poetry" (542). The book ends with a blatant, if oblique, denunciation of Napoleonic ambition, as Staël exhorts the nation never to renounce enthusiasm in favor of calculating reason; otherwise, though France might master the world, it would leave no trace of its passage.

It becomes obvious to the most perfunctory reader that Staël's book on Germany is a seditious text from beginning to end. Implicit criticism of Napoleon is sown between the lines like a series of tiny land mines. The continual denigration of French superficiality, frivolity, and barren literary imitation; the effulgent praise of France's archenemy, England; Staël's invincible admiration for Germany, a nation antithetical in every way to the French; and her not so subtle call for German unification represent a textual continuum intended to sabotage French authority, much the same subtext that underlies *Corinne*.

The premise of Staël's book, and its achievement, is to offer a considered guide to German literature, life, and thought; evaluations of individual works and writers provide an accompaniment to assist the inquisitive neophyte. As she does in *Littérature*, Staël censures imitation. The concept of continual progress makes it imperative to look forward, not back. The Germans have infused literature and philosophy with a fresh spirit; their contributions cannot be ignored. Staël emphasizes and exemplifies the benefits of cultural exchange, admiring Talma for assimilating the best of Shakespeare and Racine, singling out Herder and Schlegel for their accomplishments in the new area of comparative literature. While illustrating by her own example the importance of translation, she stresses language study as essential to comprehending foreign works and culture.

Far more than *Corinne*, *Allemagne* is a preromantic text.[8] Its rehabilitation of the Middle Ages and distinction between "romantic" and "classical" poetry mark a division between the new age and the old. Staël's opposition to the traditional rules that govern classicism and impede the free flight of inspiration prepares the romantic emphasis on individual avenues of creativity. The book is suffused with an aura of melancholia, which stems from the author's personal experience of solitude and suffering, imposed from within (her love entanglements) and from without (her enforced exile and obligatory travels). The isolation and anguish she associates with the harsh climates of northern lands are also characteristics of the romantic concept of genius, which Staël consigns (as in *Corinne*) to a special category exempt from the restrictions that govern ordinary mortals. "Provided it respects religion and morality, genius may go as far as it wishes; it is expanding the empire of the mind" (*OC*, 10:205). Unlike mere talent, genius is never envious, selfish, nor vain: "True genius inspires gratitude and modesty: for we realize who bestowed it, as well as the limits the giver set" (227). The person of genius is innately good (11:402), while the products of genius are a joyful manifestation of divine inspiration. Whereas Staël still considers the man (and woman?) of genius as belonging to a masonic fellowship who recognize one another at a glance and from a distance, her concept of genius working in splendid isolation—as exemplified by German thinkers—is not far removed from Vigny's Moses or Hugo's Olympio.

Second to genius is the ability to recognize and appreciate it—a crucial definition of Staël's approach to criticism, which must enter into the spirit and mentality of the creative artist in order to achieve objective force. Just as admiration and identification animated her evaluation of Rousseau, so an enthusiastic subjective response is her criterion of criticism in *Allemagne*. Emotion and reason are as indissolubly linked in her critical view as they were when she wrote in *Littérature*, ten years before: "I cannot separate my thoughts from my feelings. . . . Affections modify our opinions in all matters. . . . We especially admire certain writings because they alone have roused all the moral forces of our being" (*OC*, 4:600). Not disposed to observe objective rules of criticism, Staël continues the attack she first launched in *Littérature* against the tyranny of literary rules and prescribed taste.

Though she once said, according to Sainte-Beuve, that she would travel 500 leagues to converse with a man of wit but would not open her window to view the Bay of Naples (Bersaucourt, 166 n. 2), Staël has become increasingly aware of and receptive to nature. Her chapter on the contemplation of nature puts her squarely among the romanticists, for whom nature either harmonizes or contrasts with human moods. She is also alive to the affective powers of music, a wordless language that communicates with the listener's soul: "Luther considered it an art akin to theology, a powerful means of inculcating religious feelings in the human heart" (*OC*, 11:5). A gratuitous gift from God, it reflects our deepest emotions: "Because music alone is of noble uselessness, it moves us profoundly; the further removed it is from any purpose, the closer it approaches that intimate well-spring of thought whose flow is restricted when it is applied to some goal" (292). Only enthusiastic persons are capable of that pure appreciation of music[9] that partakes of spiritual communion: "Is there music for those who are incapable of enthusiasm? . . . Has their entire being vibrated like a lyre when, in the middle of the night, silence was suddenly broken by song? . . . Did they then sense the mystery of existence in the feeling of pity that unifies our dual nature, blending senses and spirit in a common rapture?" (11:541).

Staël's conception of religion has evolved since *Delphine*'s strictures against the hypocrisy of Catholic ritual and the moral bigotry of a Matilde. Having softened her attitude considerably in *Corinne*, she now achieves a genuine ecumenical stance in calling for the ultimate abolition of religious distinctions in favor of a single Christian denomination. "Some day a cry for unity may arise and Christians everywhere aspire to the same theological, political, and moral religion; but before this miracle is accomplished, all men . . . will have to respect one another mutually" (*OC*, 11:453).

Allemagne elicited an enthusiastic and enduring, though controversial, reaction. The first edition of October 1813 sold out in three days. When the book appeared in France in May 1814, after Napoleon's defeat, it was an instant European success. Within the next five years, four complete editions were published in France alone. Every French, German, Swiss, Italian, and English periodical hastened to print reviews, complete with lengthy citations (Pauline de Pange, 140–42). At first, *Allemagne* profited from the general reaction to imperial tyranny, of which Staël was viewed as an illustrious victim. It was not long, however, before the French detected an underlying spirit at odds with their pride in the pre-eminence of French literature. A chorus of protests ensued, led by the xenophobic critic François-Joseph Dussault, who had already discredited *Littérature* in the *Journal des Débats*, and the enraged classicist Charles-Dorimond de Feletz. Staël's detractors denounced her theories as unpatriotic, chaotic, and destructive of the glorious French literary tradition.[10]

By 1818, the same year that Régnault de Warin devoted two volumes to celebrating Staël's work, Charles Nodier published a series of articles on *Allemagne* in the same *Journal des Débats* that had excoriated her. In 1821 the publication of Schiller's and Shakespeare's plays in translation—an event directly ascribable to the influence of *Allemagne*—marked a turning of the romantic tide. Staël's importance increased during the following years. Her insistence on the significance of foreign literatures enabled the editors of the *Muse Française*, founded in 1822 by Emile Deschamps, to enlist the collaboration of Hugo and Vigny. Staël's ideas were further propagated in the *Globe*, which began publication in 1824.

Hugo's preface to *Odes et ballades* (1826) expresses almost word for word Staël's views on genius and freedom from imitation. Abel Villemain, a longtime admirer, recapitulated her theories in the course on French literature he taught in 1829 at the Sorbonne. Reading *Allemagne* prompted Byron to pronounce Staël "the most eminent woman writer of this or indeed of any century."[11] In "Les Destinées de la poésie" (The Destiny of poetry, 1834) prefacing his *Méditations*, Lamartine expressed his generation's debt to Staël and Chateaubriand: "There are very few of us who do not owe them what we were, what we are, or what we will be" (Pellegrini, 70).[12] *Allemagne* crossed the Atlantic to influence New England transcendentalism in the 1820s and 1830s.[13] Few books of the era—whether written by men or women—enjoyed such a broad and persisting influence.

Chapter 8
Miscellany

Only a few loyal friends dared brave Napoleon's ire by visiting Staël after she returned from Vienna in 1807. Her chief diversion at this time was acting on the Coppet stage in plays of her own devising, unintended for publication. Auguste de Staël suggests that the five plays he included in the *Oeuvres complètes* cannot possibly produce the same effect when read as in his mother's rendition.

Agar dans le désert (Hagar in the desert, 1806) retells the familiar biblical tale of the handmaid's expulsion by Abraham, her wandering in the desert with her son Ishmael, and their final rescue by an angel of God. Stressing the quality and strength of Hagar's love for her child, Staël presents her expulsion as a life-threatening and undeserved exile that puts her religious faith to the test. On the point of death, Hagar evokes her homeland with nostalgia. Mother and son are saved by a supernatural agent[1] which, belying her pessimism, proves the power of prayer and maternal love.

Geneviève de Brabant (Genevieve of Brabant, 1808) takes its subject from a popular medieval legend.[2] As the play opens, Geneviève is preparing to leave the forest grotto where she has been living (in exile) with her small daughter for ten years. In act 2 she recounts her story to a saintly hermit. Upon leaving for the Crusades, her husband Sigefroi entrusted her to his friend Golo; in retaliation for her spurning his advances, Golo falsely accused her of infidelity. The hermit produces a signed confession from Golo exonerating her before he died. The child stops a young hunter (her brother Adolphe), who in act 3 arranges for his father to meet the girl and her mother. Sigefroi refuses to believe Geneviève's protestations of love and innocence; calling on the angel of death, she faints away at his feet. After the hermit shows him Golo's letter, the contrite husband prays for Geneviève's revival. To the sound of heavenly music, she is restored briefly to life. Once again, Staël places at center stage a maligned and innocent mother who has suffered unmerited exile—this time at the hands of a misguided man. Like Hagar, Geneviève is a paragon of maternal devotion and religious conviction who has been banished to the wilderness with her child; she, too, is succored by supernatural forces. As in some of Staël's early stories, the heroine is the victim of one man's villainy and another's lack of faith. Although properly repentant, both men are punished—one by death, the other by losing the woman he loves.

La Sunamite (The Shunammite, 1808) is another biblical prose drama centering on maternal affection and religious commitment. Inordinately proud of her beautiful daughter Semida and deaf to her sister's remonstrances that the girl is promised to God, the Shunammite prepares a feast in Semida's honor, at which the girl collapses while dancing. The distraught mother begs the prophet Elisha to cure her child, but as representative of a vengeful God, he refuses even to set foot in her house; eventually, his disciple Guehazi prevails on him to help. By act 3 Semida is dead. Guehazi announces to the Shunammite the possibility of a life to come (a mystery that was not revealed to the fathers of her people), and Elisha resurrects Semida. The women promise to dedicate their lives to God's service.[3] Mother love, so nobly depicted in Hagar and Geneviève, is here pushed to the extremes of self-gratification. The Shunammite is humbled in her hubris by the death of her beloved child. All ends happily in a burst of religious ardor as the prideful mother sees the error of her ways. Semida's death is no more binding than Ishmael's or Geneviève's demise; each is averted or reversed through the clemency of a compassionate God.

In *La Sunamite*, Staël betrays a more vitriolic anti-Semitism than in *Dix années*. Portraying Jews as venal and materialistic, she paints a picture of an implacable God and a benighted religion that fails to provide the comfort of eternity. According to Elisha: "The people of Israel, so often inclined to idolatry, care merely about earthly concerns and ask only of their God fruitful vines, abundant harvests, and long days spent in pleasure here on earth" (*OC*, 16:99). This comfort-loving, terrestrial blindness is what the vision of a (Christian) hereafter comes to correct.

Signora Fantastici (1811) is a cheerful, insubstantial diversion. The very names of the characters elicit a chuckle. Married for 25 years, Mr. and Mrs. Kriegschenmahl are quarrelsome and bored. (He speaks with a heavy German accent, she with an English inflection.) Their son Licidas, spouting verses, wishes to leave for Italy with the vibrant singer Signora Fantastici and her daughter Zéphirine. The other son, Rodolphe, furious that Licidas aspires to be an actor, agrees to guard him while their parents summon the police commissioner to send Signora Fantastici packing. Licidas tries unavailingly to interest his brother in poetry, until spunky little Zéphirine arrives and charms Rodolphe into removing his boots and saber and dancing with her. When the Kriegschenmahls return with the stuttering commissioner, Signora Fantastici promises him the role of bailiff on stage. She silences the Kriegschenmahls' complaint by inviting them also to join her troupe: he will play the noble father, and his wife can be a coquette. The humor rests on the absurd situation, puffed-up characters, and witty repartee. Staël pokes fun at Kriegschenmahl's inflated self-importance and Rodolphe's martial pomposity. Even Licidas and Fantastici are lighthearted caricatures. Only peppy Zéphirine seems to come from the real world—a world of self-confidence and joy. The denouement, in which everyone is invited to become an actor, parodies Staël's lifelong attachment to the theater.

The preposterous protagonist of *Le Capitaine Kernadec, ou Sept années en un jour* (Captain Kernadec, or Seven years in a day, 1811) is a blustering and bellicose sea captain, given to recounting his past maritime exploits. He will not hear of his daughter Rosalba's marrying the writer Derval because the young man has not seen service. The soubrette Nérine, whom Kernadec is openly courting, obtains his consent, provided that Derval first fight for seven years in seven campaigns. Sabord, the captain's valet, has a plan: he will get Kernadec drunk for 24 hours, while everyone pretends that seven years have elapsed. Sabord limps on stage in act 2 with a wooden leg he supposedly lost in battle, claiming the year is 1818 (not 1811) and that Nérine is his wife. A uniformed Derval swears and swaggers (mixing up nautical terms) to lay claim to Rosalba. Kernadec is convinced of time's passage by his wife's obvious aging until, insulted, she exposes the plot. Derval calms the irate captain with the news he has arranged for him to receive the naval cross, whereupon the delighted father gives his consent. The satirical characterizations in this lively spoof are amplified by clever lines and an amusing plot twist. Staël's capacity for humor is a deep-lying vein that gleams from time to time even in her serious polemical writing and shines joyously in a slight, lighthearted playlet like this.

In *Le Mannequin* (1811), M. de la Morlière is an expatriate Frenchman who, like Kriegschenmahl, has a heavy German accent (an obvious source of merriment for Staël's audience). Infatuated with all things French, he insists that his daughter Sophie marry the fatuous comte d'Erville[4] rather than the unpretentious painter Frédéric Hoffmann. D'Erville admits to Frédéric that he does not love Sophie, but "it is only fitting that a man like myself should marry a wealthy girl, of less illustrious birth than he" (*OC*, 16:241). Determined to make d'Erville retract his marriage proposal, Sophie hides a mannequin behind a curtain in act 2, while Frédéric informs the count of a far richer prospect, who does not speak a word of French. The high point of the play is the amusing scene in which the count interrogates the mannequin (whose answers Sophie translates). Does she read, sketch, sing, or dance? Since she does none of these things, d'Erville accounts her a truly accomplished woman and rescinds his proposal to Sophie. When he discovers he has chosen a dummy, Sophie admits she wanted to show him that a German woman could play a trick on a Frenchman. Fluffy, inconsequential, and droll, *Le Mannequin* ridicules French chauvinism, especially vis-à-vis the Germans. Whereas Frédéric is the standard ingénu, Sophie is an astute young woman determined to escape from the marriage trap in a witty way. Staël subtly undermines the assumption that women should be simpering fools. What turns d'Erville into a ridiculous clown is less his conceit and hypocritical self-importance than his reducing women to a state of nonexistence. His being bested by a woman adds a feminist zest to the play.

Sapho (Sappho, 1811) reiterates an obsessive theme for Staël—the woman of genius misunderstood and abandoned by the man she loves. Once the most celebrated poet in Greece, Sappho[5] has given up her lyre to mourn the loss of Phaon's love: "I was born for glory, and I succumb to love! The world clamored for my genius, and the scorn of a single man has withered the gift of the gods" (*OC*, 16:290). She agrees reluctantly to participate in a poetry contest for the priestesses of Apollo, in act 2. Her improvisation extolling the joy of creativity wins Apollo's crown, which she blasphemously spurns. In act 3, after declaring his love to the unwitting Cléone, Phaon begs Sappho's forgiveness, but she sends him away: he has not suffered as much as she. To ensure that his happiness derives from her (shades of Corinne), Sappho makes Cléone admit her secret love for Phaon, in act 4, and promises to sing at their wedding from the top of a rock. Outwardly calm but inwardly agitated, Sappho presides at the marriage in act 5. She sings of love and death, of the brevity of life and the ephemeral nature of talent; the only reality on earth is sorrow. Her song ended, she throws herself into the sea. The essential ingredients of *Corinne* are repeated on a reduced scale: the woman of genius who loses her talent when her lover deserts her, then sings a swan song inspired by suffering; the advent of a younger woman who marries the beloved; the self-destructive denouement. Other elements hark back to *Sophie*: the older woman who must cede her place to youth; the young girl who first hides, then confesses her love to her rival-confidante. Suicide for love is a constant in much of Staël's work, from *Jane Gray* and *Mirza* to *Delphine* and *Corinne*.

Although composed in 1811, *Réflexions sur le suicide* (Reflections on suicide) did not appear until 1813. The preface tones down any possible harshness in Staël's condemnation of suicide by expressing her empathy for anyone wretched enough to contemplate taking his or her life. Resignation to fate is of a higher moral order than revolt against it. She presents her arguments under three headings: the effect of suffering on the spirit; Christian laws governing suicide; human dignity. "If . . . the ways of Providence contain a hidden or manifest justice, we cannot consider suffering as either accidental or arbitrary" (*OC*, 3:311). The purpose of suffering, in Staël's revised view, is to develop spiritual qualities to the fullest.

In attempted suicide, as in all extravagant acts, there is a dose of rage that dissipates with time. Even grief over the loss of a loved one is not sufficient reason to take one's life: "We must not allow the ephemeral to thrust us into eternity" (*OC*, 3:319). Although people kill themselves over financial ruin and dishonor, time might have altered their perspective. Life can either be measured in worldly goods or regarded as spiritual preparation for the world to come. Suicide is incompatible with a religious frame of mind. Christ came to earth to preach charity, patience, and faith: charity teaches us our duties toward others; patience offers us consolation; faith announces our recompense. He taught repeatedly that the purpose of misfortune is to purify the soul. Staël compares the peaceful death of Louis XVI (previously invoked in *Passions* and *Considérations*) to the death of Christ—the mightiest example of resignation to suffering. When life's tribulations have taught us the vanity of human pretentions, our religious abnegation precludes self-destruction.

Staël lauds the courageous example of Socrates, whose death has been revered for 200 years, while thousands of suicides have left no trace. Although she admires Sir Thomas More for sacrificing his life to his moral conscience, she considers England's high suicide rate to be a function of the British temperament and climate; conversely, suicide is rare among southern peoples, for the very air they breathe is conducive to loving life (a contrast highlighted in *Littérature*). Excoriating for many pages the 1811 suicide pact between a German officer and a married woman, Staël repeats her prescription of *Allemagne*: instead of dwelling on analysis and sophistry in their writings, the Germans should expend their abilities on political renewal. Although the French commit suicide with customary intrepidity and insouciance, countless émigrés have endured cruel privations with serenity, including exile from their homeland—a fate with which Staël can well empathize. She ends, as she often does, with hope for a reinvigorated France, a "nation that will be glorious once it knows freedom, the political guarantee of justice" (*OC*, 3:369).

There follows a "Notice about Lady Jane Gray," who was placed on the throne through the machinations of her father-in-law Lord Northumberland, then imprisoned and executed by Henry VIII's vindictive daughter Mary. Although only 18 when she died, Jane Gray was an exemplar of erudition, dignity, and gentle piety. Staël quotes a letter in which Lady Jane rejects the offer of poison against her imminent execution, explaining: "Life's unique goal is to teach immortality" (*OC*, 3:377). She also turns down a reprieve at the price of religious conversion. She has chosen death voluntarily; although she will not kill herself, neither will she live: "To give up a life that could only be purchased at the cost of one's conscience is the sole form of suicide allowed the virtuous man" (383). This quotation sums up Staël's emended attitude toward suicide.

Smitten by the genial old Prince Charles-Joseph de Ligne, whom she had charmed during her second visit to Vienna, in 1808, Staël decided to publish and furnish a laudatory preface to a slim volume that she sifted from 34 tomes of his military and literary writings and titled *Pensées et lettres du maréchal Prince de Ligne* (Thoughts and letters of Marshal Prince de Ligne, 1809). Rephrasing what people often said about her, she comments: "One always regrets not having enjoyed the intercourse of men renowned for their clever conversation, for citations provide only an imperfect idea about them" (*OC*, 17:331). Staël depicts the prince as gracious, debonair, witty, and gay; only one event ever ruffled his composure—the death in battle of his eldest son. Tactfully suggesting that his style is more conversational than profound, she offers selections from his correspondence and random thoughts as portraying his courtly character. This brief introduction is an elegant if discreet encomium of the prince that concentrates on his qualities while downplaying whatever flaws the reader may discern in his writings.

Sometime between 1811 and 1813, Staël wrote three biographical sketches of Aspasia, Luis de Camoës, and Cleopatra for Michaud's *Biographie universelle* (Universal biography, 1811–57).[6] In the case of the two semilegendary women, she attempts to revise the image of the courtesan in the light of Christian apologetics. In discussing Camoës, she empathizes with the ironic vicissitudes of the poet's life in exile and lauds his nationalistic inspiration.

Born in Ionia, Aspasia combined political and literary talent with feminine grace. Staël excuses her for becoming a courtesan on the grounds of an unjust social order, for Athenian law proscribed foreign women and did not recognize as legitimate the children they bore in wedlock (an implicit analogy with the condition of Protestants in France). Socrates was reputedly in love with her. Her greatest achievement (in Staël's adjudication) was the sincere and lasting love she inspired in Pericles, whom she also instructed in oratory. The author inserts a significant comment about women and politics: "In a monarchy, there is a repugnance for women who meddle in political matters and seem to rival men by usurping their career; but in a republic, where politics is men's main concern, they cannot have a deep relationship with women who do not share this interest" (*OC*, 17:340).

The lyric poetry of Luis de Camoës is closer to the (romantic) vein of Christianity and chivalry than to the classical genre of his native Portugal. After losing an eye in battle, he wrote an epic poem glorifying Portuguese exploits but was exiled to Macao for satirizing colonial abuses. While living in solitude, he composed his famous patriotic poem *Os Lusiadas* (1572), which celebrates Vasco de Gama's expedition to the Indies. Finally recalled from exile, he was shipwrecked and had to swim to safety, holding his precious manuscript above the water. After persecution, imprisonment, and the loss of his royal benefactor, he ended up writing poems about poverty, while his servant begged for food. Fifteen years after his death in 1579, Camoës was acknowledged as the master of Portuguese literature.

At 17, after declining to rule with her brother, Cleopatra had herself wrapped in a rug and deposited before Caesar; her ruse won the heart of the Roman arbitrator, who placed her on the throne of Egypt. She soon bore him a son. Caesar incensed the Romans by placing golden statues of Cleopatra in the temple. After his death, she set sail for Tarsus on Mark Antony's orders. People lined the banks of the river to watch the gilded ship with purple sails glide by. When she invited Antony to supper, she inflamed a love even more violent than Caesar's. Although he married Octavia in Rome for political reasons, Antony did not stop loving Cleopatra. Some years later, he returned to Egypt, leading a dissolute life while the power of his rival Octavius grew. Cleopatra built a tomb near the temple of Isis, where she hid when Octavius defeated Antony; the latter died in her arms, and she disfigured herself out of grief. To prevent Octavius from exhibiting her triumphantly in Rome, she ordered flowers brought that concealed an asp; after dying from its bite, she was buried with Antony. In spite of its familiar details, this account reflects the author's predilections and prejudices. She cannot restrain admiration for Cleopatra as a beleaguered queen and captivator of men. She half-identifies with those irresistible charms that supposedly compensated for a lack of beauty. Nonetheless, she disapproves of the Egyptian queen's heathen whims, extravagant coquetry, and corruptive influence on Antony. Cleopatra's suicide is presented as a fact, which Staël neither castigates nor defends. In the end, the Egyptian queen is redeemed by love.

Staël wrote two fiery sermons against slavery—a cause she had championed since youth.[7] The first text is her "Préface pour la traduction d'un ouvrage de M. Wilberforce sur la traite des Nègres" (Preface to the translation of a work by Mr. Wilberforce on the Negro slave trade, 1814), a book favoring abolition. She calls Wilberforce a distinguished member of the House of Commons, well read in literature and religious philosophy, who spent 30 years fighting to end slavery. After amassing evidence of cruelty, he introduced a motion in Parliament in 1787 to abolish the slave trade; although supported by Pitt, Fox, and Burke, he was defeated by "all those who divide the human species into two parts, one of which, in their opinion, must be sacrificed to the other" (*OC*, 17:370). Wilberforce repeated his motion yearly until it was finally adopted in 1807, under Fox's ministry. After this hymn to English humanitarianism, Staël turns her ammunition on the French. English politicians and speculators proffered the same arguments that French colonials and merchants voice today—that ending slavery would be their ruination. Their fears have proved groundless in the seven years since England put an end to the slave trade.

This preface also serves as an introduction to the next piece, "Appel aux souverains, réunis à Paris, pour en obtenir l'abolition de la traite des Nègres" (An Appeal to the sovereigns meeting in Paris, to obtain the abolition of the Negro slave trade, 1814). Staël begins by eulogizing England's humanitarian achievements during a period of war and political crisis, when adversarial parties joined to implement a moral decision. Repeating the argument that abolishing the slave trade seven years before in no way impaired the prosperity of the British colonies, Staël notes that England made abolition a condition of its peace treaty with Denmark. After depicting the horrors of the slave trade—the sufferings of transit, the greed and cruelty of chieftains who export their people— she recommends that Europe repay its 25-year debt to England by adopting the humane act that England advocates. Abolition would be a meaningful monument to commemorate the downfall of humanity's oppressor (Napoleon).

Two other pieces are oriented toward literature. In her acerbic "Réponse à un article de journal" (Response to a newspaper article,

1814), Staël goes from refuting one reader's criticism of *Suicide* to indict-
ing French criticism in general because it consists primarily of misquota-
tions used out of context. In contrast, she opposes the depth, talent, and
knowledge of English and German critics, whose accuracy gives them
the right to pass judgment. "De l'esprit des traductions" (The Spirit of
translation, 1816), composed during Staël's second trip to Italy,[8] asserts
the importance of translating masterpieces from one language to another—a notion stressed in *Allemagne*. The circulation of ideas is the most
advantageous type of commerce. Good translations renew language and
preserve a country's literature from banality and decadence. In singling
out Monti's translation of Homer, Staël defines her concept of the translating art: "Translating a poet does not mean taking a compass and
copying the dimensions of the edifice; it means animating a different
instrument with the same breath of life" (*OC*, 17:395). Plays in translation can be even more effective than poetry, "for the theater is truly the
executive branch of literature" (396). Revitalizing ideas contained in
Littérature and *Allemagne*, heralding romantic ideology, Staël stresses
originality of inspiration over classical imitation and preaches a cross-pollination of national literatures, each of which has something innovative
and beneficial to offer the others. True intellectuals welcome the ideas
and beauties inherent in other cultures, thereby enriching their own.

As if to exemplify her dictates, Staël executed a number of verse translations from Italian, English, and German—a lugubrious sonnet by
Minzoni on the death of Christ, another by Vincenzo da Filicaia decrying
the conquest of Italy, Goethe's "Der Gott und die Bajare," "Der Fischer,"
and "Geistes-Gruss" (1774), which she (or her posthumous editor) erro-
neously attributes to Schiller (*OC* 17:448), and Schiller's "Das Siegesfest."
Although somewhat labored and pedestrian, these translations bespeak a
valiant attempt to capture the poetic essence of the original.

"Henry et Emma," a ballad imitated from Matthew Prior, disclaims
women's reputation for inconstancy by telling the tale of a heroine with
a pure and courageous heart. When her lover apprises her that he has
been condemned to death and must flee, she replies that she will follow
him to the ends of the earth. The poem is divided into stanzas titled
"Henry" and "Emma," in which Henry paints increasingly gruesome
pictures of the life that awaits him and Emma reiterates her willingness
to remain with him, no matter what befalls. His final test is to tell her he
loves another woman; even this knowledge fails to discourage Emma. At
the end, Henry reveals that he is really the country's ruler. Emma cares
as little about splendor as about danger; beside him, she will always be

queen. Her fidelity convinces Henry that the old saws about flighty hearts are untrue. Whereas Henry is a scoundrel in toying with Emma's love and fears for his safety, she emerges as an unblemished heroine who invariably comes up with the right answers to prove her constancy.

Staël's "Imitation d'une élégie de Bowles, sur les eaux de Bristol" (Imitation of an elegy by Bowles on the waters of Bristol, 1791) proceeds from a consideration of nature's awakening at sunrise to a sympathetic description of scarlet-cheeked consumptives facing death but still bravely clinging to life, and ends with an exhortation to banish melancholy, hold steadfast against one's enemies, serve one's friends, and believe in life.

These varied pieces, written at different periods of the author's life, attest to her abiding infatuation with romantic love (invariably stronger, more tenacious, on the part of woman), her moral-religious proclivities, and her lifelong crusade for inspired, enthusiastic literature. It is to be noted that this remarkable woman was not averse to trying her hand at translation and entering the lists with the likes of Goethe, Schiller, and Minzoni. There was almost nothing Staël did not think she could accomplish. Her achievements in every genre give the lie to those critics who perceive her as apprehensive and insecure.

Chapter 9

Postmortems

The political works discussed in chapter 3 were written in the heat of the moment, in the hope of influencing the course of events. Others were composed after the fact, with a view to affecting contemporary perceptions of past events. Benefiting less from the objectivity that comes with time than from the corrective lens of hindsight, they constitute a remedial postmortem performed on the historical figures, events, and personal experiences the author describes.

Partly a minuscule political and historical recapitulation, partly a subjective depiction of her own bereavement, Staël wrote "Du Caractère de M. Necker et de sa vie privée" (On the character of M. Necker and his private life) immediately after his death and published it in February 1805 as a preface to the *Manuscrits de M. Necker, publiées par sa fille* (Monsieur Necker's manuscripts, published by his daughter). This piece—an intensive apology for his career and writings and an oedipal encomium of his private person—is a panegyric to the most incomparable of men. Her stated reasons for offering this book to the public are the general interest accruing to her father's role in "History" and his instructive example of honesty in office and equanimity in adversity. Marveling at his rare combination of financial and literary talent, Staël blames invidious courtiers for his ouster and therefore, by implication, for the disaster that befell the country: "If he had remained minister, he might have averted the Revolution by maintaining financial solvency" (*OC*, 17:31). She will renew this hindsight vision in *Considérations sur les principaux événements de la Révolution française* (Considerations on the principal events of the French Revolution, 1818).

As virtuous in private as in public life, Necker spent his retirement writing and developing "a celestial spirit and a character that became purer, nobler, and more sensitive by the day" (*OC*, 17:71–72). The pieces she is publishing herewith, composed the preceding winter, contain his sagacious reflections on human nature and reveal the acuity of his social observations. The collection ends with a novel—a love story of passion and delicacy—that her 70-year-old father wrote in response to her challenge. Now she is overcome with grief at his death: "I was to lose . . . my protector, father, brother, and friend, the man I would have chosen as the love of my life had fate not put me in another generation from his!" (105). A patently prejudiced appraisal that emphasizes Necker's merits with scant attention to any flaws, Staël's preface is persuasive in its reasoning and poignant in its yearning to burnish her father's portrait for posterity. This concern accounts for the persistent undertones of much of her writing, ending with a ringing reevaluation in *Considérations*.

This book, like *Dix années d'exil* (Ten years of exile), was written many years after the event and published posthumously. Staël began writing *Dix années* in 1811 and *Considérations* in 1812. Probably sensing that her time was short, she directed Schlegel and her son Auguste to oversee publication after her death. Although they found the manuscripts in various stages of composition, they refrained from tampering with the text except for minor stylistic changes. *Considérations* appeared separately in 1818; *Dix années* was included in Staël's *Oeuvres complètes* in 1820.

Considérations is titularly a historic overview of the causes leading up to the Revolution and the events that denatured its original goals and eventuated in Napoleon's Empire—in Staël's eyes, a retroactive revival of the worst monarchical abuses and a betrayal of revolutionary ideals. In point of fact, the book is a rehabilitation of Necker, in line with the regret expressed in *Allemagne*, that a great man in retirement is both forgotten and reviled. The conclusion lauds the free and peaceful government of England—an example Necker had invoked in prerevolutionary days. Implicit throughout is Necker's clairvoyance. Time and again, Staël points to the moment when the Revolution might have been arrested if his advice had been heeded. Robespierre's Terror and Napoleon's Empire are the deplorable but inevitable consequences of Necker's fall from power, as the Restoration is the glorious if belated incarnation of his hopes and plans. In demythicizing Napoleon, Staël again responds viscerally. There is scarcely an act he committed, a victory he gained, or a reform he enacted that she does not invalidate retroactively. Napoleon's attempt to muzzle his most vociferous critic backfires, as she retaliates for years of censored silence.

Staël stands behind the scenes, witness to and commentator of history—a history both selective and subjective, its events chosen to prove a preconceived thesis. Occasionally, she emerges from the wings to play a bit part in her re-created drama. She watches the riots at Versailles (symbolically, from a window), survives near-massacre on the Place de Grève, saves assorted friends from death, steps sadly into allied-occupied France. At other times, her very absence is significant. She downplays her role in the 18 Fructidor coup, makes no mention of manuevering to place Bernadotte on the throne, and conceals the frequent relationship between her public and private life.

Part 1 is a summary of European history, with a fortified version of Necker's career under Louis XVI. Part 2 recounts the Revolution, part 3 traces the Terror, and part 4 follows the consolidation of Napoleon's power. Part 5 is a reserved salute to the Bourbon restoration of Louis XVIII. Part 6 raises to the level of idolatry the prized British political example. Throughout, the author blends fact, reminiscence, and bias into a unique reconstruction of history. Freedom is ancient, she claims, and tyranny new. The nobility restrained royal might throughout medieval Europe. The Reformation unleashed a spirit of free inquiry that leads necessarily to representative government. Accusing Louis XIV of indirectly causing the Revolution by his cult of absolute power, Staël inveighs against the 1685 revocation of the Edict of Nantes, which deprived Protestants of property and civil rights.

Two decades after his execution, she is still unflinchingly loyal to Louis XVI, whose errors she attributes to a weak character and inept advisers—all save Necker, whom she extols continually. As director general of the royal treasury, his objective was to curtail expenditures rather than raise taxes. He managed to borrow on the strength of his personal credit and finance war for five years without new taxation. He sought invariably to limit ministerial power, including his own. A result of libel and resentment, his "disgrace" in 1781 was met by a public outpouring of respect and regret. The work he then wrote, *De l'administration des finances de la France* (On administering the finances of France, 1784), sold 80,000 copies and contained all the tax reforms since adopted by the Constituent Assembly.

Pressured by nobility and clergy, the king promised to convoke the Estates General in May 1789. (Every revolution, Staël claims, must be initiated by the upper class.) Together with the parliaments (the origins and evolution of which she traces), the Estates General traditionally limited royal authoritarianism; in contrast, the bicameral British parliament combines the legislative authority of both these bodies. By his own account, Necker's recall in 1788 came too late. The Third Estate, which by now numbered 90 percent of the nation, asked that its deputies equal those of clergy and nobility combined. Necker delayed his decision to double the Third until he could sample public opinion. To alleviate a wheat shortage in Paris during the winter of 1788–89, he contributed half his fortune to the royal treasury. When the Estates General opened on 4 May 1789, the procession of 1,200 deputies was an imposing sight. Staël describes the Third Estate, not as a ragtag mob but as a stately group of men of letters, businessmen, lawyers, and some aristocrats. Its deputies called for vote by head count, the nobility and clergy for vote by order. The provincial nobility—petty, pretentious, pedantic—were more intractable than the old-line aristocrats in opposing Necker's compromise. While the privileged orders were bogged down in debating their own interests and power, abbé Sieyès proposed that the Third constitute itself a National Assembly of France and invite the other two orders to join. Because its assembly hall was closed to prepare for the royal reception, the Third Estate thought it was barred from meeting; for this reason, its deputies gathered in the Jeu de Paume to swear an oath to uphold their rights.

The declaration that Necker prepared for Louis XVI on 23 June 1789 is almost identical to Louis XVIII's proclamation at Saint-Ouen on 2 May 1814, Staël asserts; the bloody circle of the intervening 25 years could have been avoided by consenting at once to the people's wishes. When the king's council changed his proclamation to favor the privileged elements, Necker resigned. Kept in the dark about the king's secret plans to assemble foreign troops, Necker obeyed his sovereign's order to leave France secretly on 11 July. When his removal became known, all Paris rose up in arms. People wore green *cocardes*, the color of Necker's livery, and medals were struck with his likeness.[1] As barricades were erected, the people formed an army 100,000 strong. The Bastille, citadel of arbitrary government, was stormed on 14 July 1789. (Staël recounts these events as if they were a direct result of Necker's dismissal.) Forced to condone a revolution he could not arrest, the unfortunate king begged Necker to return. After quoting comte de Lally-Tollendal's lengthy encomium of her father, Staël describes the crowds of citizens pulling his carriage, the women kneeling in the fields as he passed, and the crowds standing on Paris rooftops to greet him.

As part 1 details events leading up to the Revolution, part 2 traces the Revolution's course after the Bastille was stormed. Staël devotes the first chapter to the comte de Mirabeau, a vain and immoral demagogue, whom she contrasts with Necker as the evil and good geniuses of the age. True to her lifelong vision, she sees the early days of the Revolution as a time of unity and shared fervor for freedom, with La Fayette as a model of sacrifice for high-minded ideals. Before analyzing how the Revolution went off course, she lists the positive achievements of the Constituent Assembly: it abolished torture, proclaimed freedom of religion, outlawed lettres de cachet, introduced the English criminal justice system, inaugurated a free press, and opened military rank to all citizens. Still inspired (like Necker) by the British example, she condemns adoption of a unicameral legislature. Not only is an upper house a necessary intermediary between king and deputies, but it provides the only possibility of eradicating the second-class nobility (her frequent bête noire).

In a stirring eyewitness report, Staël describes the populist march on Versailles of 5 and 6 October, when ruffians broke into the palace, massacred the queen's guards, and brought the king and royal family forcibly back to Paris. This event marked the rise of the Jacobins and the Revolution's change of focus, as the lower class gained dominance over "the class called on by its talents to govern" (OC, 12:349). Patriotic Paris arrived en masse for the 1790 Federation, at which national guardsmen swore allegiance to the new, still incomplete, constitution, Talleyrand celebrated mass, and La Fayette pledged fealty to king and nation. Dubious about the general rejoicing, Necker resigned on 3 September 1790 and set out brokenhearted for Basel by the same road along which he had been borne in triumph 13 months before.

In a breach of Staël's oft-vaunted separation of powers, the Assembly seized executive authority to quell provincial disturbances during the winter of 1790–91. After his injudicious flight to Varennes, the king was kept prisoner in the Tuileries pending a new constitution, the provisions of which Staël criticizes. Robespierre struck down the property-holding condition, which she deems essential in order to "confine election to the class that has an interest in maintaining order" (OC, 12:422).[2] Where the Assembly provided for a two-stage electoral process, she argues in favor of direct election by the people (who should nonetheless choose representatives from the upper class). The king could scarcely reject the wretched Constitution of 1791 since it terminated his captivity. Although the Revolution seemed over, Staël descries the doom of constitutional monarchy in the exclusion of the propertied class and the aristocratic emigration that followed (part 3).

A "political Fénelon" (OC, 13:11),[3] Necker spent the last 14 years of his life defending the ideals of English government vis-à-vis the Constituent Assembly, Convention, Directory, and Bonaparte. His prophetic *Du pouvoir exécutif dans les grands états* (Executive power in large nations, 1820–21) predicted the Terror that would stem from Jacobin power and the military dictatorship to follow. After the new Legislative Assembly toppled the throne on 10 August 1791, the Convention of Pilnitz marked the start of a bloody conflict that was to tear Europe apart for a generation. In December the Legislative Assembly entrusted the war department to Narbonne,[4] "a great lord, a clever man, a courtier and philosopher" (38), whose colleagues conspired to have him dismissed. When Louis XVI vetoed two unacceptable decrees proscribing the clergy, 20,000 men of the lowest class broke into the Tuileries and forced him to don the red bonnet. Despotism of the vilest sort arose from the vulgar classes like vapors from a pestilential swamp. The most rabid men in France poured into Paris for the 14 July celebration of 1792, at which the king walked slowly down the Champ-de-Mars, like a sacrificial victim. His next public appearance would be on the scaffold.

Staël's personal anecdotes are vivid and compelling. On the night of 9 August, she heard the tocsins tolling as people from the faubourgs advanced under Antoine Santerre; no one expected to survive the night. Early next morning, having heard the erroneous report that her constitutionalist friends had been slaughtered, she set out to find them. It took her coachman two hours to cross the Seine. Drunken men armed to the teeth cursed hideously as she passed. She took the risk of hiding Narbonne in the Swedish embassy; if discovered, he would have been killed on the spot. One day, a group of men belonging to the dregs of humanity paid her a dreaded "home visit," as it was called. Staël warned that they were violating the rights of a powerful nation (Sweden) poised on the French border to strike if provoked. Ignorant of geography, the intruders left. She also saved Jaucourt and Lally-Tollendal from execution by persuading Communard Louis-Pierre Manuel to set them free: "Save up a sweet and consoling memory for the day when you may perhaps be proscribed yourself" (*OC*, 13:68). Manuel was indeed guillotined 14 months later.

Having promised to meet the proscribed abbé de Montesquiou on 2 September and take him, in servant's dress, to Switzerland, she set out in a coach drawn by six horses with servants in full livery (a mistake—she should have avoided attention) and was attacked by a mob. Staël describes the old women who seized the horses' bridles, shrieking that she was carrying off the country's gold; her whispered warning to his servant to alert Montesquiou; the chaotic scene at the faubourg assembly; the missing servant on her passport; the frightful drive across Paris to the Hôtel de Ville amid a crowd clamoring for her death, despite her pregnant condition; the screaming horde that filled the commune presided over by Robespierre; the timely arrival of Manuel, who spirited her away at nightfall through the unlit Paris streets. Armed with a new passport, she left for Switzerland next day.

While the royal family was kept captive in the Temple, a national convention proclaimed France a republic. After Necker published a memorandum in the king's favor in October 1792, his property in France was sequestered. Although the king chose Guillaume de Malesherbes as his advocate, Necker's defense is a worthy historical document (from which Staël quotes amply to prove the king's innocence). Appalled by the disrespect to Louis XVI during his trial, she blames political fanaticism for the monstrous events that ensued. The assassination of the queen and Mme Elisabeth, the king's sister, caused even greater horror than the king's execution. Emigration under the Terror became a life-saving necessity. As the Committee of Public Safety spewed forth atrocities, Robespierre's austere fanaticism frightened even his cohorts. Staël met him once at her father's house in 1789, when he was only a small-time lawyer from Artois, with plebeian features, a pale complexion, green veins, and radical ideas. Colleagues and conventionalists teamed up against him to end the Terror. Lying bloodied on the same table where he had signed countless death decrees, Robespierre in defeat was a symbol of divine justice.

While the conventionalists held power after Robespierre's fall, the populace endured famine and currency depreciation with astonishing fortitude; if the French kings had subjected them to half these hardships, they would have rebelled. Although people were appealing right and left for the return of their émigré friends, Staël found it strange that Deputy Legendre denounced her to the Convention for the same activity. "Golden salons" opened, in which Jacobins were solicited for favors; a new court was in the making, with the same abuses as the old.

After the Paris sections were repulsed on 13 Vendémiaire (4 October 1795) by General Bonaparte commanding the Convention army, five regicide directors were named, with power to exile, imprison, or deport any persons they deemed loyal to the ancien régime. The Directory lasted from November 1795 to 18 Fructidor (4 September) 1797; despite initial achievements (financial stability, restoration of a free press), its last four years were marred by warring factions. Although on the émigré death list, Necker published in late 1796 the four-volume *Histoire de la Révolution* (History of the Revolution), containing two extraordinary predictions: the struggle between the Directory and legislature, and the military dictatorship he felt certain would follow.

Deprived of legitimate executive power, the Directors turned to Bonaparte for support. Staël defends herself against charges of promoting the 18 Fructidor coup[5] when General Pierre d'Augereau's troops took over the Council of Five Hundred; to the contrary, she professes that securing Talleyrand's appointment proves her wish to prevent it. Before execrating Bonaparte's actions, she flagellates his character— stony, willful, intimidating, unfeeling. He treated people as objects to help or hinder his rise. Because he was short, he looked best on horse-back: "In everything, it is war, and war alone, that suits him" (*OC*, 13:197). Although the Directory wanted him to attack England, Bonaparte chose Egypt as a more flamboyant target. Needing funds, he made unpardonable plans to seize the treasury of Berne. Staël describes watching with her father from the balcony at Coppet after he invaded Switzerland in January 1798. Because Necker faced an automatic death sentence as an émigré on French-occupied territory, the first order of business was to have him erased from the émigré list—an act the Directory voted unanimously.

Although she cannot deny the truth of Bonaparte's assertion that "the French crown lay on the ground, and I picked it up" (*OC*, 13:219), Staël concentrates in part 3 on inculpating him on every level. By sending his grenadiers into the Council of Five Hundred on 18 Brumaire, Bonaparte sapped the authority of the people's delegates. Playing on fears of Jacobin resurgence, he instituted a consular constitution that abrogated popular suffrage and retained revolutionary laws like extraordinary tribunals, press censorship, and the power to exile. Although irreligious, he courted the Catholic clergy so that it would second his ascent to the throne. To celebrate his concordat with the Vatican, Bonaparte ordered a splendid ceremony at Notre-Dame in April 1802—presided over by the archbishop who had anointed Louis XVI at Reims—and arrived in the king's coach with full regal pomp. After the concordat, the French priesthood menaced with damnation anyone who failed to embrace his regime.

Because Necker's *Dernières vues de politique et de finances* (Final views on politics and finance, 1802) disclosed Bonaparte's plan to head a reinstated monarchy, the book was pilloried by the press. The first consul refused to consider restitution of Necker's two million–pound loan or to sanction his daughter's return to Paris. Staël was the first woman whom Bonaparte exiled. She views indiscriminate exile as even more tyrannical than illegal imprisonment. Her punishment was aggravated by compromising her friends. Both Mathieu de Montmorency and Juliette Récamier were exiled for having visited her. Staël observes with unaccustomed irony: "This coalition of two women on the banks of Lake Geneva appeared so formidable to the master of the world, that he was ridiculous enough to persecute them. But as he had once said, *Power is never ridiculous*; he certainly put this maxim to the test" (*OC*, 13:302).

By crowning himself emperor, Bonaparte completed a counterrevolution. He reinstated monarchy, clergy, and nobility, established a police state, and reintroduced torture. Worst of all, he fragmented countries like Poland, Italy, Greece, and Germany. None of the projects he completed—the highways necessary to his plans, the monuments consecrated to his glory, improved jurisprudence, public education, or scientific encouragement—compensated for the degrading yoke he laid on the vanquished. In denigrating Bonaparte's accomplishments, Staël belies his renowned military prowess. She chides him for turning fervid revolutionary troops into a crass mercenary lot and risking his soldiers' lives for personal gain. His civil government was rife with corruption. Extraordinary tribunals suspended legal safeguards in political cases. Police surveillance was ubiquitous. Imperial censorship dictated official opinions on politics, religion, literature, mores, and personalities. Some writers were faced with the kind of harassment that forced the author to escape and take refuge in England.

Absolute master of 80 million men, meeting no impediments to his ambition, Napoleon was nonetheless incapable of founding a durable institution. Regarding high-minded ideals as hypocritical, he once said to the Duke of Melzi: "There is only one thing to do in this world: keep acquiring more and more money and power. All the rest is an idle dream" (*OC*, 13:384). Abetted by willing sycophants, the disastrous Russian campaign confirmed his appetite for conquest. Staël tells of fleeing across Russia ahead of his troops. Someday, she says, she will write about this little-known country,[6] with its hospitable peasantry and enlightened emperor. After his Russian defeat, Bonaparte returned to Paris to recoup his forces. Miraculously, the nation created a new army to march on Germany. Even self-interest cannot explain his subsequent actions, including his insensate refusal to make peace in March 1814. When the allies entered France, Staël voiced the hope that Bonaparte would end up victorious, but dead. Not having touched on his private life because it bears no relation to national interest, she flatters herself that she has judged him impartially.

Part 5 is a muted paean to constitutional monarchy as embodied in the Bourbon restoration of Louis XVIII; as such, it is a further refutation of Napoleonic autocracy. The editor's note of 1818 reminds the reader that Staël did not have a chance to revise this section, which was published as found. Just as the experience of the Terror tempered her republicanism, so the Napoleonic Empire has revised her ideas about legitimacy. She now advocates a hereditary regime on the British order, recommending an old-line aristocracy over an upstart nobility.

The constitutional charter granted by Louis XVIII in 1814 contained most of the guarantees of freedom that Necker had proposed to Louis XVI in 1789, before the Revolution. (In other words, France had come full circle: the suffering of the intervening years could have been avoided if Necker's prescient counsel had been followed.) While analyzing the failure of Louis XVIII's initial reign, Staël prescribes measures that should have been taken. Most of her recommendations repeat past, unheeded advice. For example, the house of representatives should have been enlarged to enhance its importance, the house of peers confined to old-line nobility and men prominent in military and civilian life. Public education should have been encouraged and a free press preserved. Above all, the king should not have surrounded himself with former Bonapartists but with "friends of freedom." Bonaparte signed his second abdication on 22 June 1815; foreign troops entered the capital on 8 July. During this brief interval, the legislature voted what Staël enthusiastically calls a "bill of rights" on the English model. Here end the author's historical considerations. So long as it is occupied by foreign armies, France does not exist.

Part 6 presents a final, full apology for the English system of government that Necker championed and Staël adopted in his wake. An overview of English history purports to prove that violence and despotism can ultimately give way to law-abiding government. Present-day England enjoys widespread prosperity, which Staël attributes to confidence in a free government and, in true Neckerian spirit, to the credit possibilities of a responsible regime. The guarantee of individual rights is the premise of freedom, she states. The British criminal system protects the defendant with humane safeguards, most important of which is trial by jury. Although civil procedures are expensive and protracted, Staël expects them to improve over time, "for what especially characterizes the English government is the possibility of its being perfected without upheaval" (*OC*, 14:219). The coexistence of ministerial and opposition parties is essential to freedom, for despotism lurks when men always agree. There is no danger of rebellion if members of the opposition possess property, wealth, rank, and above all, knowledge. Staël reiterates the concept of a propertied and intellectual elite that she recommended in *Circonstances*.

A country's enlightenment can be gauged by its healthy political system and the general level of its science and literature. The British people's participation in public affairs favors intellectual progress. A large number have studied ancient languages. Private libraries and public schools abound. Both English and Scots have written major works of philosophy, jurisprudence, and political economy, because they know their ideas can be put into practice. English poetry—rich, lively, and imaginative—is not threatened with decadence like most European literatures. Staël cites William Cowper, Samuel Rogers, Thomas Moore, Thomas Campbell, Walter Scott, and Lord Byron as examples of the "second age of poetry . . . being reborn in England," where enthusiasm is unstifled and concepts of "nature, love, and country" prevail (OC, 14:256–57). She also singles out certain outstanding women writers, like Miss Edgeworth,[7] Mrs. d'Arblay,[8] Mrs. Hannah Moore [sic],[9] Mrs. Inchbald,[10] Mrs. Opie,[11] and Miss Bayley [sic].[12]

Although she praises British political freedom, justice, commercial integrity, and domestic morality, one senses that Staël would never have wished to live among them. For one thing, she has an aversion to huge social gatherings, which are unconducive to conversational repartee. In addition, she finds the position of English women barely tenable. They have no influence on popular elections, parliamentary debates, or legislation, nor is there any precedent for a woman's making political prescriptions (as Staël does here). Excluded from male conversation, women live on the fringes of society. Staël's ideas about life for an English woman, especially in the provinces, have not changed since her devastating picture of Corinne in Northumberland.

Naturally shy and ill at ease, the English have difficulty forming close bonds. They cherish the concept of "home"—which is probably why they detest exile or arbitrary arrest. Staël suggests that their love of travel may stem from a desire to escape the constraint of their customs as well as their country's fog. In most other nations, social pleasures are confined to the upper, or leisure, class. In England, lords and businessmen alike prefer physical sports to conversation. Nowhere does one find as many "eccentrics." Truthfulness is the country's predominant trait: "The habit of perfect honesty can only exist in a country where dissimulation leads nowhere except to the discomfiture of discovery" (OC, 14:277).

Despite her overall admiration, Staël is vehemently opposed to British presence on French soil. Violating the integrity of their neighbor compromises English doctrines of freedom, risks provoking new warfare, and poses the danger of acquiring a militaristic mentality. The present situation notwithstanding, she points out the necessity for modeling any constitutional monarchy on the British system (a position she had argued while Louis XVI was still alive). After a revolution, a constitutional monarchy is the only government that can reconcile hereditary interests with enlightened politics. Repeating Necker's assertion that a conservative element is essential to freedom and order, she argues in favor of an upper chamber.

Staël concludes this long and complex work with a luminous appeal for "love of freedom," a deep-rooted attachment from which she has never deviated. Three groups at present oppose freedom in France: the nobility, who align their interests with the king; men disgusted by revolutionary ideas; and Bonapartists and Jacobins, who lack a political conscience. She demolishes their reasoning point by point. Liberty encompasses everything we love and honor. Liberty alone can stir human hearts and souls. She ends with a tribute to the lineage of men who have cherished freedom in all ages and nations.

More than a factual history or narration of events, *Considérations* is a series of philosophical, political, and subjective reflections marshaled in the service of a thesis. Intended originally as a panegyric of Necker, the book expanded into an overview of French history from Charlemagne to Louis XVIII, with emphasis on the scourge of tyranny in every form. In the process of proving the validity of Necker's doctrines, Staël has her own political axe to grind. She despises authoritarianism in every guise, be it the absolutism of a Louis XIV, the cruelty of a Robespierre, or the colossal ambition of a Bonaparte. Not only does she propose the British example at every juncture of French revolutionary history, but she devotes the final section of the book to justifying the British political system as evinced by the happiness and prosperity of its people. She has reclaimed Necker's dream.

The 60,000 copies of *Considérations* that appeared in 1818 were sold out within a few days. A second edition came out immediately, a third in 1820. The work was reprinted in Staël's *Oeuvres complètes*, also in 1820, and again in 1836 and 1838; three further editions came out in 1843, 1862, and 1881.[13] Benjamin Constant equates *Corinne* and *Considérations* as the two works that best illustrate Staël's character and views. "The first created a new era in French literature, so to speak, and . . . the other elevated the most durable monument that had yet been erected to the principles of liberty proclaimed in 1789" (Bornecque, 252). As is only to be expected, Stendhal and Lamartine reviled *Considérations*. The former called it "a contradictory and puerile work" (Correspondence, 1: 941), while Lamartine was disappointed by its condescension to the intellectual weaknesses and banalities of its time.[14] Though not pub-

lished until 1876, Stendhal's *Vie de Napoléon* was a heated counterattack
against *Considérations* (Godechot, 39). As usual, Sainte-Beuve is lavishly
laudatory. Calling Staël the Restoration's "historical and political muse,"
he claims she cannot be properly appreciated until 1818, with the publication of this splendid posthumous work on the French Revolution.
"Mme de Staël is complete only as of that date; the full influence of her
star rose above her tomb" (Sainte-Beuve, 85). *Considérations* achieved its
influence and received its full justification, not under the Reformation,
but under Louis-Philippe's July monarchy, which put into practice the
tenets of the author's political prescription: "government in France by an
elite of property-holders and men of talent, illuminated by the judicious
light of liberalism" (Diesbach, 546). To crown Staël's posthumous triumph, her son-in-law Victor de Broglie, a spokesman for her liberal
principles, was appointed prime minister by Louis-Philippe in 1835.

Her second historical postmortem—even more autobiographical and
outspoken—was *Dix années*, her bitter account of exile. Staël's correspondence and writings reverberate with laments about this worst of all
fates. "Exile is not a simple matter," she wrote Joseph Bonaparte on 3
December 1803, "and the ancients were right to find it as painful as
death" (Jasinski, 5:128). To Adrienne de Tessé she complained on 30
June 1806: "Even the people dearest to me do not understand what suffering exile causes me. . . . Strong men like Cicero, Bolingbroke, and
Ovid faced death more bravely than banishment" (Solovieff, 325–26).
"No one has any idea what exile means," she wrote Juliette Récamier on
14 April 1809. "It is the hundred-headed hydra of suffering" (Levaillant,
183). To conjure this source of torment and to vent her wrath at
Napoleonic injustice, Staël undertook to write about the ordeal of which
she had been victim.

Composed intermittently between 1811 and 1816, *Dix années*
remained unfinished at the author's death. Although the title indicates a
ten-year time span, in fact, the narration begins in 1800, stops in 1804
(the year of Necker's death), resumes in 1810, and ends abruptly with
her arrival in Sweden in 1812. Staël judges Napoleon with even greater
severity in this work, when imperial power was at its height, than in
Considérations, written after his defeat. The first part is a step-by-step
account of Bonaparte's rise to power and parallel hostility toward her.
The second part is the narrative of her flight across Europe. It is also a
tour guide to Russia and the Russian people—a diminished echo of the
exercise in *Corinne* and *Allemagne*.

The first chapter of part 1 displays a rare subjectivity as Staël discourses on "the causes of Bonaparte's animosity towards me." Because of his minute and inflexible persecution, she claims to have divined the first consul's tyrannical nature and ambition long before anyone else. She faults the European powers for capitulating too readily at Marengo in June 1800: "[Bonaparte's] great talent is to frighten the weak and utilize the unscrupulous. When he comes up against honesty, his guile is foiled, as the devil is conjured by the sign of the cross" (*OC*, 15:23). This is not the first or last time she will compare Bonaparte to Satan.

After inveighing against his arbitrary deportation of 130 Jacobins following an abortive assassination attempt in November 1800, she condemns his duplicity in breaking a peace treaty to imprison Toussaint Louverture. His methods are like the workings of an infernal machine: "We watch astonished as the will of a single man propels the turbulent machinery of a great forge, whose hammers and rollers seem like . . . devouring beasts that would annihilate us if we struggled against their power. This apparent pandemonium is nonetheless under control and the mechanism activated by a single motor. For me, this image represents Bonaparte's tyranny" (*OC*, 15:43). As in *Considérations*, she blasts the first consul for assuming the trappings of royalty—using the royal "we," creating a pretorian guard, encrusting his sword with the crown diamonds. She criticizes his conduct, character, and appearance as confirmation of similar defects. "His clothes were all of gold and his hair lay flat; he was short in stature and had a large head; awkward and arrogant, disdainful and diffident, he combined the ill grace of an upstart with the audacity of a despot" (48–49).

Staël admits to frequent meetings with General Bernadotte and his liberal cohorts; had their plans been discovered, she would have been lost, for Bonaparte had already criticized her to his inner circle, and he was accustomed to having his conversational wishes carried out: "If he had insinuated that such and such a person should be hanged, I believe he would have found it insubordinate if . . . the subject had not bought a rope and built a gallows" (*OC*, 15:61). By autumn, she thought he was so absorbed by his planned attack on England that he had forgotten about her. To the contrary, she was denounced, arrested, and deported 40 leagues outside Paris. When attempts to intercede on her behalf failed, she left for Germany. Praise of the Prussian king gives Staël an opportunity to reiterate her belief in constitutional monarchy and to underscore Bonaparte's subversion of the Revolution. She tells of awakening early one morning in Berlin to learn that the duc d'Enghien had been abducted and summarily shot. Horrified by this heinous crime, she explains Bonaparte's motives: to prove himself a revolutionary by shedding Bourbon blood and to terrorize the opposition before seizing the crown. Necker's last written words denounced this assassination. (Staël devotes a chapter to her father's illness and death and her own inconsolable sorrow.)

The first consul soon orchestrated a plebiscite to be named emperor. Staël mocks the courtiers he created overnight as multiple replicas of Molière's *bourgeois gentilhomme*. The fete of 14 July 1804 celebrated the Empire's supposed consolidation of revolutionary gains. Shortly after his coronation, Bonaparte disclosed his true purpose: "People joke . . . about my new dynasty; in five years, it will be the oldest in Europe" (*OC*, 15:123). What benefits could he offer the Europeans, Staël asks: "He came to exchange their tranquillity, independence, language, laws, wealth, blood, and children for the misery and shame of being destroyed as nations and despised as men. He introduced universal monarchy, the greatest scourge to menace the human species and the unequivocal cause of everlasting warfare" (125–26).

The editor fills in the interval between parts 1 and 2 with a summary of Staël's life from the time of Necker's death in 1804 until the suppression of *Allemagne* and a renewed exile order in 1810. Not unexpectedly, he demonstrates the same bias toward his mother that she exhibited toward her father—a purified explanation of motives and achievements. The account is suffused with filial compassion for Staël's tribulations, pride in her courage, and delight in her undiminished wit. Dismayed when Schlegel was banished for preferring Euripides' to Racine's *Phaedra*, she comments: "It was exceedingly discerning of a Corsican monarch thus to take up cudgels over the slightest nuances of French literature" (*OC*, 15:162). Harping on Napoleon's foreign origins, she complains of being forced to flee like a fugitive by order of a man who was less French than she, "for I was born on the banks of the Seine where tyranny alone naturalized him" (203).

After eight months of indecision, Staël resolves to depart secretly, her ultimate destination England. Setting out in her carriage on 23 May as if for an afternoon ride with her son, daughter, and Rocca, she meets up with Schlegel at a farm outside Berne. The interspersed travel commentary intensifies as she visits more remote regions, so that by the time she tours Russia, Staël will be issuing insights into native character, landscape, social customs, and literary tastes, while her antagonism toward Napoleon will persist.

Stymied in Vienna by passport predicaments and hounded by police spies, she discovers that permission is needed for travel to the nearest Hungarian town, only six leagues away: "Indeed, one could not help thinking that Europe, which used to be open to all travelers, has become a wide net under . . . Napoleon that tightens with every step" (*OC*, 15:222–23). Forced to make a detour of 2,000 leagues to escape his rule, she opts to travel via Galicia, a country she finds unrecognizable under Austrian domination. Education has been neglected, industry is nonexistent, and Jews monopolize commerce. (Staël's infrequent allusions to Jews are distinctly anti-Semitic.) A placard warning against her hangs in every police station, and gendarmes line the road to the capital to make sure she does not linger. This once-powerful and noble monarchy has been reduced by Napoleon to the lowest rung among nations.

Entering Russia on 14 July,[15] Staël feels she has come full circle since the Revolution. In this empire, falsely labeled "barbaric," she is welcomed hospitably by aristocrats and commoners alike. Rapidly crossing Volhynia, a province "inundated with Jews, like Galicia" (*OC*, 15:248), she feels strange having to flee before the advancing French forces, who may force her to detour via Odessa to reach Constantinople, where she plans to document her project about Richard the Lion-Hearted: "This poem is destined to depict the nature and mores of the Orient and to glorify a great era of English history, when the enthusiasm of the crusades gave way to enthusiasm for freedom" (251).[16]

With her visit to Kiev, Staël is ready to embark on descriptive generalizations about landscape, customs, and character. She finds the Ukraine a fertile but disagreeable area, with enormous wheat fields that seem cultivated by invisible hands. Because the wooden houses catch fire easily, she imagines the inhabitants ordering a new house in the forest the way most people buy food in the marketplace. Rising among these huts are great palaces and churches, whose splendid gilt domes reflect the rays of the sun. Staël prefers the Russians' colorful Oriental garb to European-style dress, precisely to avoid "that grand uniformity of Napoleon's despotism, which presents every country with military conscription, then with war taxes and the Napoleonic Code, so that entirely different nations may be governed the same way" (*OC*, 15:255).

Having chosen Greek orthodoxy because it granted him spiritual as well as temporal powers, the eleventh-century ruler Vladimir[17] baptized thousands of subjects in the Dnieper River, which flows through Kiev. Staël is partial to the beautiful chants of the Greek religion, which she considers less prejudiced than Catholicism: "Poetic and sensitive . . . [it] seems to capture the imagination more than it guides behavior" (OC, 15:257). Noting that all denominations are tolerated in Russia, she makes hearty pronouncements about the native character. Patient and active, melancholy and gay, the Russians are immune to fatigue or physical pain. In fact, they resemble Orientals: "Their court manners are European, . . . but their nature is Eastern" (260).

Russian conditioning to hardship amazes her. Fruits and flowers are grown in greenhouses, vegetables are unheard of, and English "comforts" are totally lacking. Immense wealth has not made the Russians effete. They are public-spirited, energetic, proud, devoted, religious-minded, and xenophobic. Staël disagrees with Diderot's representation of Russia as a corrupt court with an enslaved populace. In her view, the Russians are not remotely like the French. Extremely taciturn, they betray none of their feelings or opinions in conversation. Their idea of a social gathering is not a circle of intelligent men and women who enjoy conversing together; they assemble in large groups to savor fruits and rare comestibles from Asia or Europe, listen to music, and gamble. Poorly educated, they take no pleasure in serious conversation and no pride in witty repartee. Poetry, eloquence, and literature are as yet unknown.

Nine hundred versts separate Kiev from Moscow. Although Staël's driver drives swiftly, he appears to make no progress, so uniformly barren is the landscape: "This country seemed like the image of infinite space which it took eternity to cross" (OC, 15:264). She finds Moscow an enormous mixture of huts, houses, palaces, Oriental bazaars, churches, public buildings, lakes, woods, and parks—a patchwork of the diverse cultures that compose the nation. Asiatic opulence is evidenced in the gold, silver, and ruby ornaments adorning the churches. Some palaces are made of wood so that they can be constructed and torn down quickly. Others are built and richly decorated for one day's celebration. The Kremlin resembles a Turkish minaret. After visiting the apartments of the former czars, Staël climbs to the top of the church steeple, from which she can look out over the palace and many of Moscow's 1,500 churches. She imagines Napoleon gazing from the same vantage point as she. The city would lie in ashes a month later.

No modern nation is as close to savagery as the Russian people, whose basic nature has not changed since Peter I[18] tried to introduce civilization: "They are still what we would call barbaric, that is, led by an instinct that is often generous, always involuntary, and concentrates on the means without examining the goal. . . . I use the term ["barbaric"] to denote a certain primitive energy which alone can replace the concentrated power of freedom in a nation" (*OC*, 15:289). Staël finds a dearth of educated persons in Russia, where students attend university solely to prepare for a military career. The few literary attempts are French imitations, to which she naturally objects, counseling the Russians to seek poetry in the recesses of their own souls—an echo of *Littérature*.

Sorry to leave Moscow, she journeys on to Novgorod, a former republic, which is now a ghost city that recalls its once prosperous past. Marshland separates Novgorod from Saint Petersburg. Suddenly, "you arrive in one of the world's most beautiful cities as if, with a wave of his wand, a magician had conjured up all the marvels of Europe and Asia out of the dry desert" (*OC*, 15:296). The inhabitants remind Staël of southerners condemned to live in the North and battle a climate alien to their nature. The nobility have the same tastes as southern aristocrats. Their country houses built on an island in the middle of the Neva are adorned with tropical plants, Oriental perfumes, and Asiatic divans. Russian hospitality is legendary. The day after her arrival, Staël dines with one of the city's foremost businessmen, who extends a mass invitation to all his friends by raising the flag on the roof of his house. The wealthy proprietor of Strogonoff Island keeps his home open every day of the year; often, he does not know half the people at dinner. Many houses in Saint Petersburg have the same custom, which she finds incompatible with spirited conversation.

Staël speaks kindly of the imperial family. Though an absolute monarch by custom and law, Czar Alexander[19] is a moderate ruler by choice. When they meet, she is impressed by the simplicity with which he discusses questions of vital European concern. Willing to overlook and even palliate his absolutism, Staël tells the czar (with typical courtly flattery) that his character serves as his country's constitution and his conscience as its guarantee. She does not concede that her enthusiasm is based on his being the last barrier against Napoleon (and on the warm welcome he extends her). After meeting with Alexander, Staël visits his mother, traversing the colossal hall built by Prince Potemkin[20] on her way. This sight causes her to reflect on the Russian aristocracy's capricious uses of power and wealth and on its generosity, savagery, unbridled passions, and superstitious religiosity. Civilization has not yet penetrated deeply in Russia. The nobility may ape European manners, but they are Russian at heart: "[This] constitutes their strength and their originality, love of country being, after love of God, the finest sentiment that human beings can harbor" (*OC*, 15:317–18).

After visiting the estate of the court chamberlain Narischkin—an easygoing, affable, and urbane man—Staël extrapolates Russian defects and qualities from the customs of the high-ranking nobility. Constantly on the move, Narischkin is avid for intellectual stimulation, which he finds in things, not books. His estate is an oasis in a barren and swampy countryside. During dinner, served in a Moldavian-style hall, Staël is again struck by the southern customs of this northern people. The table is covered with fruit, while servants bring meat and vegetables to each guest. Narischkin keeps several Kalmucks—opinionated Tartar slaves whose intractability amuses their master. A fervent abolitionist, Staël considers this spectacle repulsive: "Amidst all the pomp of luxury, I seemed to see an image of what man can become when he is deprived of the dignity afforded by religion or law" (*OC*, 15:323).

While spending too little time in Saint Petersburg to achieve any insight into family life, she receives the impression that there is virtually no sentimental love among this pleasure-oriented people. According to Asiatic custom, the husband manages the household; the wife receives the guests he has invited. Russian men and women fall in love impetuously but are naturally fickle: "For these whimsical and violent temperaments, love is more a celebration or a frenzy than a deep, deliberate affection" (*OC*, 15:326). A long habit of despotism has accustomed the Russians to circumspection and manipulation of the truth. They refrain from broaching controversial subjects and maintain a prudent reserve. When a ruler has unlimited power to exile, imprison, or send people to Siberia, it requires heroism to defy persecution, and heroism is not a universal trait.

Enthralled by new sights and experiences, Staël almost forgets about the war. Although Russian courtiers are too secretive to report military reverses, a foreigner informs her that Smolensk has been taken and Moscow is in danger. In contrast to the Russian coverup, she vaunts British forthrightness: "Noble candor of a government as sincere toward the people as toward its monarch, recognizing the same right for both to know how public matters stand." Strolling sadly through the beautiful city of Saint Petersburg, she fears it may be destroyed by the arrogance of a single man who would say, like Satan atop a mountain, "The kingdoms of earth are mine" (*OC*, 15:336).

Visiting a school for deaf-mutes and another for the blind, Staël has her own prescriptions for improving Russian education. Schools should be opened throughout the empire to provide the people with rudimentary instruction. Less learned than Catholic curates or Protestant ministers, Greek prelates should not serve as teachers. Russia needs a center of learning whose rays can spread to all parts of the empire. The Russians will acquire creative, rather than imitative, skills in art and literature "when they have found a way to express their native character in language, as in action" (*OC*, 15:341).

Staël saw Alexander once more after his meeting with Bernadotte at Abo, where they agreed never to make peace with Napoleon—a resolution that she says led to the ultimate liberation of Europe. Leaving Saint Petersburg at the end of September, she provides a passing description of the Finns: blond and fair-skinned like the Germanic peoples, their honesty and simple customs stem from their Protestant upbringing. Finland is a country of rocky crags and endless forests, with sparse vegetation, few cities, and brisk winds that fan frequent forest fires: "Man has difficulty in every way fighting nature in these glacial climes" (*OC*, 15:352). When Czar Alexander seized Finland after the treaty of Tilsitt, he respected Finnish freedom, as well as tax privileges and recruitment, and he generously assisted the burned cities: "To a certain extent, his favors compensated the Finns for the rights they possessed, if free men can ever voluntarily accede to such an exchange" (353). It is obvious that Staël is treading a tightrope in praising the Russian czar, whose opposition to Napoleon atones for any and all failings. The manuscript ends with her apprehensive departure on the watery crossing to Sweden. The editor adds that she composed the present journal during eight months spent in Stockholm, then continued on to London, where she published her book on Germany.

Autobiographical though this narrrative may appear to be, like *Considérations*, it omits crucial aspects of the author's life. She makes no mention of her clandestine marriage to Jean Rocca, the birth of their baby, or his accompanying her throughout her flight. She plays down her relationship with Benjamin Constant and her maneuvers to install Bernadotte on the throne of France. In fact, she attenuates all political participation.[21] Staël tends always to omit the private revelations that might taint her moral persona, impinge on her credibility, or detract from her self-styled stance as an objective (or persecuted) witness to history. Of course, it is impossible to conjecture to what extent her son may have airbrushed her narrative. In light of the pains both Auguste and Albertine took to gather and burn their mother's private correspondence, it is not inconceivable that the extant version of *Dix années* has been gussied up from the original in numerous unavowed ways.

While a more personal, less pontificating and ambitious work than *Considérations*, this book provides a unique outlook on the then little-known land and people of Russia, whose alliance Staël considers essential for the recent overthrow of tyranny. Because it concentrates on Napoleon with such virulence, *Dix années* naturally provoked attacks from his most ardent supporters. Others, like Constant, were more even-handed. While lauding Napoleon's military genius, he cannot help considering "the long and obstinate persecution he laid on Mme de Staël as one of the least excusable acts of tyranny during his reign" (Bornecque, 286). Staël's excoriation of Napoleon is not a mere personal vendetta. It reflects and repeats her execration of totalitarianism in every form. It is part and parcel of her never-wavering championship of freedom—freedom to think, to write, and to speak the truth without incurring exile, a fate worse than death.

Chapter 10
Critiques and Contributions

Few people today read Staël for profit or pleasure. The political problems over which she agonized have long since been settled, superseded by global concerns that seem far more compelling at the end of the twentieth century. The moral questions she tackled appear quaintly outdated. *Delphine* and *Corinne*, which brought tears to nineteenth-century eyes, are too prolix and sentimental for modern taste. Although still read chiefly in the context of French literary evolution, Staël is regarded increasingly as a precursor of feminist thinking.

In considering critiques by contemporaries, we will discover a male-female bias that sought to undermine her achievements by denigrating her person. The mores of the day denounced any woman who dared lay claim to independent thinking; she was "unfeminine" or "virile"—an indefensible insult. Even her close friends were wont to dismiss Staël as too masculine. Although Byron called her "the most eminent woman author of this, perhaps of any century," he noted in his journal that "she should have been born a man."[1] Enthusiastic about her intellectual (ergo, male) prowess, Benjamin Constant noted in his *Journaux intimes* on 9 January 1803: "What a man's mind, with the wish to be loved as a woman,"[2] and again on 26 January: "Germaine could make ten or twelve distinguished men."[3] But in a peeved moment, he wrote, on 26 October 1806: "I am tired of the *homme-femme* whose iron hand has enslaved me for ten years" (Bornecque, lxii).[4]

If Staël's intimates impugned her femininity, how much more so did her enemies. The outpouring of vituperation aimed less at her writings than her gender. The *Actes des Apôtres et des Martyres* labeled her "hermaphrodite" and "prostitute" (9 July 1797), the *Censeur des Journaux* compared her on 8 August to a witch emerging from a sabbat (Jasinski, 4:83), and *L'Ami des Lois* likened her on 8 July 1799 to "a crow" that "always announces something sinister by her croakings" (Gutwirth, 98). The *Quotidienne* of 5 August 1797 painted an unflattering portrait that had nothing whatever to do with her work: "Born without grace, beauty, or nobility, Mme de Staël has not compensated for these lacks by any attempt at self-improve-ment. . . . Her conversation is biting, her dress slovenly, her look brazen, and her amorous leanings depraved" (Gwynne, 41).

Staël's defamers did more than sully her in the press. After Narbonne accompanied the king's aunts abroad, a comedy entitled *Les Intrigues de Mme de Staël à l'occasion du départ de Mesdames de France* (Mme de Staël's intrigues upon the departure of Mesdames de France, March 1791) depicted her as a democratic Circe and the baron de Staël as a rather asinine cuckold (Jasinski, 1:421). Félicité de Genlis barely disguised her as "Mélanide" in a fierce onslaught on Staël's vanity, eccentric appearance, and misplaced coquetry: "Her person and manners were so affected and bizarre as to draw unwarranted attention. . . . Her ludicrous and illusory pride was betrayed by the *masculine assurance* of her bearing and by her intrepid and overpowering demeanor."[5] Chafing at the impossibility of responding to her attackers in kind, Staël vented her frustration to Adélaïde Pastoret on 10 September 1800: "It is a pity to have as much wit as the next person and to be condemned by one's accursed woman's dignity not to make use of that gift. It would appear that being a woman elicits the greatest ridicule and permits the least response: you are like the bull's-eye that is riddled by arrows it can never return" (Jasinski, 4:322).

Male critics, from her father to Anthony West, have been sexist toward Staël in varying degrees. Lamartine prefaces and ends his generally favorable discussion in the "Cours familier de littérature" (Informal course in literature) with the admonition that women remain by the hearth to bear and nurse children, for a woman who seeks equality extinguishes love, and a woman writer deprives her husband of that which she gives to the public (26:86, 88–89). However vociferously he professes to be "both a royalist and a passionate admirer of Mme de Staël" (272), Lamartine's relegation of women to domesticity diminishes his praise of Staël as an exception to her sex.

The same misogynistic bias has persisted through the nineteenth century and into the present day. In an article mocking women intellectuals as a whole and Staël in particular as the "camp mother" of all Bluestockings, Barbey d'Aurevilly manages, with typical literary irrelevance, to incriminate her turban, the size of her feet, her Swiss origins, her love affairs, and her frustrated yearning to be a beauty.[6] Within the scant space he devotes to Staël and "*Dix ans d'exil*," the historian Jules Michelet emphasizes her coarse features, obese figure, and masculine mien: "Standing in front of a fireplace, her hands behind her back, she dominated a salon with a virile attitude, a powerful word, that contrasted mightily with the comportment of her sex and caused some doubt whether she was a woman."[7]

Dripping with sarcasm, Henri Guillemin persists in calling the writer "Germaine" and in ascribing hypocritical or vengeful motives to her actions. Also referring to her with contemptuous familiarity, David Glass Larg attributes "Germaine's" literary output to the disordered overflow of a "sentimental life in perpetual ferment" and nullifies her religious and political views in *Circonstances*: "It would be playing a trick on Mme de Staël to take her seriously. . . . It is understandable why sober-minded thinkers sent this woman to the devil."[8] The insidious double meaning of Christopher Herold's title *Mistress to an Age* is as sexist as his imaginative rendition of the subject's hysterical outbursts and the emphasis he places on her amatory defeats.

There is perhaps no more disparaging and inaccurate modern appraisal of Staël than Anthony West's *Mortal Wounds* (1973), which skews the facts in order to diminish her accomplishments, sneer at her feminist perspective, and reduce her to the dimensions of a depressive, controlling, and mercenary neurotic. Like other male detractors, West takes a perverse pleasure in detailing Staël's physical unattractiveness: "The portrait Madame Vigée-Lebrun had painted . . . depicting her as Corinne, tells most of the story, giving one a little less than the truth about the buck teeth, the weakly greedy mouth, the bulbous nose, and the protuberant eyes, but achieving a complete, and devastating, frankness about the slack spread of the deteriorating stomach, the beefy thighs, and the tremendous width of the hips."[9] Has any male writer been condemned for his complexion or corpulence? As Noreen Swallow points out, the prejudicial remarks that dwell on Staël's supposedly mannish appearance have perpetuated the caricature of "a creature monstrously overblown, at once a muscular virago riding to glory over the bodies of her victims, and a blowsy buffoon blissfully unaware of her own vulgarity."[10]

In addition to gender-related taunts, contemporaries considered Staël a perennial outsider. As a Swiss woman—if not by birth, then by descendance—married to a Swede, she was viewed as a foreigner, despite her vehement protestations to the contrary.[11] She was an outspoken Protestant in a Catholic country and a member of the opposition in every government from the Convention to the Empire. To add fuel to the fire, she championed innovative and unpopular causes.

On the asset side, countless contemporaries appreciated Staël as a popular novelist and prized her as a political iconoclast. We have already noted the widespread readership of *Delphine* and *Corinne* and the international impact of *Allemagne*. We have seen their author lionized throughout Italy, Germany, and Russia. Nor should we forget the immense influence of her salon. Staël was one of the few hostesses under the Directory who welcomed proponents of all political persuasions. "She was pardoned because of her sex, wit, talent, and ideals. . . . Perhaps no [woman] since the Fronde had exercised so marked a political influence," wrote Antoine Thibaudeau in his memoirs (Gwynne, 30).

This open-minded assemblage predated the liberal and nonpolemical tenor of Coppet, which became a nucleus of political and literary ferment during Staël's exile. In Switzerland, outside the sphere of Napoleonic control, Coppet was a mecca for the intelligentsia of Europe—what Sainte-Beuve called "the intellectual Elysium of an entire generation" (Levaillant, 8)—where men and women of all backgrounds, "nationalities,"[12] and religious credos could assemble for a productive interchange of ideas. Stendhal dubbed Coppet "the Estates General of European opinion," a gathering place for 600 of the top minds of the continent. "Voltaire never had anything like it at Ferney."[13] The chatelaine supervised a beehive of creative productions and translations, which served as a means of cultural communication and influence.[14] According to Bonstetten, "More wit is expended at Coppet in a day than in the rest of the world in a year" (d'Andlau, 63). Like Staël, her guests were united by their common hatred of tyranny, opposition to Napoleon, and crusade for free expression. The liberal spirit that infused the "Groupe de Coppet" with ecumenical and international perspectives, resuscitation of Shakespeare, Calderón, and medieval culture, the conviction that writers have a political mission, an aspiration toward individual freedom, and a celebration of creative genius was a dynamic force that would reshape European literary and cultural values.

As a daughter of the Enlightenment, Staël synthesizes certain aspects of eighteenth-century philosophy with romantic tenets.[15] Her entire work manifests a confidence in rational argument and understanding inherited from the thinkers who frequented her mother's salon. She also imbibed from the eighteenth century the inflexible belief in human progress and perfectibility that illuminates her writing. Nor did she ever deviate from the ideals of freedom and morality bequeathed by Necker.

Littérature is the first of Staël's works to reconcile humanity's past achievements with its future possibilities. In rehabilitating the Middle Ages and exalting northern literatures, Staël not only stressed the cross-cultural fertilization that would come to full flower in *Allemagne*, she also introduced a strain of melancholy and meditation, a background of historic nationalism, and a stress on individual striving that would find analogous expression in the works of Hugo, Lamartine, Vigny, Stendhal, and Baudelaire. Her apologia for suicide in the lineage of *Werther*— beginning with *Rousseau* and illustrated in her short stories and novels (although later emended)—prefigures the nineteenth-century *mal du siècle*.[16] By rejecting the imitation of classical models and predicating new creative stimuli and modes of expression, Staël liberated literature from the petrification of a thousand years and prefigured innovations in subject and style that would proliferate during the nineteenth century. Aware that the poetic impulse can be activated by solitude, reverie, religious ecstasy, and self-exploration, she nurtured the sensibilities of her romantic successors. By introducing the literary productions of other nations, urging language study, and validating translation, she toppled French literature from its self-erected pedestal and opened up avenues of approach to unknown or unappreciated cultures.

Corinne and *Allemagne* expand on the preromantic elements of *Littérature* by abandoning classical modes and adopting a liberal, cosmopolitan outlook. As early as *Delphine*, Staël had noted the correlation (and occasional discrepancy) between natural phenomena and human moods. In *Corinne*, with landscape and nature playing a greater part than in any other work, Staël emphasizes the romantic equation of self and surroundings. Her evocation of Rome parallels Hubert Robert's pictorial "melancholy of ruins" that would dominate romantic imagery from Chateaubriand on. Her guided tour of the country, with its sentimental concurrences, would nourish the cult of Italy that inflamed the imagination of Lamartine, Musset, and Stendhal. The sibylline qualities of Corinne encapsulated the divine inspiration of the romantic muse. The concept of the solitary and suffering genius would become integrated into the romantic psyche. The analogy of sensory "correspondences" antedated Baudelaire by 50 years.

More than any other work, *Allemagne* was a direct antecedent of and impetus for the French romantic movement. Staël accomplished the incomparable feat of introducing German literature to France and demolishing the myth of French cultural supremacy. She presented an image of Germany that lasted until 1870 and won the hearts of the young romantic generation. For Lamartine, *Allemagne* was more than a book: "It was a European manifesto against the materialism of eighteenth-century philosophy and the brutality of French despotism" ("Cours familier," 185). Furthermore, "in . . . *Allemange*, Mme de Staël inaugurated a new force in the domain of intelligence and art. She created . . . the republic of genius" (201). *Allemagne* stresses enthusiasm as the sine qua non of creative activity—a doctrine the romanticists would adopt with fervor. Passion, sentiment, and sensitivity—Staël's inborn traits—would be cornerstones of the romantic ego.

Allemagne does more than embellish *Littérature*'s reclamation of northern literature. By analyzing the ramifications of an entire culture, from behavior to philosophy to mores to music, and offering reasons why a people thinks and acts in certain ways, it anticipates the discipline of sociology. It also sounds a clear call to revolution in literature. Like *Corinne*, it carries an encoded message for a parallel political insurrection. Just as Staël preaches reverting to native roots in literature, she makes the strong subliminal suggestion that a nation's glory can be achieved only through unification.

Her relentless opposition to tyranny in general and to Napoleon in particular—implicit in *Delphine*, *Corinne*, and *Allemagne*, explicit in *Considérations* and *Dix années*—made Staël an undisputed martyr to progressive ideology. Her defiance of despotism stamped the entire generation of late Restoration liberals to which her son-in-law, Victor de Broglie, belonged. Her tendencies in religion and politics inspired Barante, Guizot, Soumet, Chênedollé, and Nodier, who wrote about her in 1818 in the *Journal des Débats*. After 1820 Staël was consulted like a Bible and supported by the *Muse Française* and, after 1824, by the *Globe*.[17] If we are to equate romanticism with liberty—with *"liberalism in literature,"* as Hugo does in his preface to *Hernani* (1829)[18]—then Staël played a decisive role indeed in the literary and political orientation of the romantic movement.[19]

What remains open to controversy is the extent of Staël's "feminist" awareness and activity. Was she a closet feminist, a precursor of today's women's liberation movement? Was she a female Uncle Tom, who paid lip service to the patriarchal position toward women? Or was she an early Simone de Beauvoir, willing to analyze woman's lot while shielding herself from membership in the group? In gauging interpretations of Staël's feminist orientation, we are not contending with misogynistic perceptions of female achievement. We are entering the ranks of contemporary feminist scholars in their admittedly uneven assessments. It should be noted that the lists of feminist articles on Staël and feminist editions of her works are constantly swelling.[20]

Emphasizing Staël's empathy with women's plight and her willingness to take on the "establishment," Simone Balayé asserts that she has finally begun to assume her rightful place in constructing a new critical system (9). Madelyn Gutwirth, another eminent Staëlian, is more impatient with her kowtowing to societal convention, less assured of her role as a claimant for women's rights.[21] Some feminist writers, ambivalent about Staël's contributions to women's awareness, tend to assess her in the light of their own more liberated era rather than situating her in the restrictive climate of her age. Even Gutwirth, who calls Staël "timid" as an "overt feminist," excuses her and other contemporary women writers because their efforts to combat the "profoundly misogynistic climate" in which they lived "could only have been limited, halting, and mitigated by a self-doubt shared by their women readers, a doubt intensified by the suspicions of the men" (296).

It is our contention that Staël was an extraordinarily feminist-minded writer, who pushed to the limit her advocacy of women's education, male fidelity in marriage, a single sexual standard for men and women, the opportunity to divorce, freedom from social constraint, and greater self-fulfillment for women. As fearless in championing women's causes as she was in preaching an unpopular political message, she expressed herself with a forthright conviction that stopped just short of alienating her readership altogether.

From the beginning to the end of her literary career, Staël had woman's condition in mind. Her early defense of Marie-Antoinette, predicated on compassion for the queen's essential femaleness and motherhood, is addressed to a coalition of women readers as most likely to be fair-minded and judicious. Although a fervid admirer of Rousseau, Staël rejects his theories on women's education, denigration of women's capacity to love, and insistence on their domesticity and social inferiority; instead, *Rousseau* makes a brief for equal education for women and sustains that women writers possess greater perceptivity, sincerity, and sensibility than men. By granting the novel equal status with other genres, *Fictions* endorses the one field appropriated by women writers and tacitly encourages their self-realization. *Passions* underscores woman's loyalty in love, questions her emotional dependence on man, and acknowledges with lucid forebearance the problems facing her if she strives for glory in men's domain. As *Littérature* makes clear, ancient cultures suffered from the exclusion of female society. By granting women equality with men, Christianity enabled them to introduce concepts of tenderness, love, sympathy, and philanthropy that revolutionized modern literature. Nonetheless, Staël decries their subservient social position, demands equal civil and educational rights, and stresses the importance for the social order of an informed, innately sensitive, female constituency.

In works like *Réflexions sur la paix*, *Paix intérieure*, *Considérations*, and *Dix années*, Staël enters the political combat zone, hitherto a male preserve. Through precept and example, she is a committed feminist ready to breach barriers, transgress taboos, incur enmity, and conquer contempt in order to preach and justify equal opportunity for women. *Delphine* is as subversive a text as *Corinne* or *Allemagne* or *Dix années*. A severe incrimination of society and its treatment of women, it ridicules the pontiffs who decree what female behavior should be and provides a sympathetic portrayal of every conceivable destiny for woman—each thwarted, dwarfed, or warped in a different way. For the first time in literature, *Corinne* dares to introduce a woman of genius as a fictional heroine. The fact that Corinne renounces her talents and pines away for love is not a devaluation of her gifts but a denunciation of social conformity, which not only fails to recognize the intrinsic needs of genius but, far worse, immolates genius to convention.[22]

Corinne was one of the most popular books of the nineteenth century[23] throughout Europe, England, and America. Its influence on women's lives was without parallel. Isabel Hill's English translation, published in 1807, "promptly became a troubling intrusion into all Anglo-Saxon communities. It was perpetually denounced from middle-class pulpits and assiduously read by middle-class daughters in their chambers at night."[24] Jane Austen and Mary Godwin Shelley were among *Corinne*'s early readers. In the filiation of Corinne, Ellen Moers remarks European writers like Charlotte Brontë, Fanny Kemble, George Sand in *Consuelo* (1842–43), George Eliot in *The Mill on the Floss* (1860) and *Middlemarch* (1871–72), and Elizabeth Barrett Browning in her narrative poem *Aurora Leigh* (1857). In America, Elizabeth Stuart Phelps's *Story of Avis* (1877) continues the *Corinne* tradition, as does Willa Cather's *Song of the Lark* (1915) and Anna Jameson's novel *Diary of an Ennuyée* (1826). Staël's most decisive influence in the United States was on Margaret Fuller and her friend Lydia Maria Child, who went on to write Staël's biography.[25]

Staël covered an astounding variety of subjects in a gamut of genres, including drama, fiction, essay, sociological and psychological study, literary criticism, autobiography, historical survey, philosophy, theology, science, and political treatise. In the breadth of her interests and knowledge, the scope of her subject matter, and the polemical intent of her works, she stands in direct contrast to her female contemporaries, most of whose writing was limited to poetry and romance.

She was as courageous in her personal life as in her literary output. Unafraid to speak up in inappropriate times and places to voice her political convictions, she exerted a forceful impact on Constant, Schlegel, Sismondi, Bonstetten, and other habitués of Coppet. An astute business-woman who managed the affairs of her father's estate with diligence and acumen,[26] she brought up three children with exemplary dedication. Staël was an early superwoman who not only juggled marriage and children with a career but produced a significant and enduring body of work. She stood fast in a period of political turmoil; more important, she channeled her beliefs into action. She had an extraordinary effect on her contemporaries and a lasting influence on posterity. While a true precursor of feminist consciousness, Staël is too protean to be confined within any single classification. The fact that her feminist reclaim is only one element in her total social, political, and literary commitment to freedom points up the polymorphic universality of her outlook. Is it conceivable that, ready and able to meet men on their own intellectual ground, she may incarnate, generations ahead of her time, Beauvoir's impossible dream of a woman who "has taken the weight of the world upon her shoulders"?[27] Will Germaine de Staël finally receive the long-withheld recognition that is her due?

Notes and References

Chapter One

1. Carmontelle engraving conserved in Coppet archives, reproduced in comtesse [Béatrix] d'Andlau, *Madame de Staël* (Geneva: Droz, 1960), 7; hereafter cited in the text.

2. Ghislain de Diesbach, *Madame de Staël* (Paris: Perrin, 1983), 15; hereafter cited in the text.

3. "Notice sur le caractère et les écrits de Mme de Staël," *Oeuvres complètes* (hereafter cited in the text as *OC*), 17 vols. (Paris: Treuttel et Würtz, 1820–21), 1:xxiii; hereafter cited in the text. Necker de Saussure's was the first appraisal of Staël's life, works, and character. All translations from the French, whether primary or secondary sources, are my own, except for quotations from Blennerhassett (see ch. 1, n. 12).

4. Necker's grandson, Auguste de Staël, would many years later marry a Vernet.

5. Even after 30 years, Necker wrote his wife: "The love I bear you surpasses all expression. It is my blood flowing in your veins and yours flowing in mine. When I think of being separated, I feel the universe collapsing around me" (comte [Othenin] d'Haussonville, *Madame de Staël et M. Necker d'après leur correspondance inédite* [Paris: Calmann-Lévy, 1925], 58–59).

6. Staël signed her childhood letters "Minette," a pet name reserved for her father, her husband, and Benjamin Constant; Constant would also call her "Biondetta," the name of the demon metamorphosed into a woman in Jacques Cazotte's *Le Diable amoureux* (1772).

7. J. Christopher Herold suggests she may have suffered from manic depression (*Mistress to an Age: A Life of Madame de Staël* [New York: Bobbs Merrill, 1958], 31; hereafter cited in the text).

8. Catherine Rilliet Huber, "Notes sur l'enfance de Madame de Staël," *Occident et Cahiers Staëliens*, 5–6 (30 June 1933; March 1934): 5: 42; hereafter cited in the text.

9. Quoted in Simon Schama, *Citizens: A Chronicle of the French Revolution* (New York: Knopf, 1989), 89; hereafter cited in the text. Recent research into Necker's papers at Coppet has led to a more balanced and sympathetic evaluation of his administration (90).

10. Staël wrote to her husband on 15 May: "This work of my father's is the greatest event of our lives in terms of glory, fortune, and happiness" (quoted by Simone Balayé and Marie-Laure Chastang, "Un Ouvrage inconnu de Mme

de Staël sur M. Necker," *Cahiers Staëliens* 12 (June 1971), 23; hereafter cited in the text as "Ouvrage inconnu."

11.   *Le Journal de jeunesse de Mme de Staël*, in *Occident et Cahiers Staëliens*, 1–3, (15 October, 1932) 1930:236; hereafter cited in the text as *Jeunesse*. Comtesse Jean de Pange explains in the introduction that the text of this journal, conserved in the family archives and first revealed to the public by comte d'Haussonville, is incomplete; Staël admitted to having destroyed its principal passages.

12.   Lady [Charlotte Julia von Leyden] Blennerhassett, *Madame de Staël: Her Friends and Her Influence in Politics and Literature*, 3 vols. (London: Chapman & Hall, 1889), 2:179; hereafter cited in the text (quoted in translation).

13.   "[T]he student of Staël cannot but wonder, contemplating this momentous purchase, how many male writers await public approval and the death of a parent before feeling that they have the right to use a desk" (Charotte Hogsett, *The Literary Existence of Germaine de Staël* [Carbondale: Southern Illinois University Press, 1987], 133; hereafter cited in the text).

14.   Vicomte [Othenin] d'Haussonville, *Le Salon de Mme Necker*, 2 vols. (Paris: Calmann-Lévy, 1882), 2:46–47.

15.   Germaine de Staël, *Correspondance générale*, 6 vols., ed. Béatrice W. Jasinski (Paris: Jean-Jacques Pauvert, 1962–74 Hachette, 1985; Klincksieck, 1993), 1:42–43 n. 4; hereafter cited in the text.

16.   Daughter of the maréchal de Noailles, and an old acquaintance of Staël's.

17.   Comtesse [Béatrix] d'Andlau, "Mathieu de Montmorency: Réflexions sur Mme de Staël," *Cahiers Staëliens*, 14 (September 1972), 7.

18.   Benjamin Constant, "De Mme de Staël et de ses ouvrages," in *Adolphe*, ed. Jacques-Henri Bornecque (Paris: Garnier, 1963), 249; hereafter cited in the text as Bornecque.

19.   [Charles-Augustin] Sainte-Beuve, *Portraits de femmes*, ed. Albert de Bersaucourt (Paris: Editions Bossard, 1928), 98; hereafter cited in the text as Bersaucourt.

20.   Mother of Elzéar de Sabran and Delphine de Custine.

21.   Staël's biographers differ over the precise date of birth. Jasinski opts for 22 July, probably at the Neckers' home in Saint-Oven (1:202).

22.   Staël-Holstein's father and grandfather were named Matthias; he recognized this son and his wife's two other children as his own (Jasinski, 2:369).

23.   Georges Solovieff, ed., *Choix de lettres de Mme de Staël (1778–1817)* (Paris: Klincksieck, 1970), 84; hereafter cited in the text as Solovieff.

24.   Staël described to the princesse d'Hénin (17 June 1794) her scheme of sending a Swiss man or woman with a valid passport who resembled and changed places with the person to be evacuated (Jasinski, 3, pt. 1:30–31).

25.   After fighting in the American War of Independence, Montmorency became the youngest deputy to the Estates General, where he

introduced the motion to abolish titles of nobility. His later clandestine activities for the church and his attachment to Staël would bring about his exile. He would enjoy a distinguished political career under Louis XVIII and, after Staël's death, would become her children's legal tutor (Solovieff, 230).

26. Gruesome hospital experience prompted her to write a tract protesting the frequency of premature interments (Jean-René Bory, "Le Tombeau de Mme de Staël," in *Mme de Staël et l'Europe: Colloque de Coppet {18–24 juillet 1966}* [Paris: Klincksieck, 1970], 120; hereafter cited in the text as *Colloque*).

27. "The man who would count most for her (after her father) was a red-head of the petty nobility, myopic with green spectacles, as seductive as a freshly dug-up carrot" (Françoise d'Eaubonne, *Une Femme témoin de son siècle: Germaine de Staël* [Paris: Flammarion, 1966], 52; hereafter cited in the text). A precocious youngster who studied at Oxford at age 13, Constant was chamberlain to the Duke of Brunswick when in 1789 he married a vile-tempered lady-in-waiting, Wilhelmina von Cramm. He soon fell in love with a married woman, Charlotte von Hardenberg, who would pursue and finally marry him 12 years later. An aspiring public figure and writer of political tracts, he was dubbed "Constant the Inconstant" for his political about-faces. His novels *Adolphe* (written 1806, published 1816) and, especially, *Cécile* (written 1811, published 1951) are semiautobiographical accounts of his love affair with Staël.

28. In October 1805, August Wilhelm von Schlegel would pen a similar document of submission, declaring himself Staël's property, to dispose of as she wished (Solovieff, 317–18).

29. Furnishing reasons why their meeting could not have taken place before the summer of 1799, Jasinski claims the women's celebrated friendship did not commence until 1800–1801 (4:213–14 n. 8).

30. Juliette Récamier's loyalty was tested and proven when, having refused Napoleon's offer to be maid of honor to Josephine, her defense of Staël provoked the emperor's wrath, her own exile, and her husband's bankruptcy. Staël wrote Récamier on 1 October 1809: "You made me aware, dear Juliette, of a new feeling. . . . You taught me what is truly sweet in a woman's tenderness: the union of two feeble creatures who face their oppressors together" (Maurice Levaillant, *Une Amitié amoureuse: Mme de Staël et Mme Récamier* [Paris: Hachette, 1956], 202; hereafter cited in the text).

31. A well-educated woman, Albertine Necker de Saussure had studied Greek and Latin, philosophy, science, and music. When early deafness shut her off from society, she devoted herself to composing a book on the education of women, *Etude de la vie des femmes* (1838).

32. Like Staël, Albertine kept a youthful journal, much of it concerning her mother, in whom she could find no fault. She wrote on 15 August 1810: "I love HER with all my power of loving, but I should like to possess more, for it seems to me that happiness would consist in devoting my life to her, loving her if possible even more than I do, and proving it to her at every moment" (comtesse Jean [Pauline] de Pange, "Extraits d'un journal d'enfance d'Albertine

de Staël," *Revue d'Histoire Littéraire de la France* 66, no. 1 [January–March 1966]: 9).

33. Although most critics, beginning with Blennerhassett, have held this woman to be Félicité de Genlis, Staël apparently told her father, on 7 October 1803, the person was Mme de Vaines (Jasinski, 5:52).

34. Napoleon never responded to the letters Staël wrote him, imploring clemency, between 1803 and 1810. Five have been published, the others destroyed or unedited.

35. Jasinski identifies him as Lt. Antoine Gaudriot, in command of the gendarmerie at Versailles (5:63).

36. With his brother Friedrich, Schlegel had founded the *Athenaeum*, a review representing the new romanticism. Acquiring a scholarly reputation for his literary lectures and superb translation of 16 Shakespearean plays, he would later translate Staël's *Allemagne* and *Considérations* into German.

37. A future historian of the dukes of Burgundy and author of a book on eighteenth-century French literature, Prosper de Barante would be a constant visitor during Staël's final illness and become a close friend of Albertine and Victor de Broglie (Solovieff, 314).

38. Herold estimates Staël's wealth in 1808 at some 2,400,000 francs, or $600,000 in the currency of the time, not counting her father's outstanding loan to the French government, 80,000 francs owed by Constant (never repaid), and 35,000 acres in Saint Lawrence County, New York (Herold, 274, note).

39. Cf. *Lettres à Narbonne*, ed. Georges Solovieff (Paris: Gallimard, 1960), and *Lettres à Ribbing*, ed. Simone Balayé (Paris: Gallimard, 1960), the latter hereafter cited in the text as *Lettres à Ribbing*.

40. Comtesse Jean [Pauline Laure Marie Broglie] de Pange, *Le Dernier amour de Madame de Staël* (Geneva: La Palatine, 1944), 96.

41. In *Dix années*, 15 May is cited. Rather than relying on Staël's indications, we will use the dates Jasinski has meticulously researched.

42. His father, a constitutionalist of 1789, had been guillotined, his mother rescued from the Terror by Staël. After serving the Empire, Victor de Broglie would be summoned to the House of Peers under the Restoration and become a leader of the Doctrinaire party.

43. Constant made no effort to disclaim his paternity, noting in his journal on 20 September 1804: "My Albertine is a charming child. I have never seen more spirit nor more of my spirit, which to me is a great merit." Charlotte von Hardenberg, Constant's wife, also knew he was Albertine's father, as evinced in a letter of 22 February 1810 berating Staël for claiming that "she was more your wife than I, who assures anyone who wants to listen that you are the father of her daughter" (Bournecque, xxxiii, xxxiv).

44. For a moving description of Staël's degenerating physical and moral condition, read Sismondi's letter of 5 July 1817 to his future bride, Jessie Allen (Robert de Luppé, "Lettres inédites de Sismondi sur la mort de Mme de Staël," *Cahiers Staëliens*, 8 [April 1969]: 27).

45.   For a painstaking account of the perambulations of Staël's correspondence and its fitful publication, see Jasinski (Intro., 1:vii–xiv). Solovieff reconstructs the scene in December 1830 when Charlotte von Hardenberg, as per her late husband's instructions, handed over for incineration by the duchesse de Broglie all the letters Staël wrote Constant in her lifetime, after which Albertine drew up a testimonial (conserved in the Broglie archives) that she received and burned same (ix–xi).

46.   The Berg Collection of the New York Public Library possesses 142 A.L.S. (autograph letter, signed) from Staël to Narbonne written between August 1792 and May 1794, apparently entrusted by Narbonne to his friend Alexandre d'Arblay, husband of Fanny Burney. On the outer wrapper appear the words *"Lettres brûlantes, à brûler.* A fine moral lesson, too."

47.   The convoluted branches of Staël's ancestry and offspring are traced in Arnaud Chaffanjon's genealogical study *Madame de Staël et sa descendance* (Paris: Editions du Palais Royal, 1969).

Chapter Two

1.   These include such varied texts as *Eloge de M. de Guibert, Rousseau,* the preface to her collection *Manuscrits de M. Necker* (1805), *Circonstances, Considérations,* and, peripherally, *Littérature, Passions, Corinne,* and *Dix années.*

2.   Letter to Staël-Holstein of 19 November 1790. Staël read her completed play—no copy of which has been found—to audiences in her Paris salon in early 1791 (Jasinski, 1:397, 421).

3.   The heroine's name recalls Olympe de Gouges's play *Zamore et Mirza, ou l'Heureux naufrage,* performed at the Comédie Française in 1789. Author of the "Déclaration des droits de la femme," de Gouges was a champion of Necker's fiscal policy.

4.   Whereas Staël may have named her heroine after Adélaïde Pastoret, she may also have had in mind Mme Adélaïde, daughter of Louis XV and protectress of Narbonne. Adélaïde can be compared with the self-sacrificing Adèle (note the similarity of name) in "Epître au malheur," whose lover Edouard bears the same name as the hero of *Histoire de Pauline.*

5.   The names Orfeuil and Orville suggest the opposition between country (*feuille*/leaf) and town (*ville*/city).

6.   The opposition uncle/aunt is duplicated in the conventional symbolism: city/country = vice/virtue.

7.   Staël may have named her heroine for her good friend Pauline de Beaumont, who had lost her entire family under the Terror.

8.   Staël changes her age within the space of the first paragraph.

9.   Both Mirza and Fernand enjoyed a European upbringing, which enables them to surpass their native compatriots. Staël clearly maintains an elitist attitude toward European—particularly French—culture.

10.   Already used to signify the budding woman of genius, the name Mirza is given here to a featureless rival.

11.   Diesbach submits that it would have been impossible to print any work without the knowledge and permission of the daughter of someone as powerful as Necker (82).

12.   Calling this disclaimer false, Hogsett suggests that *Rousseau* is the work of "a young person who had every intention of becoming a writer, who had a life's work in mind, and who was with this short book announcing and setting out on that work" (36).

13.   Belying this caveat is Staël's expressed admiration for women writers like Fanny Burney, Maria Edgeworth, Marie-Madeleine de La Fayette, Isabella de la Charrière, Juliana von Krüdener, et al. (most of whom have not stood the test of time as well as she).

14.   "The entire education of woman must be relative to that of man. To please him, to be useful to him, to raise him when he is little, to take care of him when he is grown, to counsel him, to console him, to make his life cozy and agreeable, these are the duties of woman in all times and they must be taught her from childhood on. . . . Woman was created to yield to man and to bear even his injustice" (quoted from book 5 of *Emile*; Madelyn Gutwirth, *Madame de Staël, Novelist: The Emergence of the Artist as Woman* [Urbana: University of Illinois Press, 1978], 6; hereafter cited in the text).

15.   Among the habitués of her salon, only Condorcet and Talleyrand proposed public and equal education for women (G. E. Gwynne, *Mme de Staël et la Révolution française: Politique, philosophie, littérature* [Paris: Nizet, 1969], 177; hereafter cited in the text).

16.   Georges Poulet, *La Conscience critique* (Paris: José Corti, 1971), 16.

17.   "To anyone familiar with [Staël's] manner of writing, her feelings, and her enthusiasm for her father, it is apparent from the very first pages that this text is indeed hers" ("Ouvrage inconnu," 25). It was Simone Balayé who discovered this text in the Bibliothèque Nationale.

Chapter Three

1.   Toward the end of her life, she confided to her daughter that "involvement in politics combines poetry, religion, and morality" ("Notice," cccvii).

2.   Like the second panel of a diptych, this pamphlet was almost a pendant to Necker's *Réflexions présentées à la nation française sur le procès intenté à Louis XVI* of the previous year (Jasinski, 2:468).

3.   On 21 August a band of armed revolutionaries burst into the Swedish embassy, seized Staël's personal papers, and arrested her valet and her husband's secretary (Jasinski, 2:468). Diesbach finds a direct connection between this violation of diplomatic immunity and the *Procès de la reine* (138).

4.   Influenced by Staël's persuasiveness, Pitt's political opponent Charles Fox was to ask Parliament to free La Fayette, who would later express his gratitude to Staël (*Lettres à Ribbing*, 156 n. 2).

5. In a note to *Passions* (*OC*, 3:296), Staël expresses her pride at this public sign of approbation.

6. Simone Balayé, preface to *Des Circonstances actuelles qui peuvent terminer la Révolution et des principes qui doivent fonder la république en France*, ed. Lucia Omacini (Paris and Geneva: Droz, 1979), ix; hereafter cited in the text as *Circonstances*.

7. The manuscript of *Circonstances* was entrusted at some point to Juliette Récamier and later donated to the Bibliothèque Nationale by the latter's niece and heir. First discovered in 1899 by Paul Gautier, who used it for his doctoral thesis, *Mme de Staël et Napoléon*, the text was not published until 1906 by J. Viénot, who claimed it to be the lost second half of *Passions*. Even if this hypothesis were true, Omacini suggests that Staël's project soon changed from a theoretical exercise to a utilitarian program: "*C.A.* [*Circonstances*] is one of the most pragmatic and practical books that [Staël] ever wrote, a composite text combining immediate political concern . . . with the fondness for grand theoretical generalizations evinced in the later works" (*Circonstances*, lxiii).

8. Diesbach, d'Eaubonne, Gautier, Gutwirth, and Hogsett fail to mention this work at all.

9. Among them, Gautier, Herold, and Gwynne (*Circonstances*, lx).

10. Staël is referring to the precondition of property, without which a citizen has no vested interest in government.

11. Another scientific conception, to be likened to the mathematical proof of morality.

12. George Steiner has noted the crucial relationship between language and political inhumanity. For example, by endowing certain words, like "the final solution," with nightmarish meanings, the Nazis invalidated the authenticity of the German language and used it to enforce untenable falsehoods (*Language and Silence: Essays on Language, Literature, and the Inhuman* [New York: Atheneum, 1970], 99).

13. This is one of the first expressions of Staël's internationalism, which would find a focus and a *foyer* when she became a political outcast at Coppet.

14. On reading Condorcet's *Essai sur l'application de l'analyse à la probabilité* . . . in 1785, Staël wrote: "He submits all moral ideas to algebraic calculations: triangles and angles are poetical figures with which I want henceforth to embellish my discourse" (*Circonstances*, 299 n. 7).

Chapter Four

1. Probably composed the preceding year (Simone Balayé, *Mme de Staël, Lumières et liberté* [Paris: Klincksieck, 1979], 51; hereafter cited in the text). Goethe wrote Schiller in October 1795 about the difficulty of translating this work, which he reproduced in the periodical *Die Hören* in 1796 (Blennerhassett, 3:2).

2. As Enzo Caramaschi points out, it was commonly said that women wrote fiction because it was inconsequential, and fiction was inconsequential because it was written by women ("Le Point de vue féministe dans la pensée de Madame de Staël," *Saggi et ricerche di letteratura francese* 12 [1973]: 314–15).

3. Although Staël used different classifications in *Rousseau*, the earlier piece also points up fiction's moral purpose.

4. First read, we may recall, in Mme Necker's salon.

5. An actress and the onetime wife of the well-known actor and dramatist Antoine François Riccoboni, she was the author of several sentimental epistolary novels.

6. Constant's early protector and mistress.

7. Written by Constant's uncle, Samuel de Constant.

8. The first mention of this work occurs in a letter to Narbonne (24 September 1792): "To take my mind off a thousand and one sorrows that would kill me if you were not there to sustain me, I am writing a treatise on the *Influence of passions on happiness*. It is the only topic dear enough to my heart for me to endure this occupation" (Jasinski, 2:28–29).

9. Staël recants this idea totally in *Réflexions sur le suicide* (1811) when she states that even the death of a loved one is insufficient reason to take one's own life.

10. Echoing Zulma, Staël complained to her lover Ribbing on 18 April 1795: "A man should be as true and faithful in his promises to a woman as to his comrade-in-arms" (Jasinski, 3:304).

11. She has suggested in the introduction that no one read her book before this age (*OC*, 3:39).

12. Staël wrote Goethe on 29 April 1800: "Reading *Werther* marked a personal epoch in my life. I consider this book and *La Nouvelle Héloïse* to be the two greatest masterpieces of literature" (Solovieff, 172).

13. Because enduring literary beauty presupposes "perfect taste," she says she invented the word *vulgarity* to denote (and proscribe) "all forms of inelegant imagery and indelicate expression" (*OC*, 4:11).

14. In this supremely heretical statement, Staël shows herself to be more of a feminist even than George Sand (d'Eaubonne, 57).

15. Staël borrows the premise of a scientific or mathematical basis for morality from ideologues like Condorcet, Destutt de Tracy, and Pierre Cabanis. Gwynne provides a detailed account of the filiation between ideologue philosophy and Staël's political and philosophical ideas (84 et seq.).

16. A lengthy note specifies the circumstances under which a writer may create a new word: it must appear "necessary" and natural, render the underlying idea precisely, and prove "harmonious" to the ear (*OC*, 4:51–53). Jasinski has made an extensive list of Staël's own neologisms, some 150 in toto (1:xlvii, et seq.).

17. C[harles]-A[ugustin] Sainte-Beuve, *Chateaubriand et son groupe lit-*

téraire sous l'empire (Paris: Calmann-Lévy, 1889), 194; hereafter cited in the text as Sainte-Beuve.

Chapter Five

1. Although Simone Balayé credits *La Nouvelle Héloïse* and *Werther* as providing Staël with forceful examples of epistolary fiction, she fails to mention Richardson's *Pamela* (1740–41) and *Clarissa* (1747–48) or Choderlos de Laclos's *Liaisons dangereuses* (1782) as other probable models (*Delphine*, 2 vols., ed. Simone Balayé and Lucia Omacini [Geneva: Droz, 1987–90], 1:12).

2. Staël gave Charles de Villers yet another reason (3 June 1803): "For the struggle between prejudice and reason, there is no more favorable period than the French Revolution" (Jasinski, 4:628).

3. Adélaïde, Pauline, Delphine, and Corinne are all orphans; Corinne alone has been shaped by a mother's influence. All but Corinne have been married and widowed young; all are independently wealthy. Their married status (for Corinne, her exceptional prestige as a poet) and personal fortune endow these heroines with the freedom of action that would be unthinkable for an unmarried woman or an impecunious widow at the turn of the nineteenth century.

4. Not only does the concept of a paternal husband reflect Staël's subconscious wish; it mirrors the real-life example of her intimate friend Juliette Récamier.

5. Staël acknowledged to Suard on 4 November 1802 that her novel was slightly "anti-Catholic" because the plot places "the heart's religion above Catholicism" (Jasinski, 4:570).

6. Louise is supposedly modeled on Benjamin Constant's hunchbacked cousin Rosalie.

7. The antinomy of a binational upbringing will resurface in the conflicts of Corinne's character.

8. This scene is a precise rendition of Staël's rescue at a reception by Delphine de Sabran (see ch. 1).

9. Despite lack of evidence that Staël ever read Laclos's *Liaisons dangereuses*, both Hogsett and Gutwirth detect resemblances between this novel and Staël's work. Hogsett sees a similarity between Théodore's seduction of Pauline and the seductions in *Liaisons* (20 n. 12), while Gutwirth discerns a basic correspondence between Sophie de Vernon's and Mme de Merteuil's autobiographical backgrounds (119 n. 13).

10. Staël finds it important to endow even Corinne, the freest spirit she has engendered, with domestic capabilities.

11. This scene recalls Edouard's threat to kill himself unless Pauline vows to wed him; she, too, faints away.

12. Cf. letters to Narbonne of 2 and 23 October 1792 (Jasinski, 2:37, 53).

13. Elsewhere Staël emphasizes nature's indifference to human emotions. When Delphine visits the waterfall of the Rhine, she is struck by the contrast between her private sorrow and the majestic, impassive movement of the waters (*OC*, 7:151–52). She is again horrified by the brilliant sun shining on the morning of Léonce's execution.

14. According to Diesbach, this scene is a replay of Staël's impassioned defense and rescue of Jacques de Norvins before General Lemoine under the Terror (200–01).

15. Noreen Swallow maintains that the heroine's death marks the ultimate stage in the repressive process by which patriarchal society undermines her independence, fragments her identity, and nullifies her personality: "In feminist terms, Delphine's death is . . . the total eradication of a woman of intelligence and sensitivity whose qualities have been constantly devalued and whose potential has been destroyed. It is the establishment's final triumph" ("Portraits: A Feminist Appraisal of Mme de Staël's *Delphine*," *Atlantis* 7, no. 1 [Fall-Automne 1981]: 75; hereafter cited in the text).

16. The Belmont ménage reverses the sex roles of the principals: "In the 'perfect union' of the Belmonts, the wife plays precisely the sort of role which society had always assigned to the male partner in marriage: she provides for his needs, and her whole life, intellectual and moral, is filtered through her" (Gutwirth, 126).

17. "Delphine is Mme de Staël as she conceived herself to be morally and as she would have liked to be viewed physically" (Diesbach, 245). Staël's description of herself to Ribbing in a letter of 1 December 1793 tallies with Delphine's character: "All my thoughts and feelings slip out in spite of myself, and my only strength lies in the truth" (Jasinski 2:510).

18. Gutwirth considers Suzanne Necker a far more important source: "The sole importance Talleyrand has as a model was as an inspiration for the depiction of perfidy in a charming and dearly loved friend" (118). Jasinski detects a resemblance between Sophie de Vernon and Narbonne, especially in connection with her flippant wit and love of gambling (2:xviii).

Chapter Six

1. For a brief comparison of Sand and Staël, see Eve Sourian, "Madame de Staël and George Sand," in *George Sand Papers, Conference Proceedings, 1978* (New York: AMS Press, 1982), 122–29. Marie-Jacques Hoog states: "[Staël] is Corinne as Sand will be Lélia" ("Ces Femmes en turban," in *Women in French Literature*, ed. Michel Guggenheim, Stanford French and Italian Studies 58 [Saratoga, Calif.: Anma Libri, 1988], 121).

2. After a detailed comparison of Corinne and Staël, Geneviève Gennari concludes that "Mme de Staël is Corinne in her entirety" (*Le Premier voyage de Mme de Staël en Italie et la genèse de "Corinne"* [Paris: Boivin, 1947], 244; hereafter cited in the text). In 1807 Vigée-Lebrun painted Staël as Corinne—

bareheaded, with curly hair, holding a lyre; the original hangs in the Bibliothèque Publique et Universitaire in Geneva.

3. Constant's description of Corinne fits the author to a tee: "Corinne is an extraordinary woman, enthusiastic about art, music, painting, and especially poetry; of exalted imagination and excessive sensitivity, [she is] both volatile and passionate; containing within herself every means of being happy, but also open to every kind of distress; avoiding sorrow only through distraction; needing applause . . . but needing love even more" (Bornecque, 255).

In order to denigrate Staël's Swiss background and Germanic affinities, *La Quotidienne* published a poem on 28 June 1814 apostrophizing her as Corinne (Carlo Pellegrini, *Les Idées littéraires de Mme de Staël et le romantisme français* [Ferrara: "All'Insegna del Libro," 1929], 21; hereafter cited in the text). At least one admirer likened Staël to Delphine. When *Delphine* appeared in Germany, Villers wrote the author on 4 May 1803: "You are Delphine, you are infallibly she" (comtesse Jean [Pauline Laure Marie Broglie] de Pange, *Mme de Staël et la découverte de l'Allemagne* [Paris: Edgar Malfère, 1929], 24; hereafter cited in the text as Pauline de Pange).

4. Not only were both women intelligent, sensitive, attached to their fathers, and insatiably in need of reassurance, but both were subjected to misogynistic attacks. Moreover, Fuller's story of "Miranda," an *improvisatrice*, bears a close resemblance to *Corinne* (Paula Blanchard, "*Corinne* and the 'Yankee Corinna': Madame de Staël and Margaret Fuller," in *Woman as Mediatrix: Essays on Nineteenth-Century European Women Writers*, ed. Avriel H. Goldberger [New York: Greenwood Press, 1987], 39–46).

5. Ellen Moers, "Performing Heroinism: The Myth of Corinne," in *Literary Women: The Great Writers* (Garden City, N.Y.: Doubleday, 1976), 177. She traces *Corinne*'s influence on George Eliot, Charlotte Brontë, Harriet Beecher Stowe, George Sand, and Willa Cather. Elizabeth Barrett wrote, at age 26: "[*Corinne*] is an immortal book, and deserves to be read three score and ten times—that is once every year in the age of man" (173).

6. Consult Gennari for a comprehensive evaluation of the relationship between Staël's trip and the evolution of *Corinne*, including the respective influences of Schlegel, Sismondi, Bonstetten, and Monti in altering Staël's ideas about Italy.

7. Until the end of the nineteenth century, the Bibliothèque Nationale listed *Corinne* as a travel guide (Marie-Claire Vallois, "Voyage au pays des doubles: Ruines et mélancolie chez Mme de Staël," *L'Esprit Créateur* 25, no. 3 [Fall 1985]: 76; hereafter cited in the text).

8. According to Vallois, Italy represents the heroine's "metaphoric double." The enigma of the title is repeated in the plot, where the mystery of Corinne's background and patronymic motivates a search that mirrors the quest for Italy (77).

9. For a detailed account of the praise heaped on *Corinne*, see Blennerhassett, 3:183–87.

10.   Don Pedro de Souza, one of the models for Oswald, had recently lost his father, like Staël, and was wont to commiserate with her over their mutual grief.

11.   During her Italian travels, Staël had occasion to hear celebrated "improvisers"—appreciated for their extemporaneous versification—like abbé Biamonti, professor of eloquence at Bologna (Gennari, 59), the beautiful Isabella Pellegrini (77), and signora Mazzei, whom she found extraordinary, if physically unattractive (Solovieff, 311).

12.   This description of Corinne corresponds in many respects with Staël, who invariably wore a turban and high-bosomed dress, took pride in her beautiful arms, knew herself to be stocky, and likened herself to a sibyl.

13.   Corinne's resemblance to the sibyl is stressed in her appearance, her semidivine inspiration, the location of her home in Tivoli, and the Domenichino painting to which she is compared. Guibert's "portrait," we recall, likened Staël to the priestess of Apollo. In relating Mary Shelley's visit to the cave of the Cumaean Sibyl, Gilbert and Gubar define the sibyl as possessing "a goddess's power of maternal creativity, the sexual/artistic strength that is the female equivalent of the male potential for literary paternity" (Sandra M. Gilbert and Susan Gubar, *The Madwoman in the Attic: The Woman Writer and the Nineteenth-Century Literary Imagination* [New Haven: Yale University Press, 1979], 97).

14.   Oswald's resentment of Corinne's social success echoes the feelings of both Théodore and Léonce.

15.   Friedrich and August Wilhelm von Schlegel are generally credited with inspiring Staël's observations on art and aesthetics in *Corinne*. While the latter accompanied Staël through Italy, the former was to translate *Corinne* into German in 1817, the year of Staël's death.

16.   Staël's "Epître à Naples" (Epistle to Naples, 1805) is a poetic paean to Italy as the land of love, enchantment, and indolence, but also of volcanic eruptions and death. Evoking the undying heroes of the past, she exhorts Italy to overthrow its yoke and regain its former greatness (*OC*, 17:415–20).

17.   This scene is memorialized by François Gérard in his famous painting of Staël as Corinne at Cape Misenum, lute in hand and eyes raised to heaven (see frontispiece portrait).

18.   Despite Staël's disclaimer in a footnote (*OC*, 9:166), critics agree that Maria Madellena Morelli (Corilla Olimpica), the most celebrated woman poet of her time—also crowned at the Capitol—was an important model for Corinne (Gutwirth, 173 n. 38).

19.   Cf. letters to Narbonne of 8 November and 25 December 1792 (Jasinski, 2:59, 94). Gilbert and Gubar theorize that early women writers felt so anxious and guilty about their creativity that they often utilized images of illness and insanity; they feared that by wanting to write they were quite literally mad (58–61).

20.   To reinforce the resemblance, Staël gives the child the name of the character Corinne portrayed at the apogee of Oswald's love.

21.   Oswald's weakness and indecisiveness recall Adolphe, Constant's fictional alter ego.

22. Although a note says the dance was modeled on that of Mme Récamier (*OC*, 8:193), Juliana von Krüdener supposedly invented the famous "shawl dance," which was later popularized by Mme Tallien (Levaillant, 32–33). Frederika Brun's daughter Ida and Albertine de Staël were also proficient at this dance (Solovieff, 327).

23. Staël's more mellow attitude toward Catholicism can be traced to the loss of her father, the influence of Kant, her friendship with Schlegel, and the broad-minded cardinals she met in Italy (Gennari, 158–59).

24. Simone Balayé, "Corinne et les amis de Mme de Staël," *Revue d'Histoire Littéraire de la France* 66, no. 1 (January-March 1966): 140. There is abundant testimony that the novel caused men and women alike to weep.

25. Necker de Saussure learned from her son of *Corinne*'s reception in Edinburgh: "All of society was electrified; metaphysicians, geologists, professors in every discipline stopped each other on the street to ask where they were in their reading" ("Notice," cxxxix n. 1).

26. Thomas Moore, *Letters and Journals of Lord Byron*, 3 vols. (London: John Murray, 1833), 1:502, note.

27. Stendhal [Henri Beyle], *Correspondance*, 3 vols., ed. Henri Martineau and V. del Litto (Paris: Galliard, 1962–68), I, 578; hereafter cited in the text as Stendhal *Correspondence*.

28. Stendhal, *Oeuvres intimes*, ed. Henri Martineau (Paris: Pléiade, 1955), 1034–35.

29. Charles Nodier, *Mélanges de littérature et de critique,* (Paris: Raymond, 1820), 2 vols. I: 387; hereafter cited in the text.

30. "Rome and you are inseparable in my memory . . ." Staël wrote de Souza on 14 May 1805. "My imagination had not yet populated the desert; I loved you, and everything came alive for me: art, nature, even those memories of the past that troubled me but that I learned to enjoy" (Solovieff, 310).

31. Gutwirth proposes Jacques Necker as a model for Oswald (232). Gennari provides an entire list of keys to various characters (123), among them, Talleyrand as the prototype of Maltigues.

32. As early as 30 July 1791, Staël wrote her husband: "I shall never be what people call an English wife. Perhaps time will prove that nature has endowed me with certain gifts that excuse me; but if anyone tried to force me . . . I would throw myself into the lake on whose banks they tried to shackle my life" (Jasinski, 1:471).

Chapter Seven

1. Staël had already determined the tenor of this work. She wrote Friedrich Heinrich Jacobi on 1 January 1804: "On returning from Germany, I intend to write a literary and philosophical travel book about this country" (Pauline de Pange, 53). She informed Joseph-Marie de Gerando on 26 February

1804 that she was studying German philosophy and esthetics: "I have no intention of writing a metaphysical work; but to provide an idea of the German character and the distinctive spirit of their literature, I have to offer a simple and popular notion of their philosophical systems" (52).

2. Footnotes scattered through the text pinpoint passages the censors suppressed, especially the chapters on enthusiasm in book 3 and the final section.

3. From her breezy account of this slapstick situation, it is difficult to agree with Simone Balayé (107) that Staël derived the idea for *Corinne* from this farce.

4. In spite of this demurral, she chooses a similar conceit in her comedy *Le Mannequin*, composed almost simultaneously with *Allemagne*, in 1811.

5. During her clandestine stay in Paris in 1806, Staël made sure to see Talma perform in *Manlius Capitolinus* by Antoine de Lafosse. Showered with favors by Napoleon, Talma probably declined Staël's invitation in 1809 to perform in Geneva for fear of displeasing the emperor (Solovieff, 384).

6. One of the models for Corinne's famous shawl dance.

7. Staël had already propounded this notion in *Circonstances* (147, 245–52).

8. It engages the romantic battle seven years before Lamartine's *Méditations* (1820), ten years before Stendhal's *Racine et Shakespeare* (1823–28), and fourteen years before Hugo's preface to *Cromwell* (1827).

9. Similarly, Staël states that only enthusiastic persons are able to commune with nature (*OC*, 11:539).

10. Heinrich Heine published a blasting refutation in 1833, *Zur Geschichte der Religion und Philosophie in Deutschland* (*Madame de Staël et l'Europe*), cataloged by Simone Balayé and Marie-Laure Chastang [Paris: Bibliothèque Nationale, 1966], 107; hereafter cited in the text as Balayé and Chastang).

11. Victor de Pange, "Le Rêve anglais de Mme de Staël," in *Colloque*, 180; hereafter cited in the text.

12. Most of the data concerning the reception of *Allemagne* are taken from this important work, which traces Staël's influence on the nascent romantic movement.

13. Kurt Mueller-Vollmer, "Staël's *Germany* and the Beginnings of an American National Literature," in *Germaine de Staël: Crossing the Borders*, ed. Madelyn Gutwirth, Avriel Goldberger, and Karyna Szmurlo (New Brunswick, N.J.: Rutgers University Press, 1991), 141–58; hereafter cited in the text.

Chapter Eight

1. Juliette Récamier usually played the part of the angel.

2. Genevieve of Brabant, wife of comte Siegfried of Treves, supposedly lived in the early eighth century. Many hagiographies refer to her as a saint. She has been the subject of numerous popular songs and prose narratives as well as of a "marionette" opera by Erik Satie.

3. When the play was staged in Vienna in 1808, Staël played the mother and Albertine her daughter. Friedrich Tieck made a pencil sketch the same year of Albertine as Semida (Balayé and Chastang, 92).

4. The name—like the character—is reminiscent of comte d'Erfeuil in *Corinne*, whom Staël originally called "d'Erville." She is fond of names ending in "——ville" (Sainville, d'Orville, Valville, Mondoville, Fierville, and, of course, Nelvil).

5. Little is known about the life of Sappho, the greatest woman poet of ancient Greece, who was probably born of an aristocratic family in Lesbos around 600 B.C. The popular story of her passion for Phaon and her leap from the Leucadian rock is almost certainly fictitious.

6. These pieces appeared respectively in volumes 2, 6, and 9. It is also believed that Staël "ghosted" the pieces on Jacques and Suzanne Necker in that same compendious reference work.

7. In her bulletin to King Gustav of Sweden on 11 November 1786, she had already expressed her aversion to the slave trade and her enthusiastic hope that it might end: "What glory for a century would be the abolition of slavery! If a single man were responsible, he would have accomplished more good than any man could ever do" (Jasinski, 1:141).

8. Translated by Pietro Giordani, this piece appeared in 1816 in the Italian journal *Biblioteca italiana* (Paul-Emile Schazmann, *Bibliographie des oeuvres de Mme de Staël* [Paris: Victor Attinger, 1938], 94).

Chapter Nine

1. These can still be seen at the Musée Carnavalet, in Paris.

2. Staël had said much the same thing in *Circonstances*, in greater detail.

3. It will be recalled that Suzanne Necker's thwarted ambition was to write a book on Fénelon.

4. Staël omits any mention of her own part in this nomination.

5. In spite of Staël's denials, several critics, most notably Gwynne, are convinced that Staël played an active role in precipitating Bonaparte's coup (39–40).

6. A reference to *Dix années*, which she had already begun writing.

7. Maria Edgeworth (1768–1849), author of over 20 books, collaborated with her father, Richard Lovell Edgeworth, on the treatise *Practical Education* (1798) and completed his memoirs in 1817 after his death.

8. Fanny [Frances] Burney (1752–1840), the novelist and diarist, published *Evelina* (anonymously, 1778), *Cecilia* (1782), *Camilla* (1796), and *The Wanderer* (1814). Staël met Burney in Surrey in the spring of 1793, but her friendship was rebuffed.

9. Hannah More (1745–1833), a successful dramatist and letter writer, was a member of the Bluestocking Club and a friend of Dr. Johnson, Samuel Richardson, Joshua Reynolds, and David Garrick.

10.   Elizabeth Simpson Inchbald (1753–1821), a novelist, actress, and dramatist, is chiefly remembered for two prose romances and several plays.

11.   Amelia Alderson Opie (1769–1853) was a prolific poet and novelist; her *Adeline Mowbray* (1804) is based on the life of Mary Wollstonecraft.

12.   Probably Joanna Baillie (1762–1851), the Scottish dramatist, poet, and friend of Sir Walter Scott. Between 1798 and 1812, she published three volumes of *Plays on the Passions*, each of which focuses on the effect of a particular passion (a concordance to be compared with Staël's *Passions*).

13.   Jacques Godechot supplies these figures in his introduction to *Considérations sur la Révolution française* (Paris: Tallandier, 1983), 32; hereafter cited in the text. While basically laudatory, he makes the unjust accusation that Staël sought liberty only for the privileged classes. Like other misogynists, he traces her hatred of Napoleon to an amorous defeat and, in the biographical section, calls her "Germaine."

14.   Alphonse de Lamartine, "Cours familier de littérature," *Revue Mensuelle*, 1856–69, 26:249; hereafter cited in the text as "Cours familier."

15.   Auguste de Staël's footnote reminds us of "destiny's mysterious coincidence" (*OC*, 15:246); his mother died on 14 July 1817.

16.   From this brief notation, we can surmise Staël's intention of introducing the Orient to her French readership, while again upholding the perennial English model of freedom.

17.   Vladimir I (ca. 956–1015), the first Christian ruler of Russia, ascended the throne and seized Kiev from his brother in 980, after his father's death.

18.   Peter the Great (1672–1725, czar after 1682). Following a 16-month trip incognito through Europe (1697–98), his attempt to introduce Western customs resulted in a kind of cultural revolution in Russia.

19.   Alexander I (1777–1825, czar of Russia from 1801), was reared by his grandmother, Catherine the Great, and educated along Rousseauesque lines. He initiated reforms in education, administration, science, and serfdom before becoming reactionary in the latter years of his reign.

20.   Grigori Aleksandrovich Potemkin (1739–91), soldier, statesman, and recognized paramour of Catherine the Great.

21.   An inveterate detractor of Staël, Henri Guillemin disparages her deletion of imploring letters to the emperor and her misrepresentation of her position as a principled adversary, claiming more than once that "*Dix années d'exil* is not veracious" (*Mme de Staël, Benjamin Constant et Napoléon* [Paris: Plon, 1959], 61).

Chapter Ten

1.   Victor de Pange, *Colloque*, 180.

2.   Stendhal wrote his sister Pauline on 22 March 1806: "She . . . wanted to be loved like a woman, after having shone like a man" (*Correspondence*, 1:315–16).

3. Georges Solovieff, "Mme de Staël vue par ses contemporains," in *Revue d'Histoire Littéraire de la France* 66, no. 1 (January-March 1966): 132. Providing comments about Staël by Rilliet Huber, Genlis, Gibbon, Fanny Burney, Constant, Schiller, Goethe, Humboldt, Metternich, Bonstetten, Sismondi, Byron, and others, Solovieff concludes that more than half of her contemporaries judged Staël favorably, a small number expressed serious reservations, and nearly a third held a distinctly negative opinion.

4. Even Staël's beloved British found her too political and loquacious, especially in monopolizing after-dinner conversation, when most women knew enough to leave the men to their pipes (Victor de Pange, *Colloque,* 178–79).

5. Cousin d'Avalon, *Staëlliana, ou Recueil d'anecdotes, bons mots, maximes, pensées et réflexions de Madame la Baronne de Staël-Holstein* (Paris: Librairie Politique, 1820), 39.

6. *Le Nain Jaune* (7 February 1866), in *Le XIXe siècle: Des oeuvres et des hommes,* 2 vols., ed. Jacques Petit (Paris: Mercure de France, 1964), 2:73–74.

7. Jules Michelet, *Les Femmes de la Révolution: Héroïnes, victimes, amoureuses,* ed. Pierre Labracherie and Jean Dumont (Paris: Hachette, [n.d.]), 88.

8. David Glass Larg, *Madame de Staël: La Vie dans l'oeuvre (1766–1800)* (Paris: Champion, 1924), 55, 186.

9. Anthony West, *Mortal Wounds* (New York: McGraw-Hill, 1973), 159.

10. Noreen Swallow, "The Weapon of Personality: A Review of Sexist Criticism of Mme de Staël, 1785–1975," *Atlantis* 8, no. 1 (Fall-Automne 1982): 81.

11. The Coppet archives contain a "declaration of nationality" that Staël gave the mayor of Metz in 1803 to prove her French citizenship.

12. A word coined at Coppet (Balayé, 111). The term *vulgarity* was another Staël invention (Jean-Albert Bédé, "Mme de Staël et les mots," in *Colloque,* 326).

13. Quoted by comtesse [Béatrix] d'Andlau, "Mme de Staël et Coppet," in *Colloque,* 36–37.

14. Among the writings that germinated from the fertile soil of Coppet were Schlegel's *Comparaison des deux Phèdre* and *Cours de littérature dramatique*; *L'Imagination* by Bonstetten; *Le Tableau de la littérature française au XVIIIe siècle* by Barante; Constant's *Adolphe* (1816), *Cécile* (1951), and *Wallstein*; Sismondi's *Histoire des républiques italiennes* and *De la Littérature du midi*; as well as Staël's *Corinne, Allemagne,* and *Considérations* (Balayé, 113–14).

15. For Staël's reconciliation of Enlightenment philosophy with romanticism, see Roland Mortier, "Mme de Staël et l'héritage de 'lumières,'" in *Colloque,* 129–38.

16. For an analysis of the question of suicide for Staël, see Jean-Albert Bédé, "Mme de Staël, Rousseau, et le suicide," *Revue d'Histoire Littéraire de la France* 66, no. 1 (January-March 1966): 52–70; Gita May, "Staël and the

Fascination of Suicide: The Eighteenth-Century Background," in Gutwirth, Goldberger, and Szmurlo, 168–76; and Jean Starobinski, "Suicide et mélancolie chez Mme de Staël," in *Colloque*, 242–52.

17.   André Monchoux, "La Place de Mme de Staël parmi les théoriciens du romantisme français," in *Colloque*, 364. Monchoux discusses Staël's influence on Hugo, who refers to her as a "woman of genius" in the 1824 edition of *Odes*; she specifically inspired his 1826 *Odes et ballades*; his preface to *Cromwell* (1827) contains nothing she had not already said. Monchoux also details her influence on Lamartine's *Méditations poétiques* (1820) and *Nouvelles méditations* (1823), on the poetry of the young Vigny, on Hugo's lyric collections, and on poetic historians like Edgar Quinet and Jules Michelet (365).

18.   Victor Hugo, *Oeuvres complètes*, 16 vols., *Théâtre* 1 (Paris: Robert Laffont, 1985), 8:539.

19.   Paul Van Teighem, *Le Mouvement romantique* (Paris: Hachette, 1912), 85.

20.   Recent feminist editions of Staël's works include two of *Delphine*, one edited by Claude Herrmann (Paris: Editions des Femmes, 1981), and the other by Simone Balayé and Lucia Omacini (Geneva: Droz, 1987); two of *Corinne*, one edited by Claude Herrmann (Paris: Editions des Femmes, 1979), and the other translated and edited by Avriel H. Goldberger (New Brunswick, N.J.: Rutgers University Press, 1987, hereafter cited in the text as Goldberger); and new critical editions of *Littérature* (ed. Paul Van Tieghem [Geneva: Droz, 1959]), *Allemagne* (ed. comtesse Jean [Pauline Laure Marie Broglie] de Pange and Simone Balayé [Paris: Hachette, 1958–59]), *Circonstances* (ed. Lucia Omacini [Paris and Geneva: Droz, 1979]), and *Considérations* (ed. Jacques Godechot [Paris: Tallandier, 1983]). *Ten Years of Exile* was translated by Doris Beik (New York: Saturday Review Press, 1972). Karyna Smyrlo, who co-edited *Germaine de Staël: Crossing the Borders*, is currently assembling a collection of feminist-oriented essays on *Corinne*. *An Extraordinary Woman: Selected Writings of Germaine de Staël*, translated by Vivian Folkenflik (New York: Columbia University Press, 1987) is a feminist collection that provides the only English translation extant of excerpts from pieces like *Fictions, Passions, Delphine*, and the novellas *Adélaïde et Théodore, Pauline*, and *Zulma*; it is invaluable for this reason alone. Marie-Claire Vallois has written *Fictions féminines: Mme de Staël et les voix de la Sibylle*, Stanford French and Italian Studies (Saratoga, Calif.: Anma Libri, 1987). Feminist-slanted articles include Noreen Swallow's "Portraits: A Feminist Appraisal of Mme de Staël's *Delphine*" and "The Weapon of Personality: A Review of Sexist Criticism of Mme de Staël, 1785–1975"; Joanna Kitchin's "La Littérature et les femmes selon l'ouvrage *De la Littérature* de Mme de Staël" (Deuxième Congrès de Lausanne [Lausanne: Institut Benjamin Constant, 1982], 401–21); and Enzo Caramaschi's "Le Point de vue féministe dans la pensée de Madame de Staël."

21.   In "Madame de Staël, Rousseau, and the Woman Question," Gutwirth finds Staël not only unmilitant but often reactionary in her statements about women (*PMLA* 86, no. 1 [January 1971]: 101).

22.   As Goldberger points out, what Corinne sought was as revolutionary in her day as it is in ours: "Staël suggests living arrangements and attitudes that neither men nor women are fully prepared to adopt as yet. Corinne asks to be accepted for what she is. She asks to live a full life as a woman without the mutilation resulting from the sacrifice of her God-given talents. She asks that a man with gifts inferior to her own live happily in her shadow. Just as revolutionary is Corinne's insistence that love be *freely* given and exchanged, imposing no bonds outside itself on either party" (xxxix).

23.   More than 40 editions appeared between 1807 and 1872 (Gutwirth, 285).

24.   Quoted in Gutwirth, 282. Gutwirth has unearthed two poems—Elizabeth J. Easmes's "On the Picture of a Departed Poetess" and Mary E. Hewitt's "Last Chant of Corinne," in *The American Female Poets*, ed. Caroline May (Philadelphia: Lindsay and Blakiston, 1853)—that were directly inspired by Corinne's image of female intellect and beauty coupled with sacrifice for love (284–85).

25.   Most of this information is taken from Ellen Moers's chapter on *Corinne* in *Literary Women* (see ch. 6, n. 5).

26.   For an eye-opening revelation of Staël's head for business, read her letters to her business factotum Pierre Fourcault de Pavant (Jasinski, vol. 5 *passim*).

27.   Simone de Beauvoir, *The Second Sex*, trans. and ed. H. M. Parshley (New York: Vintage Books, 1989), 713.

Selected Bibliography

PRIMARY SOURCES

De l'Allemagne. Edited by comtesse Jean [Pauline Laure Marie Broglie] de Pange, with Simone Balayé. Paris: Hachette, 1958.

Des Circonstances actuelles qui peuvent terminer la Révolution et des principes qui doivent fonder la république en France. Edited by Lucia Omacini. Paris and Geneva: Droz, 1979.

Considérations sur la Révolution française. Edited by Jacques Godechot. Paris: Tallandier, 1983.

Corinne ou l'Italie. Edited by Claude Herrmann. 2 vols. Paris: Editions des Femmes, 1979.

Corinne, or Italy. Translated and edited by Avriel Goldberger. New Brunswick, N.J.: Rutgers University Press, 1987.

Delphine. Edited by Claude Herrmann. Paris: Editions des Femmes, 1981.

Delphine. Edited by Simone Balayé and Lucia Omacini. 2 vols. Geneva: Droz, 1987, 1990.

Dix années d'exil. Introduction by Simone Balayé. Paris: Bibliothèque 10/18, 1966.

Essai sur les fictions, followed by *De l'influence des passions sur le bonheur des individus et des nations.* Presented by Michel Tournier. Paris: Editions Ramsay, 1979.

An Extraordinary Woman: Selected Writings of Germaine de Staël. Translated by Vivian Folkenflik. New York: Columbia University Press, 1987.

Le Journal de jeunesse de Mme de Staël. In *Occident et Cahiers Staëliens* (1930–15 October 1932), 1:76–81, 2:157–60, 3:235–42.

De la Littérature. Edited by Paul Van Tieghem. Geneva: Droz, 1959.

Oeuvres complètes de Mme la Baronne de Staël, publiées par son fils. 17 vols. Paris: Treuttel et Würtz, 1820–21.

"Un Ouvrage inconnu de Mme de Staël sur M. Necker." Edited by Simone Balayé and Marie-Laure Chastang. *Cahiers Staëliens* 12 (June 1971): 22–54.

Ten Years of Exile. Translated by Doris Beik. New York: Saturday Review Press, 1972.

SECONDARY SOURCES

Bibliography

Schazmann, Paul-Emile. *Bibliographie des oeuvres de Mme de Staël*. Paris: Victor Attinger, 1938.

Books

D'Andlau, [comtesse] Béatrix. *Madame de Staël*. Geneva: Droz, 1960. Anecdotal biography, illustrated with portraits.

Balayé, Simone. *Madame de Staël, Lumières et liberté*. Paris: Klincksieck, 1979. First-rate critical evaluation by one of the most eminent Staëlians.

Benjamin Constant, Mme de Staël, et le Groupe de Coppet. Actes du Deuxième Congrès de Lausanne à l'occasion du 150e anniversaire de la mort de Benjamin Constant et du Troisième Colloque de Coppet (15–19 July 1980). Oxford: Voltaire Foundation; Lausanne: Institut Benjamin Constant, 1982. In-depth papers relating to Staël and Constant.

Blennerhassett, Lady [Charlotte Julia von Leyden]. *Madame de Staël: Her Friends and Her Influence in Politics and Literature*. 3 vols. London: Chapman & Hall, 1889. First, mammoth study of Staël, copiously detailed. Superannuated.

Diesbach, Ghislain de. *Madame de Staël*. Paris: Perrin, 1983. One of the best modern biographical studies of Staël.

D'Eaubonne, Françoise. *Une Femme témoin de son siècle: Germaine de Staël*. Paris: Flammarion, 1966. Atmospheric re-creation of Staël's life and relationships, larded with conjecture.

Gennari, Geneviève. *Le Premier voyage de Mme de Staël en Italie et la genèse de "Corinne."* Paris: Boivin, 1947. Invaluable insight into thematic development of *Corinne*.

Gutwirth, Madelyn. *Madame de Staël, Novelist: The Emergence of the Artist as Woman*. Urbana: University of Illinois Press, 1978. Finest study of Staël in English, limited to her fiction.

Gutwirth, Madelyn, Avriel H. Goldberger, and Karyna Szmurlo, eds. *Germaine de Staël: Crossing the Borders*. New Brunswick, N.J.: Rutgers University Press, 1991. Engaging collection of feminist-oriented articles.

Gwynne, G. E. *Mme de Staël et la Révolution française: Politique, philosophie, littérature*. Paris: Nizet, 1969. Thoroughgoing analysis of Staël's political thinking, with interesting sidelight on ideologues.

D'Haussonville, vicomte [Othenin]. *Le Salon de Mme Necker*. 2 vols. Paris: Calmann-Lévy, 1882. Fascinating account of Suzanne Necker's life.

Herold, J. Christopher. *Mistress to an Age: A Life of Madame de Staël*. New York: Bobbs Merrill, 1958. Facile account catering to popular tastes. A bestseller in its day.

Hogsett, Charlotte. *The Literary Existence of Germaine de Staël.* Carbondale: Southern Illinois University Press, 1987. Novel approach to Staël's creative output.

Jasinski, Béatrice W., ed. *Correspondance générale.* 6 vols. Paris: Jean-Jacques Pauvert, 1962–74; Hachette, 1985; Klincksieck, 1993. Vol. 6 appeared too late to be included in this study. Capital research tool. Corrects many previous misconceptions.

Larg, David Glass. *Madame de Staël: La Vie dans l'oeuvre (1766–1800).* Paris: Champion, 1924. Biased and misogynistic.

Levaillant, Maurice. *Une Amitié amoureuse: Mme de Staël et Mme Récamier.* Paris: Hachette, 1956. Well-written appraisal of the friendship between Staël and Juliette Récamier.

Luppé, Robert de. *Les Idées littéraires de Mme de Staël et l'héritage des lumières (1795–1800).* Paris: J. Vrin, 1969. Stresses influence of Enlightenment on Staël's thinking.

Mme de Staël et l'Europe: Colloque de Coppet (18–24 juillet 1966). Paris: Klincksieck, 1970. Collection of papers by distinguished scholars on the occasion of Staël bicentenary.

Necker de Saussure, Albertine. "Notice sur le caractère et les écrits de Mme de Staël." In *Oeuvres complètes,* 1:i–ccclxxii. Judicious if uniformly enthusiastic appraisal of Staël by her cousin.

Pange, comtesse Jean [Pauline Laure Marie Broglie] de. *Le Dernier amour de Madame de Staël.* Geneva: La Palatine, 1944. Absorbing account of Genevan society, Rocca's life, and his relationship with Staël.

————. *Mme de Staël et la découverte de l'Allemagne.* Paris: Edgar Malfère, 1929. Early assessment of the genesis and importance of *Allemagne.*

Pellegrini, Carlo. *Les Idées littéraires de Mme de Staël et le romantisme français.* Ferrara: "All'Insegna del Libro," 1929. Excellent analysis of Staël's proclivities toward romanticism.

Rilliet Huber, Catherine. "Notes sur l'enfance de Madame de Staël." *Occident et Cahiers Staëliens* (30 June 1933; March 1934) 5:41–47, 6:140–46. Endearing glimpse of Staël's youth by her closest childhood friend.

Sainte-Beuve, [Charles-Augustin]. *Portraits de femmes.* Edited by Albert de Bersaucourt. Paris: Editions Bossard, 1928. Generally sympathetic and enthusiastic toward subject.

Schama, Simon. *Citizens: A Chronicle of the French Revolution.* New York: Knopf, 1989. Dynamic sociological, economic, historical, and personality-oriented account of revolutionary causes and events.

Solovieff, Georges, ed. *Choix de lettres de Mme de Staël (1778–1817)*. Paris: Klincksieck, 1970. Fine selection of letters with thumbnail sketches of correspondents.

West, Anthony. *Mortal Wounds*. New York: McGraw-Hill, 1973. Contains skewed, inaccurate, and prejudicial section on Staël.

Articles and Parts of Books

Blanchard, Paula. "*Corinne* and the 'Yankee Corinna': Madame de Staël and Margaret Fuller." In *Woman as Mediatrix: Essays on Nineteenth-Century European Women Writers*. Edited by Avriel H. Goldberger. New York: Greenwood Press, 1987. Thoughtful rapprochement of Staël and Fuller.

Caramaschi, Enzo. "Le Point de vue féministe dans la pensée de Madame de Staël." *Saggi et ricerche di letteratura francese* 12 (1973): 285–352. Lukewarm evaluation.

Constant, Benjamin. "De Mme de Staël et de ses ouvrages." In *Adolphe*. Edited by Jacques-Henri Bornecque. Paris: Garnier, 1963. Glowing posthumous appraisal of Staël by her closest colleague.

Gutwirth, Madelyn. "Madame de Staël, Rousseau, and the Woman Question." *PMLA* 86, no. 1 (January 1971): 100–109. Provocative interpretation of Staël's attitude toward women.

Sourian, Eve. "Madame de Staël and George Sand." In *George Sand Papers, Conference Proceedings, 1978* (New York: AMS Press, 1982), 122–29. Well-balanced comparison of both writers.

Swallow, Noreen. "Portraits: A Feminist Appraisal of Mme de Staël's *Delphine*." *Atlantis* 7, no. 1 (Fall-Automne 1981): 65–76. Perceptive and impassioned.

———. "The Weapon of Personality: A Review of Sexist Criticism of Mme de Staël, 1785–1975." *Atlantis* 8, no. 1 (Fall-Automne 1982): 78–82. Important record of misogynistic bias toward Staël.

Index

Michelet, Jules, 140, 166n17
Middle Ages, 54, 55, 63, 105, 142
Minzoni, 116, 117
Mirabeau, comte de, 121
Misogyny, 37, 42, 140–41, 144, 145,
    159n4, 164n13
Molière, 56, 57, 132
Montesquieu, baron Charles de Seconday
    de, 1, 24, 28, 41, 53, 57, 58
Montesquiou, abbé de, 123
Monti, Vincenzo, 14, 15, 77, 89, 116,
    159n6
Montmorency, Mathieu de, 6, 9, 15, 38,
    92, 125, 150–51n25
Moore, Thomas, 128
More, Hannah, 128
More, Sir Thomas, 112
Morelli, Maria Madellena, 160n18
Morris, Gouverneur, 14
Mother symbols, 25, 27
Mozart, Wolfgang Amadeus, 100
Müller, Johannes von, 99
Murray, John, 18
Music, 32, 77, 80, 87, 88, 96, 97, 99,
    104, 106, 159n3; Italian vs. German,
    100
Musset, Alfred de, 143
Mysticism, 16, 95, 103
Myth, 47

Napoleon. See Bonaparte, Napoleon
Narbonne, Louis de, 4, 8–9, 16, 20, 49,
    68, 74, 93, 123, 140, 146n8, 153n46,
    153n4, 156n8, 157n12, 157n18,
    160n19
"Natural" aristocracy, 41, 43, 58
Necker, Anne-Louise-Germaine. See
    Staël, Germaine de.
Necker, Jacques (father), 2, 4, 5, 6, 10,
    17, 21, 23, 33, 34, 42, 46, 49, 50, 53,
    58, 60, 61, 69, 93, 119, 122, 124,
    129, 130, 132, 140, 142, 149n5,
    149n6, 149n10, 151n27, 153n3,
    154n11, 157n12, 161n23, 161n31;
    De l'administration des finances de la
    France, 120; De l'administration de M.
    Necker par lui-même, 4, 149n10; and
    American war, 3; comparison with

Rousseau, 30, 32; Compte Rendu, 4, 7;
    Cours de morale religieuse, 81; death, 14,
    130, 132; Dernières vues de politique et
    de finances, 125; Eloge de Colbert, 3; as
    finance minister, 3–4, 34, 120,
    149n9, 153n3; in French Revolution,
    7–8, 34, 119, 120–21, 125, 127;
    Histoire de la Révolution, 124; De
    l'importance des opinions religieuses, 32;
    Du pouvoir exécutif dans les grands états,
    122; Réflexions présentées à la nation
    française sur le procès intenté à Louis XIV,
    124, 154n2; retirement, 118–19, 122
Necker, Suzanne Curchod (mother), 1–3,
    4, 5, 17, 19, 21, 22, 46, 74, 149n5,
    158n18, 163n3; death, 9; education,
    1; hospital, 3, 151n26; Mélanges de
    Mme Necker, 4, 64; salon, 1, 3, 142,
    156n4, 163n3; as symbol, 25
Necker de Saussure, Albertine, 2, 5–6,
    12, 15, 20, 40, 149n3; on Corinne, 91,
    92, 161n25; Etude de la vie des femmes,
    151n31; "Notice on the Character
    and Writings of Mme de Staël," 1, 20,
    149n3
Neologisms, 58, 60, 156n13, 156n16,
    165n12
Nicolle, 16
Nodier, Charles, 91–92, 107, 144
Norvins, Jacques de, 158n14
Novalis, 103
Novel, 31, 47, 48, 55, 64–65, 86, 94, 99,
    145, 156n2

O'Donnell, Count Maurice, 16, 92
Opie, Amelia Alderson, 128, 164n11
Oratory, 44, 60, 134

Pange, François de, 38
Pastoret, Adélaïde de, 64, 140, 153n4
Perugino, 100
Pestalozzi, Johann Heinrich, 97
Peter I, 134, 164n18
Petrarch, 55, 78
Phelps, Elizabeth Stuart, 146
Pitt, William, 5, 23, 37, 38, 115, 154n4
Poetry, 48, 54, 58, 59–60, 62, 77, 78,
    80, 81, 85, 88, 91, 94, 97–98, 100,

The Author

Gretchen Rous Besser received her B.A. degree from Wellesley College, her M.A. from Middlebury College (for study at the Sorbonne under a Fulbright grant), and her Ph.D. from Columbia University, where she taught for a number of years. A Ph.D. examiner for Monash University in Australia and a member of the Curriculum Committee of the New Jersey Committee for the Humanities, she has taught at Fairleigh Dickinson University, Lehman College, and Rutgers University. Currently, she is on the faculty of the New School for Social Research in New York.

A former Fulbright scholar, Dr. Besser has translated one book and two plays. She is also the author of *Balzac's Concept of Genius* (1969) and *Nathalie Sarraute* in the Twayne World Authors Series (1979). She has contributed articles and reviews to the *Columbia Dictionary of Modern European Literature*, the *French Review*, *World Literature Today*, and other scholarly journals. In her other life, Dr. Besser is a toboggan-hauling member of the National Ski Patrol, its official historian, and author of *The National Ski Patrol: Samaritans of the Snow* (1983).

The Editor

David O'Connell is professor of foreign languages and chair of the Department of Foreign Languages at Georgia State University. He received his Ph.D. from Princeton University in 1966, where he was a National Woodrow Wilson Fellow, the Bergen Fellow in Romance Languages, and a National Woodrow Wilson Dissertation Fellow. He is the author of *The Teachings of Saint Louis: A Critical Text* (1972), *Les Propos de Saint Louis* (1974), *Louis-Ferdinand Céline* (1976), *The Instructions of Saint Louis: A Critical Text* (1979), and *Michel de Saint Pierre: A Catholic Novelist at the Crossroads* (1990). He is the editor of *Catholic Writers in France since 1945* (1983) and has served as review editor (1977-1979) and managing editor (1987-1990) of the *French Review*.

DEMCO